THE BOOK OF
BUSHIDO

*Treason doth never prosper, what is the reason? Why, if it prosper,
none dare call it treason.*

Sir John Harington (1560–1612)

The 'Book of' series

Book of Ninja: The First Complete Translation of the Bansenshukai

Book of Samurai: Fundamental Teachings (Book 1)

Book of Samurai: Samurai Arms, Armour & the Tactics of Warfare (Book 2)

The Ultimate Guide series

The Ultimate Art of War: A Step-by-Step Illustrated Guide to Sun Tzu's Teachings

The Ultimate Guide to Yin Yang: An Illustrated Exploration of the Chinese Concept of Opposites

Books on samurai, ninja and Japan

How to Be a Modern Samurai: 10 Steps to Finding Your Power and Achieving Success

Iga and Koka Ninja Skills: The Secret Shinobi Scrolls of Chikamatsu Shigenori

In Search of the Ninja: The Historical Truth of Ninjutsu

Modern Ninja Warfare: Tactics and Methods for the Modern Warrior

Ninja Skills: The Authentic Ninja Training Manual

Old Japan: Secrets from the Shores of the Samurai

Samurai and Ninja: The Real Story Behind the Japanese Warrior Myth that Shatters the Bushido Mystique

Samurai Death Cult: The Dark Side of Bushido

Samurai War Stories

Secrets of the Ninja: The Shinobi Teachings of Hattori Hanzo

The Dark Side of Japan: Ancient Black Magic, Folklore, Ritual

The Lost Samurai School: Secrets of Mubyōshi Ryū

The Secret Traditions of the Shinobi: Hattori Hanzo's Shinobi Hiden and Other Ninja Scrolls

True Path of the Ninja: The Definitive Translation of the Shoninki

Other books

The Illustrated Guide to Viking Martial Arts

The Lost Warfare of India: An Illustrated Guide

THE BOOK OF
BUSHIDO

THE COMPLETE GUIDE
TO REAL SAMURAI CHIVALRY

ANTONY CUMMINS

WATKINS

Sharing Wisdom Since 1893

This edition first published in the UK and USA 2022 by
Watkins, an imprint of Watkins Media Limited
Unit 11, Shepperton House
89–93 Shepperton Road
London
N1 3DF

enquiries@watkinspublishing.com

10 9 8 7 6 5 4 3 2 1

Designed and typeset by JCS Publishing Services Ltd
Calligraphy by Yamamoto Jyuhō

Printed in the United Kingdom by TJ Books Ltd

A CIP record for this book is available from the British Library

ISBN: 978-1-78678-605-0

www.watkinspublishing.com

CONTENTS

This book is dedicated to the Comminnauts, an intellectual group based in Commins Coch, near Machynlleth, Powys. Many of the ideas in this book sprang from this debate group formed by Robin Clifton, Vivien Clifton, Daniel Bryan and me, with many shared evenings of cake, tea and discussions of samurai ethics and morality.

ACKNOWLEDGEMENTS

Above all, I would like to give thanks to Fiona Robertson for her constant support of my work, a favourable wind sending me across the sea of my future dreams. Also, to my editor, James Hodgson, for his excellent treatment of the text. To Koizumi Mieko for her diligent checking of the manuscript and quotes. To Yamamoto Jyuho for calligraphy. To Matthew Okuhara for sharing with me his work on the samurai and their use of guns. Also, to the many others who have over the years translated old Japanese texts into English for the world to enjoy, including but not restricted to: Thomas Cleary, William Scott Wilson, Alexander Bennett, Hiroaki Sato, Tabata Kazumi, Royall Tyler and Eric Shahan, all of whom deserve credit for their contributions to Japanese history. A special thank you goes to Nicholas DeLaune of the YouTube channel The Shōgunate, who has been my historical fact checker on this mission, and who has helped to promote my work and support my approach to his fullest ability. Finally, to Robin Clifton, formerly of the University of Warwick, for his general help and his suggestion of the opening quote by Sir John Harington.

INTRODUCTION:
AN OUTLINE OF SAMURAI HONOUR

The samurai ideal:

> *What the cherry blossom is among flowers,* bushi *warriors are among men.*
>
> Japanese saying

The samurai reality:

> *Of course, honesty is a principle on the original form of the path which I learn. However, using deception in certain situations cannot be avoided.*
>
> Yoshisada Gunki (transcribed 1629)

WHO WERE THE SAMURAI?

The samurai originated in the second half of the first millennium. They served the imperial court, first as court servants and bureaucrats, then as a warrior caste who guarded the court of Kyōto and put down rebellions throughout the land. Later they seized power for themselves – yet never removing the Emperor as head of state – and placed Japan under military rule.

It would be wrong to view the samurai as a homogenous group; they comprised various types occupying different social levels, ranging from 'blue-blooded' sons of princes all the way down to peasants made good and opportunists. General terms for them include:

- *samurai* (侍) – literally, 'one who serves'
- *bushi* (武士) – 'military knight or gentleman'

- *mononofu* (武士) – alternative name for *bushi*, often used in poetry
- *musha* (武者) – 'military person'

There were also more specific terms for certain kinds of samurai, including:

- *rōnin* (浪人 or 牢人) – 'person who floats upon the wave of society' or 'prison person', these were wandering samurai who did not have a lord
- *watari-zamurai* (渡り侍) – mercenary, similar to *rōnin*
- *jizamurai* (地侍) – 'country samurai', akin to landed gentry
- *dogō* (土豪) – 'powerful land-owner'
- *suhadamono* (徒膚者) – warrior on the field of battle who had bare legs and light armour
- *koshi* (古士) – ex-knight from a family that had lost full samurai status but retained certain privileges
- *nobushi* (野武士) – bandit knight who lived in the wilds

All of these were considered as military personnel at one point or another, yet many did not fit the archetype of the noble warrior who aspired to follow *bushidō*.

The samurai was both servant to some and master to others, taking his place in a hierarchical pyramid with the apex warrior at the top. His objective in life was either to climb to the top of that pyramid or to give military service to someone else who climbed it and receive in return land rights and position. A system relying so heavily on the moral obligations of giving and receiving needed to be governed by some form of code of conduct, and that is how *bushidō* came into being.

WHAT IS *BUSHIDŌ*?

Bushidō (武士道) is the chivalric, moral and ethical system of ideas and correct behaviour developed by the samurai class. The term is made up of two parts: *bushi* (武士), 'military gentleman', and *dō* (道), which refers to the Daoist 'Way', meaning the pattern behind the universe, or the Confucianist 'way', meaning to follow a proper path. The full term *bushidō* is most commonly translated as 'the way of the warrior' or 'the way of the samurai'.

There has never been a single, official *bushidō* code. It started out as a living set of ethics and then various versions of it were set down in writing. The first known reference to a concept that can be identified as *bushidō* was in a poem written by a monk named Sogi (宗祇) in the late fifteenth century. Unfortunately, the original characters have not been recorded, but the poem can be found in Steven D. Carter's anthology *Traditional Japanese Poetry* (Stanford University Press, 1991):

> *Hakanaki mono wa,*
> *Mononofu no michi*
> *Ta ga tame no*
> *Na nareba mi yori*
> *Oshimuran*

> A thing of uncertainty
> Is the way of the warrior,
> For whose glory does a man care less for life
> Than for honour.

Although the poet uses the term *mononofu* rather than *bushi* (presumably to keep to the correct number of syllables), he is clearly referring to *bushidō*. This indicates that even at such an early date the samurai valued personal honour above life and limb.

Epic war tales such as the *Heike Monogatari* and *Taiheiki* celebrate ideals of behaviour, whether fictional or historical. By the time of the upheavals of the sixteenth century, there were ample quotations from leading samurai figures and military writers on what was considered proper conduct, even if it was not always adhered to. Takeda Shingen, Tokugawa Ieyasu, Katō Kiyomasa and others all talked about the proper way of the warrior. Therefore, it has to be understood that there are two avenues of enquiry when researching samurai chivalry: the first is to find the term *bushidō* in written use and the second is to find historical accounts of actual samurai behaviour. While they are two sides of the same coin, the search for patterns of behaviour must take precedence over the search for a term that identifies it.

House rules

Before the term *bushidō* came into being, clan rules helped establish warrior behaviour. See, for example, the sixteen maxims of the Uesugi clan (translated by Mieko Koizumi).

上杉謙信公家訓十六条
Uesugi Kenshin Kō Kakun Jūroku-jō
The sixteen family precepts of Uesugi Kenshin

1
心に物なき時は心く広体泰なり
When you do not hold worldly desire in mind, your mind will be expansive and your body will be untroubled.

2
心に我儘なき時は愛敬失わず
When you do not hold selfishness in mind, you will maintain your amiable nature.

3
心に欲なき時は義理を行う
When you do not hold desire in mind, you will engage in acts of justice.

4
心に私なき時は疑うことなし
When you do not hold selfishness in mind, you will not doubt others.

5
心に驕りなき時は人を教う
When you do not have haughtiness in mind, you will teach others.

6
心に誤りなき時は人を畏れず
When you do not have a guilty conscience, you will not fear people.

7

心に邪見なき時は人を育つる

When you do not have evil thoughts in mind, you will nurture people.

8

心に貪りなき時は人に諂うことなし

When you do not have greed in mind, you will not flatter people.

9

心に怒りなき時は言葉和らかなり

When you do not have anger in mind, your words will be gentle.

10

心に堪忍ある時は事を調う

When you have endurance in mind, accomplishments will follow.

11

心に曇りなき時は心静かなり

When your mind is clear, you will be calm.

12

心に勇みある時は悔やむことなし

When you have bravery in mind, there will be no regret.

13

心賤しからざる時は願い好まず

When your mind is free of greed, you will dislike unreasonable demands.

14

心に孝行ある時は忠節厚し

When you have filial piety in mind, you will have deep loyalty.

15

心に自慢なき時は人の善を知り

When you do not hold vanity in mind, you will understand people's strong points.

16

心に迷いなき時は人を咎めず

When you do not have hesitation in mind, you will not blame people.

Another, slightly later example is the Tokugawa family precepts collectively known as the Tōshōgū Goikun, extracts from which appear below.

人の一生は重荷を負いて遠き道を行くがごとし、急ぐべからず

Life is to meander along long pathways, there is no need for haste.

不自由を常と思えば不足なし

You will never be inconvenienced if you accept that normal life is inconvenient.

心に望み起こらば困窮したる時を思いだすべし

When desire surfaces within your mind, always remember the troubles you have had in the past [because of your desires].

堪忍は無事長久の基、怒りを敵とおもえ。勝つことばかり知りて、負くることを知らざば、害その身にいたる

Patience is the key to continuing in safety, anger is the enemy. If you have never lost, how can you know victory?

おのれを責めて人を責むるな

Blame is only ever placed on yourself.

及ばざるは過ぎたるより勝れり

To have a minimal existence is better than opulence and overindulgence.

It is a common misconception that only scrolls containing the term *bushidō* have anything to do with samurai ethics and morality. However, like all words, *bushidō* evolved at its own pace, only entering wide usage from the end of the sixteenth century. Many accounts of samurai exploits predate this period and must not be overlooked in the search for understanding of samurai behaviour.

SEARCHING FOR A WORD OR FOR A BEHAVIOUR?

Critics of *bushidō* often (wrongly) assert that the concept only came into existence at the end of the sixteenth century when Japan was about to enter a prolonged period of peace. They seem to be implying that the samurai before the year 1600 had no code of ethics and that those after the year 1600 were bogged down in Confucian morality, as if a switch had been flicked and the samurai abruptly embraced the warrior mystique of *bushidō*.

This way of thinking ignores the fact that Japan was unifying at this time. With unification came standardized thinking and centralized communication, leading to some aspects of language becoming more popular than others, and certain new terms replacing old ones. As we shall see from the recorded actions and expected conduct of pre-unification samurai, it would be a mistake to see the emergence of the new word *bushidō* as signalling the emergence of a new behaviour. Before *bushidō*, words such as *kahō* (家法), 'family rules', had been used for hundreds of years, showing that there was already a tradition of expected behaviour within warrior families.

THE UNTOLD MASSES

By the end of this book, it is to be hoped that you will have deepened your understanding of *bushidō*, by learning in particular to distinguish between chivalric ideals and historical reality. However, we must not forget that recorded samurai history tends to focus on exceptional figures whose behaviour may not be representative of the samurai class as a whole. There are untold masses of samurai whose actions are unknown and who, therefore, have not added to the story of *bushidō*.

Reading between the lines of both the commonly held ideals and the recorded actions of individual samurai, it is clear that there were many samurai who looked out for themselves, but likewise there were untold numbers who were loyal to the death and who did try to uphold warrior ethics. The idea that all samurai were stoic and loyal will be dismantled in this book, but if you could be transported back to medieval Japan you would undoubtedly come across many great examples of samurai living by *bushidō*. However, most of these would be warriors who owed their livelihood to their warlord and who saw no prospect of rising to become a history-changing individual. These men who spent their whole lives in loyal service to their clan and their lord often went unrecorded yet must not be forgotten.

WAR WAS THE EXCEPTION NOT THE NORM

Japan, for most of the time, was at peace. Even during the social upheavals of the so-called Warring States period, the average day for a samurai did not contain any fighting. Military campaigns were expensive to run and so were kept as short as possible. Instead, most samurai spent the majority of their time managing the villages under their care. This means that they might have gone many years or even decades without any opportunity to demonstrate their loyalty, courage or military prowess.

A REFLECTION OR A CORRECTION?

Another important question to consider is what made various samurai decide to write about *bushidō*. Do not assume that they were inspired by a desire to record for posterity the typical behaviour they observed all around them in their society; most treatises on a subject are designed to correct behaviour not to reflect it. If writers on *bushidō* were trying to steer their peers toward better conduct, this implies that most samurai were falling short of the standards laid out in these scrolls. A good rule of thumb when reading such documents is to understand that when a samurai says something 'should' be done in a certain way, it most likely means that the opposite was being done in real life.

A NOTE ON TRANSLATIONS AND SOURCES

This work has been founded on original Japanese texts, translated by a wide range of authors. A full list can be found after the main bibliography at the back of the book. I take complete responsibility for any translation mistakes made by me and my team, and also for any mistakes I might have failed to spot in extracts from other people's translations. I have endeavoured to bring as accurate a portrayal of samurai chivalry as I can, but I apologize in advance for any imperfections. (For example, the complexities of the Japanese dating system mean that ages, where given, must be treated as approximations.) This text is not exhaustive and is intended only to break the stereotype of the samurai in the West and open up a new dialogue on this period of Japanese history.

The widest possible research has been conducted to present a broad overview of *bushidō* across more than a thousand years of samurai history. No source has been dismissed as redundant or irrelevant; not only the canon of historical documents accepted as reliable, but also miscellaneous tales, mysteries and chronicles have been used to gauge what the people of old Japan considered chivalrous. A document does not need to be historically accurate to provide insights – exaggerations and lies, demonizations and idealizations can all be used to gain a richer understanding of *bushidō*.

PRIMARY SOURCES IN ENGLISH

Various historical texts on *bushidō* have been translated into English and other languages, enabling non-Japanese speakers to gain a first-hand understanding of the subject. Examples include: the *Hagakure*, published as *The Art of the Samurai* (Watkins); the *Bushidō Shoshinshū*, published as *Code of the Samurai* (Tuttle); various documents collected and published as *Training the Samurai Mind* (Shambhala); the writings of Yamaga Sokō, published as *Samurai Wisdom* (Tuttle); and the *Heika Jōdan*, published as *The Book of Samurai: Fundamental Teachings* (Watkins). The last of these gives a realistic view of an imperfect samurai society. For a look at the inherent violence within samurai society and the samurai's supposed obsession with death, see also *Samurai Death Cult: The Dark Side of Bushido* by Antony Cummins (Repeater Books).

THE SIMPLIFIED SAMURAI

There is nothing wrong with repackaging history to bring it alive for a wider audience. In doing this, an element of simplification is inevitable. However, oversimplification can lead to the creation of misleading stereotypes. I call this the 'Disney trap'. The hero figure is often a white knight or plucky, low-born warrior; their villainous opponent is a knight turned bad or an evil wizard. The hero is supported by his own sage adviser and band of helpers, with the good king and queen standing by as figures of purity and righteousness to either help the hero or be helped by them. The background characters include the merchant, who is a plump but jovial shop-keep or a penny-pinching hoarder, and the peasants, who are good-natured and simple or dreary and miserable depending on whether they are ruled over by a benevolent or a tyrannical lord.

The samurai are just as likely to fall victim to this treatment as Robin Hood and his Merry Men. An example is the portrayal of legendary samurai Kusunoki Masashige and his valiant band fighting to support Emperor Go-Daigo in his righteous struggle against a false pretender to the imperial throne. In reality, both emperors had legitimate claims, and Go-Daigo was at fault for breaking a hereditary agreement to share the throne with the other branches of the imperial line. Rather than reigning for his allotted time and then handing over power, he took the country to war and ordered his faithful servant Masashige to his death by interfering in battle tactics.

In most cases, the white knight and the evil schemer are myths. Historical battles tend to be fought between more or less equally legitimate forces vying for control over resources, and outright heroes and villains are rare. While history should be made accessible, it is a folly to do this at the expense of accuracy.

DISCOVERING SAMURAI CHIVALRY

The aim of this book is to pull back the curtain of fantasy from samurai chivalry and reveal a more realistic picture of how the historical samurai behaved, how they lived, how they valued their own culture and what they considered to be a warrior ethos. The simple truth is that the samurai were human beings and their behaviour was subject to the same complex emotions and motivations as we all experience. Like all warrior cultures around the world, they were responsible for violence, subjugation and warmongering, while also displaying nobility, a desire for perfection and commitment to a fiercely held set of ideals.

By reading this book, you will leave behind the image of the perfect warrior and come to understand the hardened, blood-drenched military leader who has a complex set of ideas about the world, who is tasked with leading a population in both war and peace, and whose greatest battle is to satisfy his own hunger for power while staying within the bounds of morality. This is the story of *bushidō* – the way of the warrior.

THE MYTH OF *BUSHIDŌ*

To truly know the samurai and understand what they considered as proper behaviour, we will chalk up throughout this book a tally of positive and negative actions. These will then be tested against the responses of the samurai who were either around at the time that the actions were performed or who were passing on the deeds of people from an earlier era. Through this process, it can be established what was deemed as horrific, necessary, good or excellent. This will cover areas including: the paramount importance of the clan and clan name; oaths, blood feuds and revenge; the arts; the significance of arms and armour, horses, banners and emblems; how the sword was seen in contrast to other weapons through history; hot-headed murders, cold-blooded assassinations and daredevil adventures; mystery and magic, the black arts and the macabre; war and atrocity; friendship and rivalry; blood, guts, sex, fire and sea battles.

But, before that, we need to wipe away any preconceptions of *bushidō*. Therefore, in this opening part of the book we will consider how the Western notion of chivalry can cloud our understanding of the Japanese concept of *bushidō*. We will also attempt to demythologize two influential sources of information about *bushidō* in the West: *Bushidō: The Soul of Japan* by Nitobe Inazō (1900) and the *Hagakure* by Yamamoto Tsunetomo (c1716). While these works are already well known to most people with an interest in the samurai, it serves a purpose to put them in their proper place before we set out to explore the depths of the samurai heart.

CHAPTER ONE

WHAT IS CHIVALRY?

Samurai should always wish to keep to the righteous path and try not to fall into the way of depravity, no matter what happens. Those samurai who keep on with the right path will achieve high honours with the aid of Buddha and the gods, while those who have fallen into a corrupt way will naturally meet with misfortune and be laughed at by the people of the world.

Musha Monogatari (1654)

In order to understand *bushidō* we first need a proper understanding of chivalry. In its strictest sense, chivalry is a historical ideal laid out in the courtly romances of medieval France. Originally it applied only to the chevalier class and evoked the popular fantasy of the perfect 'white knight'. However, if we think in terms of this unattainable fairy-tale ideal we will miss the point of *bushidō*.

For the purposes of this book, we will define chivalry as: 'a set of ethics or moral actions considered as a code of correct conduct for people of power, guiding the way they act toward those around them, including idealized behaviour and actions that warriors aspire to'.

WESTERN IDEAS OF CHIVALRY

Western chivalry can be understood as the attempt to achieve a good level of truth, justice, piety, hope, strength, conscience, obedience, courage, protection, physical ability, reason, reputation, honour and nobility, all to aspire to the status of the perfect knight.

In his treatise *The Book of the Order of Chivalry*, the Catalan philosopher Raymond Lull (1232–1316) refers to many of these virtuous qualities in his symbology of knightly equipment, outlined below.

- The lance represents **truth.**
- The lance head represents the power of **truth over falsehood.**
- The pennant upon the lance represents the **discovery of truth** by all.
- The sword represents **justice.**
- The hilt of the sword is the **holy cross** [and the implied virtues of Christianity].
- The misericord (dagger) represents **hope.**
- The mace represents **strength.**
- The *chapel de fer* (kettle hat) represents **shame.**
- The collar represents **obedience.**
- The hauberk represents **courage.**
- The pourpoint (gambeson) represents the **travails of knighthood.**
- The shield represents the **office of knighthood.**
- The chausses (leg armour) represent **safety when travelling.**
- The spurs represent **diligence and ability.**
- The horse bit and reins represent the **avoidance of falsehood.**
- The shaffron (horse's face armour) represents **reason.**
- The saddle represents **courage without recklessness.**
- The blazon represents a warrior's **reputation.**
- The standard represents the **honour of the lord** and his estate.
- The horse represents **nobility of courage.**

JAPANESE IDEAS OF CHIVALRY

As a point of comparison to the Western ideal of chivalry outlined above, here we summarize the way of chivalry for the samurai as laid down by Yamaga Sokō in the seventeenth century.

- To follow the **Way**
- To make ideas a **reality**
- To cultivate **will power**

- To know the difference between **righteousness** and self-profit
- To realize one's **destiny**
- To have **integrity**
- To have **honesty**
- To have **constancy**
- To **refine** the character
- To perfect one's **ability**
- To have loyalty and **filial piety**
- To have **humanity**
- To hold to **justice**
- To engage in **study**
- To engage in **self-examination**
- To have **self-discipline**
- To follow **manners and customs**
- To perform correct **ceremony**
- To have **respectfulness**
- To have **circumspection**
- To have a **good appearance**
- To have **respectable dwellings**
- To **give and receive**
- To understand the three great aspects: **humanity**, the **Way** and the **natural world**
- To study **leadership**
- To **study war**
- To follow the **rules and restrictions** in day-to-day living

THE WAY

Deriving from ancient Chinese philosophy, the Way, or Dao, is the unknowable 'thing' behind all creation and the pattern that governs everything in the universe. It was important for samurai always to follow the Way, by understanding the natural rhythms of the world and choosing the right action at the right time in the right place.

IDEALS VERSUS ACTIONS

As can be expected, both versions place importance on personal honour, devotion to religion/the universe, correct behaviour toward others, self-control and refinement. It is important to understand that Western chivalry and Japanese *bushidō* are both sets of *ideals* that are striven for. The fact that no one is able to live up to all aspects of the code does not invalidate it; chivalric rules are meant to be hard to follow. They are there to shame the powerful into curbing their violent, tyrannous impulses. As history has shown, sometimes this works and sometimes it does not.

The simple fact is that if everyone in society were principled, what would they fight over?

Heihō Hidensho (1701)

The above quote is a question posed by a real samurai. Consider, if all samurai had followed *bushidō* as we understand it today, surely there would have been no wars in Japan. We know that *bushidō* existed, but it is obvious from the history of wars in Japan that not all samurai acted in a moral or chivalrous way.

DID THE SAMURAI FOLLOW *BUSHIDŌ*?

There is no doubt that the samurai held certain actions as good and others as bad. But that does not tell us what *bushidō* actually was, or whether the samurai followed it and, if so, to what extent they followed it.

Two major points should be fixed in mind before these questions can be answered correctly:

- It is a fact that the samurai did not perfectly live up to their own codes of conduct.
- Historical *bushidō* is not wholly the same as the *bushidō* imagined today.

Chapter One

Much of our modern understanding of *bushidō* has been shaped by the two key texts *Bushidō: The Soul of Japan* and the *Hagakure*, which we will examine in the next chapter. Once we have understood how these books have, to a certain degree, mythologized *bushidō* we can go on to investigate the real, historical *bushidō*.

CHAPTER TWO

SOURCES OF CONFUSION

There is a high level of interest in *bushidō* among non-Japanese-speaking people throughout the world. Most medieval Japanese texts on the subject remain untranslated and so the modern Western world has focused its attention on two major sources: *Bushidō: The Soul of Japan* by Nitobe Inazō (1900) and the *Hagakure* by Yamamoto Tsunetomo (c1716).

The concepts and ideas from these books have made their way into all secondary samurai books, as well as movies such as *Ghost Dog: The Way of the Samurai* (1999) and *The Last Samurai* (2003) and countless games, comics and social media platforms. While the spread of Japanese culture in all forms is a positive thing, our over-reliance on these two sources has given us an idealized and fictionalized view of the samurai. The purpose of this book is to reconnect us to the historical roots of *bushidō*.

BUSHIDŌ: THE SOUL OF JAPAN

> *It is not the weapon that wins, it is the spirit of the wearer.*
> Nitobe Inazō, *Bushidō: The Soul of Japan* (1900)

This classic text on the way of the samurai was published in 1900. The book tapped into a keen interest in the West in Japanese culture in general, and military culture in particular, which grew further with the outbreak of the Russo-Japanese War four years later.

The book's author, Nitobe Inazō (1862–1933), was born into a high-ranking samurai family in Nambu in the northern Japanese province of Mutsu. However, the abolition of the samurai class in the early 1870s meant that he was unable to follow the path of his ancestors. Instead, he entered the academic world, studying English literature, economics and political science first in Japan, in Sapporo and Tōkyō, and then at Johns Hopkins University in Baltimore, USA and Halle University in Germany, where he achieved a doctorate in agricultural economics.

Having converted to Christianity in Sapporo, Nitobe joined the Christian Society of Friends, better known as the Quakers, while in America. It was in this community that he met his future wife, Mary Elkinton. He combined his writing with a successful career as an administrator, diplomat and statesman, which included periods as a professor at Tokyo Imperial University, an Under-Secretary General of the League of Nations, a member of the House of Peers in the Japanese Imperial Parliament, and the head of the Japanese delegation at the Institute of Pacific Relations. In short, Nitobe was a learned man of considerable achievement and a samurai by birth, making him more than qualified to write about *bushidō*.

While discussing morality with a Belgian associate, Nitobe was asked to explain why the Japanese were so well behaved. It was this question that inspired him to write about samurai ethics. He started his famous book while on leave in Japan recovering from the effects of stress, and completed it in the USA.

Upon publication, *Bushidō: The Soul of Japan* sold respectably not only in the West but also in Japan, despite not being translated into Japanese until 1908. It attracted famous readers such as President Theodore Roosevelt, and a copy of the book was presented to the Japanese Emperor. However, notable critics included Uemura Masahisa, another Japanese Christian, who described the work as the Christianization of samurai ideals, and the esteemed British Japanologist Basil Hall Chamberlain, who observed that it was very nationalistic.

Chamberlain's comment was borne out by the explosion of interest in the book during the nationalistic fervour of 1930s Japan, when it became popular reading for Japanese soldiers. After Japan's defeat in the Second World War, the samurai fell from favour but the book continued to be a staple for those still interested in samurai ways, especially in the West. In fact, it enjoyed a second boom in the late twentieth century when Japanese culture came into vogue once again. However, by today's standards the book is a difficult read, with archaic language and a meandering approach. While it has a place on most samurai enthusiasts' shelves, its pages often remain clean and unturned.

Nitobe's seven virtues of bushidō

Having discussed the book's history and purpose, we will now turn to its contents. One of the major aspects of *Bushidō: The Soul of Japan* is Nitobe's itemization of seven core virtues. These 'seven virtues' or 'seven precepts' of *bushidō* became central to Japanese martial arts and can still be seen listed on *dōjō* walls across the world.

We will introduce these seven virtues below before going on to test them later in the book against the reality of life in samurai times.

Rectitude

Gi (義), translated as 'rectitude' in the original book, is to act in accordance with justice and righteousness in order to follow the correct path. Related terms include *gishi* (義士), 'a gentleman of rectitude', and *giri* (義理), 'a sense of duty'. The idea is that you should do what is right in all situations, even if it is something you do not want to do or that does not appear to be in your interests. For example, you must respect the obligations of duty to your family elders or your lord regardless of any personal objections or bad blood. This leads to a respect for age over talent. One example might be a young woman selling her virginity to help extricate her family from financial difficulty. (This was a big sacrifice to make, but not quite as big as it would have been in Europe at the time, where a woman had to be a virgin in order to marry. The sixteenth-century Portuguese missionary to Japan Luís Fróis wrote about the Japanese: 'Women never worry about virginity; without it they lose neither their honour nor the opportunity to wed.')

Courage

Yū (勇), translated as 'courage plus a spirit of daring and bearing', means doing what is correct in dangerous situations – fighting to avoid an unnecessary death but accepting death when it is time to die. This kind of courage might involve enduring hunger, pain, extreme temperatures or sleeplessness with equanimity, as well as visiting haunted places, witnessing executions, venturing out at night to touch decapitated heads and being brave in battle, especially at the time of death. Courage is to act against natural urges in difficult times.

Benevolence

Jin (仁), translated as 'benevolence', is to show compassion toward other people. The phrase *bushi no nasake* (武士の情け) means 'the tenderness of a warrior'. People in power have a duty to help those less fortunate, so that goodness and mercy are passed down the ladder of society. Whatever your status, it is important to be mindful of other people's suffering.

Politeness

Rei (礼), translated as 'politeness', can also mean respect and courtesy. At one level, politeness comes from a self-interested fear of causing offence, but at a deeper level it is inspired by a true respect for others. For example, in old Japan when people met in the street to talk, the etiquette was to take off your hat or lower your parasol so that everyone present would suffer equally in the heat of the day. Another example of respect is the Japanese tendency to downplay the quality of the gifts they give in order not to suggest that the recipient is unworthy of these offerings.

Sincerity

Sei (誠), translated as 'veracity and sincerity', is the necessary companion to respect. Politeness is hollow if it is not founded on inner truth and sincerity. If a samurai gives an oath to a god or swears upon their sword, that should be enough for any obligations to be fulfilled. Nitobe uses this section to discuss how the samurai would distance themselves from the merchant class: to pursue financial gain was held as abhorrent. He rounds off the section by pointing out that, while it is dishonourable to tell a lie, sometimes it is more polite in social situations not to stick *too* rigidly to the truth.

Honour

Meiyo (名誉), translated as 'honour' in the original book, can also denote a sense of pride and shame. Dishonour is like a scar upon a tree, which becomes more noticeable as the tree grows. Therefore, personal honour should be cultivated and actions that bring *renchishin* (廉恥心), 'shame', should be avoided. However, samurai should not let their pride get out of hand. Nitobe tells the story of a samurai who, when warned by a peasant that a flea has landed upon him, instantly cuts down the peasant, because he cannot bear to be likened to the kind of beast that fleas normally favour.

Loyalty

Chūgi (忠義) is translated as 'loyalty' in the original book. Loyalty to a lord takes precedence over loyalty to the family; clan loyalty is still extremely important, but the clan as a whole directs its loyalty to the lord and the wishes of the lord come before the wishes of the clan. Nitobe tells the story of a loyal samurai retainer who has his own son beheaded in place of his lord's son, who has been sentenced to death. When the inspector arrives to confirm that the execution has been carried out correctly, the samurai beholds his son's severed head and declares it to be that of his lord's son. This is given as an example of true samurai loyalty.

AN ALTERNATIVE VERSION OF *BUSHIDŌ*

The scholar Muro Kyūsō (1658–1734) also laid out certain guidelines for proper samurai behaviour. These are:

- Do not speak falsely.
- Do not work for selfish gain.
- Keep the mind focused and honest.
- Maintain a simple appearance.
- Be disciplined and polite in bearing.
- Do not fawn over superiors or be aggressive to juniors.
- Always keep a promise.
- Take note of other people's hardships.

The education of the samurai

Nitobe dedicates a full chapter to explaining how the samurai mindset was instilled in young members of the samurai class. A samurai education valued wisdom over intelligence (intelligence being clever insights and gathering of knowledge, and wisdom being the understanding of correct action and speech). The only mathematics of value was that relating to military logistics and family accounting; Nitobe observes that samurai should avoid profiteering and striving to acquire money and luxury. He believes that samurai should lead an austere lifestyle with an emphasis on diligence, wisdom and ethical conduct. In short, samurai children were taught to be stoic, to be loyal servants to their superiors and benevolent masters to their inferiors, and to have a core focus on personal development rather than on business. Nitobe maintains that morality and virtue were instilled within samurai from a young age; whether or not this was the case will become apparent by the end of this book.

Self-control

Nitobe also discusses the importance of self-control and the maintaining of an impassive outward appearance. Samurai should refrain from displaying any emotion: no joy, no anger, no sadness. No external stimuli should affect the way a samurai behaves; they should remain solid and secure in their bearing. Also, they should not make any public displays of affection such as kissing. Nitobe makes a wry comparison between Western and Japanese manners, observing that the men of the West men kiss their wives in public and beat them in private, whereas Japanese men beat their wives in public and kiss them in private. For the samurai, demonstrating discipline was a sign of strength but betraying affection showed weakness. Samurai must hide their true intentions; their speech must be guarded and they must show their thoughts and feelings only in the most extreme circumstances. Later on, we will explore the connection between samurai and emotion and discover to what level they did or did not withhold their feelings.

Suicide

Ritual suicide, known as *seppuku* or *hara-kiri*, was performed by a person called a *seppuku-nin*. They cut open their stomach with various prescribed movements before an appointed second known as a *kaishaku-nin* beheaded the *seppuku-nin* upon instruction or when the *kaishaku-nin* judged that the time was correct. This ceremony was an important part of samurai culture, having evolved from dramatic beginnings as a final gesture on the battlefield into a highly ritualized form of self-execution.

Seppuku was performed either voluntarily – for example, as a response to a shameful situation or as a protest – or compulsorily, as a more honourable punishment than a standard execution. It was believed to be a fundamental part of samurai culture during the middle and later stages of the samurai period. We will explore later the circumstances in which *seppuku* actually took place in historical Japan.

A SPECIAL PLACE IN HELL

As a Christian, Nitobe must have had conflicting feelings about the samurai approach to suicide, which was viewed by his adopted religion not as an act of honour but as a shameful sin. Referring to Dante's vision of hell in his *Divine Comedy*, in which the second ring of the seventh level is reserved for suicides, Nitobe observes that this part of hell must be overflowing with samurai. Dante goes on to give a vivid description of the punishment meted out on the souls of suicides, which, he reports, are turned into old trees and attacked and fed upon by harpies.

The flower of the nation

Nitobe concludes his short book by pointing out that while the samurai, even at their height, made up only a small proportion of the Japanese population, their behaviour and ethical codes filtered down to the masses. Even now that the samurai have died out, *bushidō* still flows through society as a virtuous current.

He also makes a contrast between England's emblem the rose, which comes into bloom gradually and withers slowly, and Japan's cherry blossom, which appears with striking speed and dies just as quickly. This he sees as a reflection of the samurai's readiness to die young for the greater good compared to – in his view – a Western warrior's preoccupation with survival into old age. He views Western culture as being more individualistic than Japanese culture. In Japan, all people are set up to serve each other, out of loyalty to the family, the Emperor and the nation, in a single flowing system that favours groups rather than individuals.

Nitobe's work shaped the twentieth-century view of the Japanese warrior and has been the go-to source for all books and documentaries on *bushidō* for over a century. But how close is his analysis of samurai culture to the reality of historical samurai behaviour? This will become evident as we proceed.

THE *HAGAKURE*

The *Hagakure* scroll was compiled in around 1716 by a samurai called Yamamoto Tsunetomo, also known as Jōchō, who lived in the Saga domain of the southern Japanese island of Kyūshū. The full title of the scroll, *Hagakure Kikigaki* (葉隠聞書), can be read in various ways: 'sayings which are hidden below leaves', 'sayings from below the shade of trees' or 'sayings from the land of the *hagakushi* fruit'. The original, which has never been translated in full, contains eleven books in total, including later additions by the samurai Tashiro Tsuramoto, who compiled the book into its current form.

The *Hagakure* was not well known in its own day, being just one of thousands of works by samurai of the Edo period (1603–1868). It only became famous two centuries later, in the early 1900s, following in the wake of Nitobe's *Bushidō: The Soul of Japan*. During the 1930s, Japan's nationalistic government seized upon the *Hagakure*'s message '*bushidō to iu wa shinu koto to mitsuketari*' – 'the way of the warrior is found in death' – a sentiment that fitted the prevailing idea of ultimate sacrifice for the Emperor.

Parts of the scroll were first published in 1906, but a version with the most famous sections did not appear until 1935, at the height of Japanese militarism. An annotated edition followed in 1940, along with a three-volume set that was popular among the soldiers of the Japanese army.

After Japan's defeat in the Second World War, nationalism went into retreat and things samurai were abandoned. The *Hagakure*, with its emphasis on self-sacrifice and avoidance of the shame of a 'dog's death', was now seen as outdated and barbaric. However, it is important to remember that this manuscript reflected a mid-Edo-period mentality of service without question. The *Hagakure*'s original authors cannot be blamed for the way it was exploited to fire up a now-subdued military class with the daring actions of past generations. Therefore, it should be treated as a serious work of samurai literature, but it should not be taken out of the context in which it was written, no matter how famous it became after the fact.

The Hagakure *in context*

Modern scholars criticize the *Hagakure* for promoting a 'death corps' mentality in which fanatical loyalty and instinctive action are favoured over more logical reflection. The following quotations from the William Scott-Wilson translation of the *Hagakure* appear to support this assessment.

> *Although it stands to reason that a samurai should be mindful of the way of the samurai, it would seem that we are all negligent. Consequently, if someone were to ask, 'What is the true meaning of the way of the samurai?' the person who would be able to answer promptly is rare. This is because it has not been established in one's mind beforehand. From this, one's unmindfulness of the way can be known.*

> *The way of the samurai is found in death. When it comes to either/ or, there is only the quick choice of death. It is not particularly difficult. Be determined and advance. To say that dying without reaching one's aim is to die a dog's death is the frivolous way of sophisticates. When pressed with the choice of life or death, it is not necessary to gain one's aim.*

> *To die without gaining one's aim is a dog's death and fanaticism. But there is no shame in this. This is the substance of the way of the samurai. If by setting one's heart right every morning and evening, one is able to live as though his body were already dead, he gains freedom in the way.*

> *Thus, the way of the samurai is, morning after morning, the practice of death.*
>
> *Hagakure* (1716)

Sayings such as these have filtered down from the *Hagakure* and into documentaries and feature films. This, coupled with the exploits of fanatical Japanese soldiers during the Second World War, has fed the modern media caricature of a samurai death cult. Always keep in mind, though, that these isolated quotations do not give a balanced picture of the *Hagakure* and that the *Hagakure* does not give a balanced picture of the samurai class as a whole.

Those who focus on the fanatical parts of the *Hagakure* and allow them to run wild fail to take into account the historical context in which the scroll was compiled. We have to consider that it dates from a period of prolonged peace, the last major samurai action having taken place about 100 years earlier. The work reflects the thoughts of a real Japanese warrior who felt that his samurai contemporaries were no longer adhering to the chivalric code. Yamamoto was attempting to restore the moral framework of what he saw as the golden age of the samurai.

A summary of the Hagakure

The *Hagakure* is a loosely structured collection of sayings and ideas outlining the correct ways of the samurai, coupled with moral tales that exemplify correct or incorrect behaviour. Unlike *Bushidō: The Soul of Japan*, it does not present a clear set of precepts. The following breaks down Yamamoto's understanding of *bushidō* into four sections: personal traits, clan responsibilities, things deemed correct and things deemed incorrect.

Personal traits

- Be prepared to die for the lord without question.
- Focus on selflessness.
- Renounce self-interest.
- Constantly polish your character.
- Engage in correct marriage and relationships.
- Know that mistakes are acceptable if they are used to educate.
- Do not stick to strong opinions if they turn out to be wrong.
- Cultivate an impeccable personal appearance.
- Imitate great deeds of the past.
- Use positive role models.
- Have a steady mind.
- Always conduct yourself correctly.
- Be sincere in politeness.
- Use old stories and episodes to correct mistakes.
- If you want something doing, do it yourself.

- Build up courage by always trying to be better and outdo the best in any given field.
- Do not be led into difficult conversations on complex topics.
- Focus and pay attention in all conversations.
- Be confident when giving speeches and in casual conversation.
- Be proficient in literature and writing.
- Study the way in all matters and subjects.
- Push through sickness and remain functional at all times.
- Make decisions quickly.
- Acquaint yourself with people of knowledge and learn from them.
- Set yourself specific goals.
- Take all criticism with grace and politeness.
- Greet people with enthusiasm, as though it is the first time you have met.
- Endure suffering.
- Never drink too much.
- Engage in the tea ceremony to purify your body and mind.
- Do not let an external situation affect your mood.
- Display intelligence, humanity and courage.
- Maintain an untroubled expression, even in the gravest situations.
- Think before you speak.
- Find things in life that you enjoy and do them.
- Value truth above all things.
- Know that fanaticism is acceptable if the goal is correct.
- Recite and chant the name of your master as you would a saint.

Clan responsibilities
- Have absolute loyalty to the lord.
- Carry out obligations to ancestors and gods.
- Come together to make decisions so that the best ideas can be heard.
- Work as a team and correct each other's mistakes.
- Maintain healthy clan finances.
- Know that even untalented members of the clan have worth as long as they are loyal.

- If someone is unhappy, make a serious but understated attempt to make them happy.
- Always help people who have helped you.
- Never become adopted or marry into another family just for money.
- Keep and maintain military gear and make sure it is all practical and usable.
- Save clan funds for times of war.
- Never speak ill of the dead.
- Praise and respect the name of the family.
- Be mindful of fire hazards within your property.
- Follow a system of appointments based on merit not favouritism.
- Study your own family history.
- Make sure you understand the area of expertise your family is engaged in.
- Recognize that even a small amount of ability will appear great when put next to people of inability.
- Know that even the greatest houses come to an end, so if your clan is to fall make sure it goes out in style.

Things deemed correct
- Exuding a quiet strength
- Meeting any situation with direct action
- Rushing headlong into situations
- Dying in the achievement of your aim
- Gaining wisdom and talent
- Valuing the action of a person of no reputation or apparent skill who dies for a cause
- Giving advice in the correct way, at the correct time and for the correct reasons
- Being trusted by others
- Looking at people directly
- Rising early, working all day and then retiring at night
- Properly predicting future outcomes from today's evidence
- Studying and being competent in the martial and military arts
- Being first in battle

- Dying facing the front
- Retiring when it is clear you are too old or out of touch
- Pushing any correct action to the limit to show proper determination
- Putting the life of the lord above the lives of loved ones
- Keeping it simple – if things get complicated, just start killing
- Adjusting to the times you live in while never losing sight of the old ways
- Correcting your mistakes
- If society goes into a period of frenzy, retiring to your home until the tumult has blown over
- Bursting at the chest with pride in doing your duty

Things deemed incorrect

- Having skill and talent without loyalty and purpose
- Attaching yourself to a new lord or person of power when your previous lord retires or dies
- Failing to act correctly at the moment of death
- Using vulgar language
- Having strange mannerisms
- Valuing intellect over wisdom
- Incorrectly predicting future outcomes based on today's evidence
- Being found dead with unseemly attire or hygiene
- Focusing on money or sex
- Being observably relaxed in public (this will lead people to think you are lax at all times)
- Turning martial arts into an artistic display
- Verbally attacking people who are clearly under stress
- Instilling phobias and incorrect responses or traits in children
- Talking about people behind their back
- Being careless in any matter
- Getting carried away by superstitions
- Betraying fear in your voice
- Believing silly stories or legends
- Procrastinating

- Avoiding doing something through fear of blame
- Disrespecting the ways of Buddha
- Saying that Buddhism should take precedence over *bushidō*

These lists constitute the main themes in the *Hagakure* when the individual stories and anecdotes are stripped down to their bare meaning. What remains is to compare these points with other documents from across the samurai ages, accounts by Western travellers and the actual actions of historical samurai, in order to assess the extent to which the *Hagakure* is a true representation of *bushidō* for all ages in Japan.

Now we will set aside our discussion of the mythologized version of *bushidō* that has travelled to the Western world and move to an investigation of Japanese history and society. We will use as many primary sources as possible and logical debate to paint a true picture of how the samurai thought that they should act and how they actually did act.

THE SAMURAI WORLD

I fancy that there are no people in the world more punctilious about their honour than the Japanese, for they will not put up with a single insult or even a word spoken in anger.

Writings of Alessandro Valignano (16th century)

To understand *bushidō* you must first understand Japanese culture. The following two chapters will briefly set the stage for a better understanding of life in samurai times so that the actions of the samurai can be compared to what was expected of the people of Japan.

CHAPTER THREE

FOUNDATIONS OF SOCIETY

The samurai were as much a product of society as they were of the battlefield. In this chapter we will explore the defining features of Japanese life during the samurai era. How was the country governed? What role did religion play in shaping behaviour? How were the social classes organized? Where did the samurai fit in to this structure? How did the authorities maintain order?

KEY TERMS AND CONCEPTS

In this introductory section, we will touch upon some of the prevailing customs and beliefs in Japanese society during the samurai age. Some of them fell out of favour, but all of them influenced how the samurai thought, and continue to influence how Japanese people see the world today.

神国

Shinkoku

Land of the gods

Shintō gods protect the land of Japan, with the Emperor serving as heaven's representative on earth. The people believe that if they pay respect to the emperor and to the gods, heaven will guide and protect Japan.

護国の神

Gokoku no kami

Protector gods

These are gods that are given the task of watching over Japan. Some notable mortals were deified after death and joined the ranks of the protector gods.

神祇崇拝

Jingi sūhai

Worship of native gods

Worshipping the panoply of Japanese gods in their many forms binds the whole of society together. It gives the Japanese a shared understanding of their country's mythical past and unites them as 'the children of the gods'.

祖先崇拝

Sosen sūhai

Ancestor worship

The relationship between the living and the dead is particularly strong in Japanese culture. Families regularly worship and interact with the spirits of deceased ancestors, invoking their protection and guidance in family matters.

天皇

Ten'nō

The Emperor

The Emperor has not held significant political power in Japan since the twelfth century. However, his position as the spiritual leader of the nation, the link between the gods and the people, has always been unassailable. This spiritual role, akin to that of the Pope, is reflected in the Japanese term for emperor, *ten'nō*, which means 'heaven's emperor'. As a direct descendant of the gods, the Emperor could never be killed and replaced by any random samurai, although at various points in Japan's history there was competition and rivalry between different branches of the imperial line. The best any ambitious warlord could do was to become a *shōgun*, the de facto ruler of the nation, or marry his family into the imperial family and beget the next emperor; the warrior Taira no Kiyomori, for example, achieved political power in this way.

王法

Ōhō

Imperial law

The Emperor is the focal point of all Japan and the country's laws and customs emanate from him.

大義名分

Taigimeibun

Loyalty to the sovereign

All people of Japan owe obedience and loyalty to the Emperor. In previous times, the same degree of loyalty was also shown to the *shōgun*, a powerful samurai general originally appointed by the Emperor to lead the army, but who in later times undertook the overall rule of Japan.

国家守護

Kokka shugo

Military protection of the state

This concept held that the Japanese state needed strong military backing to earn the respect of other nations. It placed the samurai as the powers behind the imperial throne.

国人

Kokujin

Warriors outside of government control

Although the imperial house in Kyōto was seen as the spiritual capital of the land, many Japanese regions were ruled by samurai warlords and the Emperor had little or no direct control over them. This tension between central authority and regional autonomy was the cause of numerous wars during the samurai period.

日本語

Nihongo

Japanese language

The spoken Japanese language is native to Japan, but the written alphabet is based on Chinese characters known as *kanji*. These are supported by a series of simplified phonetics to allow the *kanji* to be spoken in Japanese. In Japan, language is a powerful signifier of hierarchy. Complex honorifics and rules govern interactions between people of different social classes and ages. Various linguistic structures are designed to humble the speaker and elevate the listener. Impersonal grammatical constructions are favoured; they can be ambiguous, but they avoid giving offence.

護国

Gokoku

Buddhism as protector of the state

Since its arrival from India via China and Korea in the sixth century BC, Buddhism has coexisted happily with the native Japanese religion of Shintō. The Shintō and Buddhist gods – some of whom have coalesced into the same figures – are seen as guardians of the lands of Japan.

仏法

Buppō

Buddhist law

Buddhism provides a code of conduct and philosophy of life and society that all Japanese people follow.

新規

Shinki

New ideas

Japan is a culture based on precedents. Historically, new ideas, referred to as *shinki* (新規), were seen as going against the old order of things. While new ideas in certain areas such as warfare might be viewed favourably, it was generally accepted that the ancient ways were best because they maintained social stability.

身分

Mibun

Birthright

The concept of *mibun* (身分), 'the circumstances of one's birth', is said to have come from China in the Song period (960–1279) and was a significant idea in Japan. Power generally went to those of the right social class who had good family connections; it was a case of who your father or grandfather was or who you were connected to.

High-born samurai using their ancestry to justify their right to govern helped to reduce social mobility and cemented the ruling powers in position. For example, the position of *shōgun* was restricted to descendants of Minamoto no Yoritomo, the first *shōgun* of the Kamakura era. Consequently, the low-born Toyotomi Hideyoshi could not be the *shōgun*; instead, he was known as *kampaku* (関白), a formal assistant of the Emperor – a position which still required a connection to the Fujiwara clan. In reality he was *shōgun* in all but name. Despite suffering in this way from the circumstances of his own birth, Toyotomi Hideyoshi sought to restore *mibun* to bring an end to the chaos of the Warring States period.

Other terms associated with *mibun* include: *seshū* (世襲), 'hereditary power'; *katoku* (家督), 'the family estate'; and *atome* (跡目), 'successorship'.

贈答

Zōtō

Giving and receiving

In Japan, gift giving was – and still is – an important part of life in general and politics in particular. To not give appropriate gifts could be damaging to a person's interests. People in lower-paid jobs but with a high degree of control over certain aspects of the lives of high-ranking people were open to receiving gifts and bribes for their help in making connections. The *Bushidō Shoshinshū* manual relates the old Japanese saying 'white jackets and officials are best when new', meaning that administrators become more corrupt the longer they are in position.

多神教

Tashinkyō

Polytheism

Japan is traditionally a spiritually inclusive country, which allows people to make their own choice from the multiple deities available to worship. A variety of religions have been imported from across the world and coexist peacefully alongside the indigenous Japanese religion of Shintō. However, although samurai were in theory free to choose their own religion, in practice they often followed the example of the provincial warlord. There have been occasional religious wars, such as Oda Nobunaga's fight against the Sohei monks of the Tendai sect culminating in the siege of Mount Hiei in 1579, but the issue at stake in most conflicts has been political power.

一夫多妻

Ippu tasai

Polygamy

At certain points of Japanese history it was acceptable to have multiple 'wives' (depending on the definition) or at least mistresses. Divorce was also permitted and, unlike in many other cultures, there was no shame in a woman having sex before marriage. Indeed, a girl's virginity was a commodity for sale in many cases. Attitudes toward homosexuality fluctuated from one era to another, but it does not appear to have been a major taboo at any time and seems to have become more common during the Edo period.

五逆

Gogyaku

The five deadly sins

The following list of offences are the ones considered most grave in Japanese Buddhism.

- Killing a father
- Killing a mother
- Killing a saintly figure

- Injuring a Buddha
- Disrupting a community of monks

CENTRES OF INFLUENCE

The capital of Japan has always been defined by the location of the imperial palace, the focus of court life. Since 1868, this has been Tōkyō, or Edo as the city was formerly known. However, for more than a thousand years before that, the Emperor resided in Kyōto. Even though Kyōto is no longer the capital, it remains the spiritual and cultural heart of Japan.

Kyōto's layout was based on that of the city of Chang'an (present-day Xi'an), the capital of China for most of the Tang Dynasty (618–907). It is aligned and positioned according to the ways of *feng shui* and is built on a grid system. It was the home of aristocrats, lesser nobility, the imperial court and high-ranking samurai. Kyōto has no fortifications, yet it has seen multiple insurrections, civil wars, arson attacks and inter-clan blood feuds.

The city's status has risen and fallen in line with that of the Emperor. During the Kamakura shōgunate (1185–1333), the *shōgun* Minamoto no Yoritomo established a rival military capital in the eastern city of Kamakura. Before then, the Emperor had free rein to appoint regional governors from among the aristocracy and samurai of noble blood, but Yoritomo forced the Emperor to award positions to his chosen men. Power shifted both from the Emperor to the *shōgun* and from Kyōto to Kamakura.

While the Emperor never regained his political authority, Kyōto became the undisputed capital of Japan once again in 1333. This is when Ashikaga Takauji overthrew the Kamakura shōgunate, founded the Ashikaga shōgunate in its place and moved the centre of government back to the imperial capital. For the next 500 years or more, any samurai with serious political ambitions had to know his way around Kyōto and the ranking system that played out there.

A notable example of the use of rank as a power play can be seen in the treatment of the sixteenth-century samurai Hōjō Ujinori when he visited Kyōto. As a punishment for defying central command in Kyōto, he was forced to take an extremely lowly seating position, well below his actual status. Toyotomi Hideyoshi, the Chancellor of the Realm, offered Ujinori a more fitting position at court among his peers in return for his compliance. When faced with a choice between autonomy in his regional base and respect in the capital, Ujinori went for the latter. This is just one illustration of how Kyōto remained the focus of politically minded warriors for most of samurai history.

THE SAMURAI CLASS

Who could and who could not be considered as a samurai was a line that shifted over time. Originally, the only people who had the right to call themselves samurai were the *jizamurai* (地侍), 'landed country samurai'. There were few, if any, city samurai in the early days other than those who served at the court of Kyōto. Certain categories of samurai such as the *dōshin* (同心), 'half-samurai', and *koshi* (古士), 'displaced samurai', were originally considered as samurai proper, but as times changed they were relegated to a station below samurai status. Similarly, there is still some debate over whether *ashigaru* (足軽), 'foot soldiers', were considered as peasants or warriors as they evolved into a permanent force.

Although in the main the samurai was a hereditary class built on clan structure, examples of people promoted into the ranks of the samurai were not uncommon. One of the most famous of these self-made samurai is Toyotomi Hideyoshi, who ended up as ruler of all Japan through his own merits. Another example is Suruga Jirō, a hunter's son who became one of Minamoto no Yoshitsune's loyal retainers, a reward for his service as a guide when Yoshitsune attacked a position called Ichi no Tan from the mountain slopes behind the fortress.

Consider also Ōkubo Nagayasu, who started out as a *nōh* actor before being elevated into the samurai and becoming a valued warlord serving the Tokugawa family. However, he converted to Christianity and was implicated after his death in a conspiracy to bring foreign troops into the country and overthrow the Tokugawa. As punishment for their father's apparent treachery, Ōkubo's sons were ordered to commit suicide.

Then there was the low-ranking samurai Toda Issai, who was promoted by Tokugawa Ieyasu after the battle of Sekigahara. This came about because Tokugawa Ieyasu was unhappy with his son Hidetada for arriving late to the battle because he stopped on the way to attempt to capture a castle. It emerged that Toda Issai had advised against delaying their march, but his words had not been heeded because he was not of a high enough status. Therefore, Tokugawa Ieyasu decided to raise his income from 3,000 to 30,000 *koku*, the level of an independent warlord, so that in future his voice would be heard.

Ironically, it was that great self-made samurai Toyotomi Hideyoshi who laid down the idea of the samurai as an exclusively hereditary caste, thereby limiting the scope for social mobility. There were still some examples of people being promoted to samurai or they might be awarded samurai-like status symbols such as the right to wear a sword or have a surname, and in some cases samurai status could be bought. What can be said is that the line between samurai and non-samurai was sometimes loosely defined and at other times fiercely restricted. You could be born as a samurai and lose that status, or start out as a peasant and become a samurai.

NON-JAPANESE SAMURAI

European traders and missionaries, accompanied by African sailors, started to arrive in Japan in the sixteenth century. There were also immigrants from the Asian mainland. Although the overwhelming majority of samurai were Japanese, a small number came from these foreign settlers.

Notable examples include William Adams, who arrived in Japan from London in 1600. Not only did he become a samurai, but he rose to the status of *hatamoto*, a close retainer of Tokugawa Ieyasu. Yasuke was an African who also rose to the rank of samurai and served next to the great warlord Oda Nobunaga in his campaigns and at his death.

The fact that these foreign men rose to such prominence shows that the rank of samurai was open to anyone who had the ability to achieve it.

RELIGION

The religions that set Japan's moral foundation played an important role in the development of samurai ethics. Before *bushidō* there was Buddhism, before samurai self-sacrifice there was Shintō, before crusades of power there was Confucianism, and before samurai domination there was Daoism. Religion and philosophy shaped the samurai as much as warcraft.

Shintō

Japan's only indigenous religion, Shintō connects the people to their landscape and their ancestors. It binds Japanese culture together, providing a link to a land created by the gods, with a god-ruler on the throne. In Shintō there is no scripture, no priests, no hierarchy of holiness, but there is divinity everywhere – in every tree, rock, river and stone. The mountains hold sacred spirits called *kami*, the water and the land too. Japan is full of divine magic.

As well as connecting the people to the land, Shintō also binds them to the Emperor and promotes loyalty to the nation. Historically Shintō has been interconnected with other religions such as Daoism, Buddhism and Confucianism, which came to Japan later, and was only separated from them after the end of the samurai era. For the samurai, Shintō was one strand in the weave of Japanese religious culture.

Daoism

Known in Japan as Dōkyo (道教), Daoism is a Chinese religion-philosophy which strives to understand the universe and the laws of nature. It can be divided into a philosophical branch, based on the writings of Lao Tzu, and a religious or magical branch, which deals with doctrine, rituals and spells.

Overall, Daoism promotes a creation theory based on the complementary yet opposing elements of *yin* and *yang* (known in Japanese as *in* and *yō*) and the five phases of earth, fire, metal, water and wood, which together create everything within the universe. The whole of creation, known as the 'ten thousand things', is then subject to either a destructive or creative relationship.

Daoism is often overshadowed by Japan's three main religions, Buddhism, Confucianism and Shintō, and it can be difficult to separate Daoist belief from Shintō and Confucianism. However, Daoist influence can be found in many aspects of Japanese life and it was instrumental in the development of Onmyōdo (陰陽道), a wide-ranging system of natural science encompassing areas such as astronomy, divination and the measuring of time.

Buddhism

Buddhism consists of the teachings of the Buddha, Siddhartha Gautama, who lived in India in the sixth century BC. The religion spread both east and west, reaching Japan via China and Korea in the sixth century AD.

Japanese Buddhism comes from the Mahayana branch of the religion, which in turn divided into multiple sects. Tendai was seen as the sect for the royal family, Shingon for the nobility, Zen for the samurai and Jōdo for the masses. All sects and branches share certain key beliefs: that life is a struggle, desire is to be avoided and perfection lies in reducing karmic debt until the soul is released from the cycle of birth and death and can migrate to nirvana.

Beyond the commonly understood ideas of Buddhism, there are concepts more specific to Japan and of particular importance to the samurai. One important example is *mappō* (末法), which is the end times when Buddhist teachings are in decline and the world is plunged into hate. The Japanese believe that this period began after the first millennium AD and that we are still living through it. Another is the idea that all dead should be honoured equally, whether friend or foe.

The ways of Buddhism were often taken up by the samurai, and it is interesting to note that some famous warriors were known not by their given names but by Buddhist titles they had been awarded. For example, Takeda Shingen (武田信玄) was originally called Takeda Harunobu (武田晴信) and Uesugi Kenshin (上杉謙信) was previously known as Uesugi Terutora (上杉輝虎). Furthermore, they were often depicted in white cowls such as would be worn by Buddhist monks. Takeda Shingen himself said, 'Pay proper reverence to the gods and study Zen.' The samurai were always aware of the karmic debt that killing incurred and they knew better than anyone the reality of suffering. However, it would appear that they did not always care enough about Buddhist principles to curb some of their more ferocious instincts.

Warrior-monks

Before the unification of Japan in 1600, Buddhist temples were heavily populated by military monks not dissimilar to the samurai. They were prone to the kind of behaviour not generally associated with pious 'men of the cloth'.

According to the *Heike Monogatari* text, the monks of the temples of Kōfukuji and Enryakuji were scuffling to place their temple plaques in the most prestigious position. Two armoured monks from Kōfukuji – one named Kannonbō, who was dressed in armour with black laces, and the other named Seishibō, who was dressed in armour with green laces – smashed the plaque of the rival temple to settle the matter. The monks from Enryakuji, shocked at this abuse of their holy plaque, retreated to contemplate their next move. Later, they charged down from their mountain in full armour and made an attack, sending the city of Kyōto into panic.

Another example of violent behaviour by monks can be seen in a letter that the samurai official Sakai Uta-no-kami wrote to some monks after they had broken into the house of one Suganuma Tōjūrō and beaten his family and attendants almost to death. The points of the letter are abbreviated below:

- Holy men should help people, but you have become militaristic.
- Beating women and children is not a rule of your order.
- You did this out of retaliation, but retaliation is not a Buddhist virtue.
- Breaking, entering and robbery are not Buddhist virtues.
- Your temple takes its name from a past emperor, whom you discredit by your behaviour.
- A man who shaves his head and puts on monk's robes but is not holy on the inside is like a bat trying to be a bird.

As these limited examples suggest, the line between samurai and monk was often blurred. Indeed, some samurai took on holy orders and brought their military skills with them. During certain periods, military monasteries constituted a real threat to samurai warlords. In the sixteenth century, Oda Nobunaga spent over ten years putting down the well-armed and well-defended Sōhei monks of Ishiyama-Honganji. This helps break down the modern notion of peaceful monks and noble warriors, and instead allows for the understanding of a much more complicated relationship between warriors, holy men, religious ideals, religious realities and the economic and political power of armed monasteries.

Zen

Zen is a form of Buddhism that focuses on meditation and the search for the nature of the self. Its emphasis on clarity of mind appealed to the samurai. Zen taught the moral virtue of not looking back once a decision had been made, alleviated the fear of death and promoted the development of an iron will, all of which were important mental attributes for a professional soldier.

Like other forms of Buddhism, Zen came from China and other parts of the Asian mainland, although it arrived later, not reaching Japan until the end of the twelfth century. It did not flourish in the imperial capital of Kyōto, but instead found a willing audience in the military seat of power at Kamakura. This surge in Zen gave rise to many core aspects of Japanese culture today, such as the idea of *wabi-sabi*, which is a mournful love of the rustic, the tea ceremony and the art of flower arranging.

The samurai embrace of Zen has led to the idea that they were stoic and centred in all that they did and that they never displayed their emotions. However, there are countless instances of samurai not conforming to that stereotype.

Take, for example, the rivalry between the Christian samurai Augustin Konishi and the famed warrior Katō Kiyomasa during the Japanese invasion of Korea in 1592. This pair were at loggerheads from the start. Konishi was first to arrive on the Korean beaches and was supposed to wait for the other forces, but instead began to race toward Seoul. Kiyomasa, furious, took a different route – samurai armies normally split up in this way – trying to beat him. The two arrived at a meeting point and argued as to who would go forward first, because to be first in battle was a great honour.

In the end, Konishi won the honour of facing the Korean resistance at a nearby river, although it is possible that Kiyomasa let him go first in the hope he would fail. Far from failing, Konishi slaughtered the Koreans. (When he tried to hold a ceremonial head inspection, the issue of too many decapitated heads and not enough time forced them to take only noses.)

At the next military meeting of these two, Kiyomasa baited Konishi by calling him a 'tradesman', implying he was low in rank or ability; the incensed Konishi started to draw his sword and had to be held back by his retainers. Interestingly, Kiyomasa was himself from a humble background, but by marrying into the family of Toyotomi Hideyoshi he was able to move in the correct circles.

It has been said that Konishi then destroyed all the boats in the area after he crossed the next river to stop Kiyomasa getting across (however, this may have been done by the Koreans) and that after Konishi had entered Seoul he embarrassed Kiyomasa by making his troops wait outside the city gates. It has even been postulated that Konishi informed the Chinese enemy – who were protecting Korea at the time – of Kiyomasa's movements to stop him from gaining more success after he had taken north-east Korea.

Konishi also incurred the wrath of Toyotomi Hideyoshi in his peace negotiations with the Chinese, during which he played the two sides off against each other (perhaps in order to stop Chinese reprisals on Japan for invading Korean soil). He told the Chinese envoys that Hideyoshi accepted the Chinese emperor as a superior and told Hideyoshi that the Chinese accepted him as a superior. Konishi's subterfuge came to light several years later when Chinese officials came to Japan to award Hideyoshi the title of 'king of Japan'. According to the Portuguese missionary João Rodrigues, Hideyoshi 'flew into such a rage that he was beside himself, he foamed at the mouth and ranted until his head smoked like it was in flames'. Hideyoshi ordered the destruction of various Korean cities as a reprisal for this slight and Konishi narrowly avoided execution.

Thus, the image of the Zen-like samurai all calmly obeying their superiors is not truly historical; tempers often flared.

ZEN AND THE ART OF WARFARE

Adherence to Buddhism and Shintō had always been a cornerstone of Japanese military life. This connection was made explicit in examples of samurai who undertook their training in the grounds of temples and shrines. However, the melding of the martial arts with Zen to the extent it is known today was a much later phenomenon, which started to be seen around the beginning of the seventeenth century. One of the most influential works from this period was Yagyū Munenori's 1632 manual on swordsmanship, the *Heihō Kadensho*. Comprising two main sections, the Life-Giving Sword and the Death-Dealing Sword, the manual owes a great deal to the ideas of a Zen monk named Takuan with whom Munenori corresponded extensively. As pointed out by Satō Hiroaki, who translated the *Heihō Kadensho* into English, the manual's philosophical approach to swordsmanship contrasted starkly with the more practical, militaristic writings of preceding generations.

Confucianism

The study of the teachings of Confucius is a Chinese philosophical system based on understanding human reason, proper manners and ethical systems. It advocates the notion of the 'superior human' and emphasizes strict social hierarchy and loyalty to the leader. Another influential aspect of Confucianism is the idea of taking the middle path between two extremes.

Confucianism was first introduced to Japan early on in Japanese history, then a second wave of so-called neo-Confucian teachings arrived in the Kamakura era during the twelfth and thirteenth centuries. However, it was not until the Tokugawa government officially adopted Confucianism to control the masses in the seventeenth century that it began to have a significant effect on everyday Japanese life. Previously, men and women and members of different social classes had been free to interact with each other to a certain extent, but Confucian values made society more rigid and closed.

THE FIVE RELATIONSHIPS

Confucianism is founded on strict notions of hierarchy within families and within society as a whole. There are five principal relationships defined in Confucianism:

1. Ruler to subject
2. Father to son
3. Elder brother to younger brother
4. Husband to wife
5. Socially higher to socially lower

In each relationship, the former party is viewed as superior to the latter and each person has certain responsibilities to the other. For example, in the relationship between ruler and subject, the ruler must be benevolent and the subject loyal.

Christianity

Christianity is often overlooked as a religion of Japan and the samurai, but for a relatively brief period it became important in Japanese history. With the arrival of the Europeans in the mid-sixteenth century, the conversion of the country was underway. After a slow start, the missionaries eventually converted hundreds of thousands of Japanese, and entire provinces took up the cross. People identified the immortal Christian soul with the Shintō *kami* spirit. However, the concept of eternal damnation was harder to sell, as it contradicted the Buddhist idea of rebirth.

The main reason, though, that Christianity did not thrive in Japan like other imported religions is that it threatened national sovereignty. Japanese Christians owed allegiance not only to the Emperor but also to the Pope. Therefore, as in the case of the Christian samurai Ōkubo Nagayasu, they were forever under suspicion of plotting with foreign invaders.

It was not long before the great persecutions began. The first martyrdom took place in 1556 when a woman was beheaded for praying to a cross; in 1597, twenty-six martyrs were crucified in Nagasaki. In 1612, fifty-two Christians were burned at the stake in Kyōto to mark the banning of the religion in Japan, and a further fifty people suffered the same fate in Edo nine years later. The culmination came in 1637 and 1638 with the Shimabara Uprising, in which tens of thousands of Christian rebels were killed. Foreigners were expelled from Japan and the country entered a period of isolation from the rest of the world, which lasted for more than two centuries.

The Christian missionaries did not help their cause by criticizing certain Japanese customs, such as sodomy and infanticide. The sixteenth-century samurai Ōuchi Yoshitaka is said to have politely listened to the sermons of Jesuits until they started to reproach homosexuality, at which point he walked away.

SOURCES

They said that committing sodomy with a boy did not cause him any discredit or his relatives dishonour, because he had no virginity to lose and in any case sodomy was not a sin.
Writings of Juan Fernandez (16th century)

But even worse is their great dissipation in the sin that does not bear mentioning [sodomy]. This is regarded so lightly that both the boys and the men who consort with them brag and talk about it openly without trying to cover the matter up. This is because the bonzes [Buddhist monks] teach that not only is it not a sin but that it is something quite natural and virtuous.
Writings of Alessandro Valignano (16th century)

> *For it is permitted that parents may sell their own children or a husband his wife, if it is necessary to fulfil his wants [because of large taxation] but the most horrible thing of all is that parents may kill their own children as they are born if they have not the ability to nourish them, or a master his slave at pleasure, without incurring any danger of the law, something which I have known committed by the parents of two young children since I came to Hirado.*
>
> Diary of Richard Cocks (1615–22)

> *They have the most peculiar form of government in the world. Each man enjoys absolute power over his family and servants and he may cut them down or kill them, justly or otherwise, as he pleases, without having to give an account to anybody. And although he may be under the authority of another lord, he is allowed to kill his own children and servants because such matters are not the concern of his lord.*
>
> Writings of Alessandro Valignano (16th century)

The sixteenth-century Jesuit Francis Xavier was careful not to condemn the Japanese out of hand. He sent only very high-level missionaries who could turn a blind eye to customs that the Church detested but could not change. Xavier's successor, Father Cosme de Torres, appears to have shared Xavier's attitude, reporting to Rome that the samurai valued honour above all things.

In the end, Christianity could not be allowed to take root, because the conversion of a single warlord could mean thousands of his subjects converting, which would diminish the power of the Emperor and cause too many problems. Thus ended Christianity in Japan.

Chapter Three

FEUDALISM

> *On account of trade and peace, many people have become rich,*
> *although the ordinary folk and peasants have become impoverished*
> *by the taxes they have been forced to pay.*
>
> Writings of João Rodrigues (late 16th/early 17th century)

The term feudalism can have a very specific meaning, but here it is used in the broad sense of a social hierarchy where overlords allot land in exchange for military service or other services or monies. Originally Japan was not a feudal society, it was a collection of clans. Later it followed the Chinese system of central government with a powerful emperor based in Kyōto conscripting armies led by warriors who were servants of the crown. However, when imperial power diminished during the Kamakura period (1185–1333), regional warlords known as *daimyō* came into being and became influential figures in a system that leaned toward feudalism.

There followed several centuries of near-constant fighting between warlords in the Sengoku period (also known as the Warring States period) until the 'great unifiers' Oda Nobunaga, Toyotomi Hideyoshi and Tokugawa Ieyasu brought Japan back under central control in the late sixteenth and early seventeenth centuries. Peace was restored and this largely continued until the civil war of the mid-nineteenth century and the rise in nationalism and militarism in the twentieth century, which culminated in the Second World War.

Social groupings

The samurai evolved into a military class in around the tenth century. Their forerunners were the *bushi* (武士), a term that is first seen in the eighth century. It is important to note the difference in characters: *bushi* is a carry-over from the Chinese 'gentleman' (士), while samurai (侍) evolved from court servants. Various warriors grouped together to form *buke* (武家), military families or clans (the word tribe is reserved for earlier Japanese family units). Some clans were autonomous, others formed into clusters, and at the times when Japan was fully unified they all paid homage to a single lord. Samurai culture was strongly hierarchical, with the most powerful leading the rest, and occasional clusters of families known as *ikki* (一揆) coming together to defend against larger forces and the ever-growing threat of a single feudal system.

The main population of Japan during the samurai era of control was divided into four sections:

1. *Shi* (士) – the gentry or warrior class
2. *Nō* (農) – farmers
3. *Kō* (工) – artisans or craftsmen
4. *Shō* (商) – merchants

This classification was not fixed; there was sometimes fluctuation between classes and also earlier systems were in place. The sixteenth-century Portuguese missionary Gaspar Vilela reported that the four classes in Japan were in fact the gentry (i.e. samurai), priests, traders and peasants.

The samurai class made up between five and ten per cent of the population depending on the period in history and whether you include foot soldiers and all men-at-arms. They were the elite caste just below the aristocracy and in some cases connected to it. They owned land and were able to divide it up among the lower classes, so it was a loosely feudal system – albeit one that sometimes strayed into militarism and despotism.

Although they were only marginally lower in status than the aristocracy, and often more powerful, many samurai aspired to nobility. For example, Taira no Kiyomori forced a marriage between his family and the main imperial line to control the succession of the throne. This rightly displeased the imperial court, because the emperor at that time was chosen from legitimate applicants; the first-born son did not automatically become emperor.

The samurai as a whole encompassed the full spectrum of society, crossing the lines of aristocrat, warrior and commoner. In the Warring States period (mid-fifteenth to early seventeenth century), lower-born samurai took control of the country away from the 'blue bloods', in an upheaval known as the *gekokujō jidai* (下剋上時代), 'the low overcoming the high'. Following the decisive battle of Sekigahara in 1600, Japan was finally unified under

Tokugawa Ieyasu, who himself was a ruler by force not birth.

The banner of the first 'great unifier', Oda Nobunaga, shows the reality of the samurai mind and their outlook on Japan's politics:

天下布武
Tenka fubu
All people under heaven, all under military rule

SLAVERY

One could argue that medieval peasants and indentured servants were slaves, because they had little or no freedom to leave their masters. But there was also a class of people in Japan who were explicitly bought and sold and owned. This practice had a long history, one that predated the samurai era. After battles, captured soldiers could be converted into slaves and sold across the world, reaching as far as Europe. Slaves were also imported from other countries; the now famous 'Black Samurai' Yasuke is thought to have been freed as a slave before joining Oda Nobungana as a retainer. We must not discount the idea of the samurai as slave master as well as warrior. Although slavery and the export of slaves was heavily curtailed by Toyotomi Hideyoshi in the late sixteenth century, it continued in other forms. The last slaves in Japan were not freed until 1872, when enslaved prostitutes were emancipated from brothels.

Taxation

The Spanish merchant Bernardino de Ávila Girón gave a detailed description of the system of taxation in Japan around the late sixteenth century. Inspectors known as *yakunin* went around the villages using a cord to measure each peasant's allocation of land. Based on that measurement, they then calculated how much they thought the land should yield. The land owners were given a tax demand based on this projection. However, the tax calculation took no account of how much the land actually did yield, which was often less than the *yakunin's* estimate, and so many families found themselves having to take drastic measures such as selling their children into slavery to pay what they owed. The punishment for not paying tax was torture and death. The Spaniard reported the case of a peasant from Satsuma who fell short of meeting his quota by the small amount of two bales of unthreshed rice. The lord showed no mercy: the man, his wife and two children were all executed.

Sometimes, however, a lord would squeeze too hard. In another account from the same period, François Caron told of a governor near the city of Edo who was stripping his people of all their wealth through taxation. When the people put forward a complaint, the government in Edo investigated and found in their favour. The lord was arrested and messengers were sent across the land with orders to round up his male relatives. Then, upon the eighth day in the eighth month when the sun was in the south, they were all forced to commit suicide. So, a whole family line was cut short for one man's crimes. Even lords and high-ranking samurai could be taken down for misconduct.

Righteous complainants did not always receive such perfect justice. Sakura Sōgorō was a village headman whose community was being subjected to crushing taxation by the local warlord, Hotta Masanobu, so he sent an appeal directly to the *shōgun*. The appeal was heard and it was found that Masanobu was indeed being excessively demanding. However, even though the case was considered valid, and the tax reduced as a result, the headman and his wife were still crucified after having to watch their three children die by beheading, because Sōgorō had been incorrect to bring a case against his own lord. In this case, 'honour' and justice did not coincide.

Total control

Broadly speaking, in old Japan each person had a specific amount of power that they could wield in life. The *shōgun* was at the very top and controlled all, while each domain leader ran their own part of the country. Within each domain, each household ran their own business and family. In short, all people owed service to someone above them. This even included the *shōgun*, who, in theory, was answerable to the Emperor (although, in practice, this was no constraint). The Emperor owed his service to Japan in a spiritual way as a form of 'pope'.

In this top-down society, each person had absolute authority over those below them. The *shōgun* could kill a lord, a lord could kill a subject, a subject could kill his wife, children or servants. In general, those higher up the chain did not interfere with executions performed by lesser people on their own subordinates.

In samurai-era Japan, all 'faces' turned to a master. Personal freedom was not a priority. Samurai felt a need to position themselves as close to the top as possible and accrue as many followers as they could to support their position. This was the framework on which samurai chivalry rested.

TOTAL CARNAGE

In his diary entry for 20 June 1618, Richard Cocks wrote of a man who had 'been possessed with the devil' and beheaded his brother, severed his father's arm, given his wife a long gash on her shoulder and then killed his house steward. Nothing was said or done about the matter, because, as the head of the family, he was in his rights to kill them all if he wanted to.

JUSTICE AND PUNISHMENT

If you survived the battles of war-torn Japan, there were still many dangers to be avoided and hardships to endure in so-called 'times of peace'. These included the inequalities of the caste system, prejudice, slavery and human sacrifice (in earlier times), extortion, banditry, over-taxation and the notoriously rough 'village justice'.

One chilling example of the Japanese justice system in action came after a visit by the samurai Kujō Masamoto to his estates in the province of Hine, during which he invited the inhabitants of one of the local villages to a feast. In the midst of the festivities it was discovered that a dagger had been stolen, and so Masamoto ordered that all the guests be taken to the temple and threatened with the 'punishment of the gods'. This involved everyone putting their hands in boiling water to reveal the thief. At this point, the actual thief stepped forward to save the other villagers from this ordeal. The samurai ordered him to give up his position as head of his estate and pass all his lands and farm to his eldest son. However, Masamoto's comparatively merciful judgement was ignored by the villagers, who banded together and killed not only the thief but also his wife and all of his sons, then raided his house and burned it down.

A similar episode involved the theft of winter supplies of treated ferns from a village storehouse. The thief was caught and killed on sight, but again the villagers went on to kill his innocent parents and children.

Much of what we know about Japanese punishments comes from the accounts of early European visitors. Francesco Carletti reported women and babies being crucified or burned alive. He also noted that samurai loved to test their swords on convicted criminals (more rarely, innocent people walking at night would also suffer this fate). In his diary entry for 3 August 1617, Richard Cocks described a man who had stolen a small amount being roasted to death; he was staked to a post and 'a fire made about him' so that he ran around in pain until he died. François Caron wrote that the lord of Hirado had some ladies in waiting impaled in chests filled with spikes for the 'crime' of speaking to some men; the men involved were made to commit suicide.

With such severe punishments for minor crimes, it is hard to imagine how a murder would have been dealt with. According to the German naturalist

Engelbert Kaempfer, writing in 1692, if there was a murder in the street, the murderer would be beheaded unless he committed suicide first. Furthermore, any people in the street at the time were boarded up in their houses for months on end as punishment for not stopping the killing. The families were at least given time to provision themselves with food and necessities to endure the imprisonment. Other families in the street who were further away from the incident were forced to do hard labour as punishment for not breaking up the fight; this included the captain of the ward.

Superstition could be another cause of unjust treatment. If someone claiming to have supernatural insight picked a person out as having been possessed by a fox then the whole of that person's family would be ostracized as a 'fox family'. The shunning would last for generations, during which the family would only be allowed to marry into other fox families.

There were other examples of outcasts, including the *eta* (穢多) and *hinin* (非人), who were outside of the four-tier caste system described previously and had almost no standing in Japan.

So, it is clear that periods of peace, or 'normal times', were by no means idyllic. Overall, however, it was a very stable environment, perhaps because the severity of the punishments served as an effective deterrent to disorder. Even during periods of war, when fortunes and social order were turned upside down, chaos was not guaranteed – art still flourished; some communities prospered.

METHODS OF EXECUTION

There was a wide range of types of death penalty available in sixteenth-century Japan, including the following:

- Crucifixion
- Inverted crucifixion
- Skewering/impalement
- Quartering by an ox
- Splitting between carts
- Roasting
- Boiling in a cauldron
- Being wrapped in a mat and thrown into the sea, set on fire or left to die
- Sawing

SOURCES

The following accounts from European visitors and native writers give a variety of perspectives on crime and punishment in old Japan.

They just as readily execute a man for stealing one farthing as for stealing one hundred thousand, because they maintain that a man who takes one thing will take one hundred if he gets the chance.

Writings of Cosme de Torres (16th century)

In Europe servants are reprimanded by whipping; in Japan they are beheaded.

Luís Frois, *Tratado* (1585)

According to how serious a crime is or is not, hiaburi [burning at the stake], nokogiribiki [death by sawing] and haritsuke [crucifixion] are used as a warning to others, each used according to the crime committed. The executions of death sentences are official business and are not those things you should casually observe.

Heika Jōdan (c1670)

When a storm is raging and you cannot see what is ahead of you, if you find something white or conspicuous anywhere on the ground, do not bend to pick it up [as it is likely to be a trap set by robbers]. If you do so without care, you will be marked and easily killed in most cases. [To see what it is,] draw your sword and check it with the scabbard and then leave it there.

Mizukagami (c1670)

Samurai are sometimes found to be without a master and wander from place to place, which is not their wish but cannot be avoided. If there is no other outlet for your martial instincts, become a yamadahi [mountain bandit]. If there is anyone else available, work together in a group. If alone, have a short sword of eight sun in length which is double edged and with no handguard; keep it inside your kimono and use it as a dagger. Wait at an appropriate place for someone to come by, grab the person by the chest, hold the dagger in your right hand in a reverse grip and quickly cut their throat. If someone else happens to pass by, stay calm and say that this man was suddenly taken ill, that he has been given medicine and that they should not worry but just continue on ahead. If no one is around, throw the body from a cliff or leave it somewhere where no one will find it.

Mizukagami Kuden no Oboe (date unknown)

A COLOURFUL SOCIETY

> *With us, colourful clothing is considered frivolous and ludicrous;*
> *with the Japanese – except men of the cloth and old men who*
> *have taken vows and shaved their heads – wearing colourful*
> *clothing is universal.*

Luís Frois, Tratado (1585)

It would be easy to form the impression that samurai society, with its strict hierarchies, near-constant warring and hideous punishments, was unremittingly serious and austere. However, there were many light-hearted and colourful aspects to life in medieval Japan that confound the stereotype of the samurai. The following are examples of these quirks of everyday life.

- The Japanese felt no shame revealing their bottoms to warm them by a fire.
- Patches used to cover up holes in clothing were not frowned upon; it was considered suitable even for the upper classes.
- Men openly used mirrors in public to groom themselves.
- Pouches and wallets were used for medicine and other daily requirements such as flint and steel; these were often held inside a *kimono* sleeve or from the belt.
- The Japanese bathed in public outside of their houses quite open to viewing.
- The higher levels of society blackened their teeth to emulate the court.
- Even high-ranking people cleaned their own tray away after eating.
- The Japanese drank with two hands.
- It was acceptable to make loud noises when eating.
- Fishing was seen as a low-level task.
- A brush stroke of ink was placed over envelopes to stop them being opened by the wrong person.
- There is one historical episode of a woman covered in de-fanged snakes dancing for the public in exchange for money, giving us a more exotic image of life in old Japan.

- Even back in medieval times, certain bars in town would pull in drunken people, especially unsuspecting foreigners, and extort them with massive bills.

While a samurai may kill his wife with impunity, he may wait to do so until she has finished sewing patches on his clothes and he has finished warming his buttocks by the fire. Then he may head into town to watch a snake dancer perform. Life in medieval Japan was richer and more complex than the traditional image would have us believe.

CHAPTER FOUR

HIERARCHY

Japanese society during the samurai era was highly structured. Everyone knew their place and was mindful to show respect to their superiors. More important than an individual's position in the pecking order was the status of their family or clan. Samurai would go to great lengths and suffer great hardships, even death, to ensure the continued success of their clan. In this chapter, we will also explore the often-overlooked role of women within the clan. The lack of references to women in samurai texts would suggest that they were considered to be of low status. While this is undoubtedly true in certain eras, the overall picture is more complex.

HIERARCHY WAS EVERYTHING

> *According to an old samurai story, there was a samurai called Machino Nagato no Kami, who served Gamō Shimotsuke no Kami of Aizu. Machino had a renowned warrior named Hattori Den'emon as a retainer, who had decapitated the head of a famous samurai whose name was Oroshi Hikozaemon. After the death of the lord, a samurai named Katō Samanosuke Yoshiaki was given the area of Aizu and came to govern there. As Hattori was then a rōnin [samurai without a master], he approached the lord to gain employment. However, when hearing that Hattori Den'emon had served Machino Nagato no Kami, Samanosuke said, 'There seems little doubt that he got Oroshi's head, but if he*

*was really right-minded in a true sense he would not have been
serving Machino Nagato no Kami as such a low-level retainer.
As he had won Oroshi's head, he should have been appreciated
as incomparably good. However, he was content with such a
position probably because he is not such an ambitious samurai.'
For this reason, Hattori Den'emon was not employed.*

Musha Monogatari (1654)

Hierarchy was overwhelmingly important to the samurai, so important that
it outweighed achievement in Yoshiaki's evaluation of the *rōnin* Hattori in the
tale above. This preoccupation with rank continued right up until the end of the
samurai era, as the following historical incident reveals.

In 1862 the English merchant Charles Lennox Richardson and his
companions were out riding near Yokohama when they encountered Shimazu
Hisamitsu, one of the major figures of the Satsuma samurai, riding with his
retinue down the road. Richardson (said to be somewhat arrogant) either did
not dismount to show respect or he tried to come through the lines of parading
Satsuma warriors and got too close to Hisamitsu.

Japanese law (*kiri-sute gomen*) allowed the samurai to strike at those lower
in rank who had shown a lack of respect. Although foreign citizens were
usually not subject to that law, still Hisamitsu considered Richardson to have
offended him and so he ordered his guards to attack the Englishman. The
other merchants having galloped away in terror, Richardson fell, bleeding to
death, from his horse and the order was given to administer a *coup de grâce*.
The English authorities in Japan were outraged by this event, which came to be
known as the Namamugi Incident. They demanded compensation and when
this did not come they bombarded nearby Kagoshima.

Hierarchy was the foundation of society in old Japan (and remains so
today). In the top slot was the Emperor, a position unattainable to all bar
legitimate descendants. Next came the *shōgun*, or the regent during periods
when the *shōgun* had no real power. After that, there was a pecking order for
everyone, right down to the lowest slave. At times there was movement in the
social order, notably during the Ōnin War (1467–77) when regional samurai

governors known as *shugo* (守護) were replaced by lower-level samurai called *kokujin* (国人).

There was also the issue of vying for position. For example, when the warlords of Japan descended upon Edo to see the *shōgun*, they paraded through the streets and each retinue jostled to have their master go first. Furthermore, seating arrangements at audiences and meals were carefully organized so that the most respected figures with the most impressive military achievements would be positioned closest to the leader and furthest from the door. The least prestigious seats were furthest from the leader and closest to the door. The prime spots were highly coveted.

Some samurai ventured on 'warrior journeys' or engaged in duels to demonstrate their superior combat skills. A famous example of this was the contest between Umezu ('the haughty') and Toda Seigen ('the saintly'). Umezu challenged Toda to a duel; Toda initially refused to engage, but his lord insisted that he accept the challenge. At the beginning of the contest, which was fought using wooden swords, Toda hit his opponent under the chin and Umezu flew into a rage. However, Toda kept his calm and won the fight convincingly. It is clear that the defeated samurai's behaviour was not considered to be in line with *bushidō*, while the unflappable victor was portrayed as an exemplar – a person superior not only in skill but in conduct.

> *A person that does not maintain calm is called a* kenkyōnin *– a flustered person.*
>
> Heika Jōdan (c1670)

MAN VERSUS MONKEY

There was a curious incident involving a monkey that had been trained to fight with a wooden sword. A *rōnin* was set up to challenge the animal and the monkey, being agile, landed its blows to the shame of the *rōnin*. In response, the *rōnin* left and returned at a later date, having trained hard to defeat the monkey and regain his honour; it is said that the monkey ran away at the sight of his determination. This was another example of the lengths to which Japanese warriors would go to gain – or regain – the respect of their peers in order to maintain their place in the hierarchy.

When Oda Nobunaga, the first of the three major unifiers of Japan, died at the hands of one of his own men, his retainer Toyotomi Hideyoshi graduated from an underling to master of all. He went on to keep the whole nation under his command until his natural death. To grasp the magnitude of this achievement, you have to remember that Toyotomi Hideyoshi was from low stock and the people he commanded were once vastly superior to him. These samurai now had to pay him homage and tribute of the highest order because he had been victorious in the battle for ultimate power. However, it is clear from the following account by a samurai of the time that some of Toyotomi Hideyoshi's former superiors resented his rapid rise:

> *Toyotomi Hideyoshi is the son of a peasant, a man born under a thatched roof and not a tiled one, and it was only through Oda Nobunaga's grace that such a lowly person rose, and now, instead of honouring the memory of Oda Nobunaga, his master, he has in fact set out to carve an empire for himself. For these reasons no one should join this upstart peasant of no family lineage.*
>
> Writings of Sakaki Yasumasa (16th century)

Sakaki Yasumasa went on to predict that those who followed this peasant-king would displease their ancient and noble ancestors in the afterlife. These scathing comments show that, beneath the surface, the samurai loved true pedigree but they would not go against someone who had superior power and who had displayed military proficiency. There is no need to labour the point; the samurai valued both hereditary pedigree and achievement through arms or cunning. Simply getting to the top and staying there gained respect, if not friendliness or love.

THE CLAN

The clan was of great importance to the samurai, more so than any personal interests. It was vital to uphold the honour of the clan in order to preserve its position, and that of its members, within the hierarchy. Successful clans could ride high for hundreds of years; others might fall down the order.

The character for clan (家) is also used to represent a house or home. Just as in the West, ruling dynasties are referred to as, for example, 'the House of Stuart' or 'the House of Bourbon', so in Japan there was 'the House of Oda', 'the House of Toyotomi' and 'the House of Tokugawa'. The term clan can be seen on two levels, as the personal clan of each samurai and the larger clan that they served. Clans could be divided into branches and different branches could end up serving different lords.

Within each clan, according to the *Bushidō Shoshinshū* document, there was a basic two-level hierarchy: samurai and non-samurai. The low-ranking non-samurai toiled all day to serve their samurai masters. However, as simple employees, they were not expected to go into battle for the lord. The samurai, on the other hand, enjoyed a life of privilege and leisure except during times of war when they had to be prepared to lay down their lives for the clan.

HOUSE RULES

Kahō (家法), 'house rules', were laws that governed the behaviour of each clan. They were generally laid down by the head of the clan and passed on for generations, sometimes adapted for new times. Examples include the house rules of Rokuhara (thirteenth century), Tako Tokitaka (fifteenth century) and Sōunji (early sixteenth century), to name but a few. As codes of chivalric behaviour, *kahō* can be seen as early examples of what evolved into *bushidō*.

Serving the clan

Japanese military history is full of episodes that demonstrate just how highly the samurai valued the honour of their clan. As in the following accounts, warriors would invariably sacrifice their own interests or feelings if that was what was required to ensure the continued success of future generations. However, it must be remembered that after a samurai has been adopted by another clan, they become a part of that other clan and therefore an outsider.

The evil emperor

Long-established clans inevitably had some bad people in their histories, and it was necessary to deal with any such figures who might otherwise threaten the continuation of the clan. Sometimes, as in the quotation from the *Bushidō Shoshinshū* below, it would be said that the bad apple had been possessed by evil spirits; in other cases, more direct earthly action was required. For example, Buretsu (489–507), tenth descendant of the great fourth-century emperor, Nintoku, was said to have engaged in all kinds of evil acts, such as disembowelling pregnant women. He was so disruptive that he was assassinated at only 18 years old, before he could produce an heir. This meant that a more suitable candidate from another line could be picked and the imperial clan could remain in power.

The house of a person of status is invariably haunted by vengeful ghosts. There are two ways in which such ghosts cause trouble. Firstly, by bringing about the untimely death through accident or illness of an upcoming warrior [...] secondly, by taking possession of a warrior who is liked by the lord and then causing the warrior to delude the lord into taking the wrong action.

Bushidō Shoshinshū (c1700)

A fatal *shinobi* mission

The seventeenth-century document *Shoka no Hyōjō* gives an example of a samurai who volunteered to die to enhance his clan's status. The samurai was part of a force attacking a well-defended castle. The attacking lord, looking for a way to break the tight bonds of trust between the defending soldiers, asked his samurai for ideas. One samurai stepped forward and said that he would create an opening for his lord. All he asked for in return was a secure future for his clan for generations to come. The lord agreed.

The samurai ventured out on a classic 'doomed spy' *shinobi* mission as described by Sun Tzu in the thirteenth chapter of his *Art of War* (*Bingfa*). Infiltrating the castle, he deliberately allowed himself to be seen, but before he was captured he burned a fake letter in a brazier. The castle guards demanded to know what was in this letter, to which he replied that they would find out soon enough, as the letter he burned was intended for a traitor within their camp. At this point he bit off his own tongue and killed himself.

The enemy samurai then became very suspicious of each other and their attention was taken up more with looking for the supposed traitor than with defending the castle, which allowed the attacking lord to take the castle. This is how the doomed samurai-spy sacrificed himself to guarantee the future prosperity of his clan.

By the sword divided

Sometimes members of the same clan would find themselves serving different lords. They would then have to put their lord's clan ahead of their own. However, when Minamoto no Tametomo and his brother Minamoto no Yoshitomo faced each other in battle, they agreed that they would spare each other's lives so as not to bring dishonour to their clan and to maintain a brotherly connection.

Brothers in arms

In contrast, the brilliant commander Kusunoki Masashige and his brother Kusunoki Masasue fought on the same side, for Emperor Go-Daigo. However, they were not spared. Having obeyed the Emperor's order to lead his army into battle, despite knowing that defeat was inevitable, Kusunoki Masashige found himself cornered in an old farmhouse with his brother and what remained of their routed forces. The two brothers killed each other in a ritual suicide pact. Kusunoki Masashige effectively gave up his own life and that of his brother in order not to shame their clan by disobeying their lord.

The golden youth

During the battle of Ichi-no-Tani (1184), Kumagai Jirō Naozane was fighting on a beach when he saw an enemy samurai with a golden sword trying to escape by dashing for a boat. Having caught up with the samurai, he engaged him in combat, defeated him and took off the enemy's helmet ready to behead him. Upon seeing the samurai's face, he discovered he was a youth of a similar age to his own son. Overcome with pity, Kumagai wanted to let the boy go, but the boy realized that they were being observed by some of Kumagai's comrades. Not wishing his captor to disgrace himself and his clan with this act of mercy, the boy knelt and allowed his head to be taken. It is said that Kumagai later became a monk out of remorse for this incident.

Diary of a family man

A samurai named Katsu Kokichi left behind an important diary of life in Edo-period Japan. Having started out as a thuggish vagabond samurai, he became a settled and orderly family man controlling a tight family unit. One of Katsu's children was Katsu Yasuyoshi, who went on to become a prominent figure in the Japanese navy and was instrumental in the transition from samurai rule to a more modern form of government.

Toward the end of his diary, Katsu Kokichi wrote that family and clan were special above all things and that family should be respected and cared for.

This fascinating account of life at the end of the samurai era was published as *Musui's Story* (edited and translated by Craig Teruko). Although it is currently out of print, it would be well worth tracking down a second-hand copy.

MARRYING OUT OF THE CLAN

The *Bushidō Shoshinshū* explains that when a member of the family-be it male or female – married into another clan they were treated as having left the clan of their birth. However, this was often just a case of keeping up appearances; while clan leaders might be cold and over-formal toward their estranged relatives in public, in private they would return to old familiarities.

LAND

In samurai society, land was the primary unit of power. The more land a clan owned, the more farmers it could support, the more food it could produce, and the more influential the clan became. Therefore, gaining and controlling land was the aim of all samurai.

The way in which land was managed and taxed ranged from the extremely lax to the extremely strict and population-crushing, but all methods of taxation were based on the principle that it was the samurai who controlled the land. Sometimes samurai lived directly off their own land; at other times they were paid in coin by a local government (in other words, their lord).

The first part of the samurai era saw the samurai as landed gentry; they owned country estates and, while some of them attended the imperial court, most stayed in their own provinces. This created a strong relationship between the clan and the wider populace over generations. There also formed a spiritual connection with the land; certain places became shrines to family gods. Therefore, when a clan lost territory, it did not only mean a loss of power and wealth but also a displacement from ancestral deities and the support and protection they gave.

Notwithstanding this spiritual attachment to the land, at certain times in history samurai leaders would order lesser samurai to move to different lands, creating displaced families. This practice came to its height during the sixteenth century and into the period of peace, when most samurai were forced to move to castle towns. The connection to ancestral fields and loyal farmers was severed and traditional samurai culture was badly damaged. Only the *jizamurai* or 'country warriors' continued in remote areas, albeit at a lower social status than their city-dwelling counterparts.

During the transition from the samurai era to modern Japan in the nineteenth century, all taxation was controlled by the new central government and military families were paid from a single fund. However, the samurai soon fell and power was centralized once and for all.

The roots of prosperity

The following sections emphasize how owning land was fundamental to success as a samurai.

A reward for loyalty

After the battle of Mikatagahara in 1572 Tokugawa Ieyasu gave his attendant Kuroyanagi Takeshige a fan with a promise of land as a reward for having faithfully stayed by his side throughout the engagement. Land produced crops, surplus crops could be sold for money and money could maintain a military lifestyle. Clans chased the dream of having ever more land and farms under their control, which of course equated to more power.

Tokugawa Ieyasu and the rare peaches

When Tokugawa Ieyasu was given a basket of peaches by Oda Nobunaga, all his retainers crowded round to admire these seldom seen delicacies. However, Ieyasu was unimpressed. He told them that the power of the samurai was built on rice paddies and that if people started growing frivolous fruit trees instead of focusing on a stable economy and proper land management then the foundation of the samurai would crumble. Reminding his men that a love of the trivial was a sure route to destruction, he told them that they could eat the peaches if they wished but he did not.

Chapter Four

Hunting and hawking

Some manoeuvres in hunting, such as advancing and retreating,
are similar to those undertaken in warfare.

Heigu Yōhō (1670)

Hunting and hawking were seen as fitting pastimes for the samurai. As in other parts of the world, game was managed by the nobility and warrior elite. Field sports were also considered as a valuable preparation for military life. Possessing great hawks was a sign of prestige, a status that bird-owning samurai advertised by using feathers from their hawks as arrow fletchings.

A sport much loved by the samurai was dog-hunting, which involved riding around an 'arena' with a bow and attempting to shoot a dog. It was excellent training in horsemanship, archery and mobile warfare. However, the sport was briefly banned by the fifth Tokugawa *shōgun*, Tokugawa Tsunayoshi, who was known as the 'dog-*shōgun*' (*inu kubō*) for his love of dogs.

Without land there could be no bushidō

Analysis of *bushidō* tends to focus on factors such as prowess on the battlefield and reputation within society. However, it is often forgotten that these aspects are inextricably linked to land ownership. Samurai were inspired to perform great deeds in battle partly by the prospect of being rewarded with more land. More land brought more wealth and more wealth enhanced a samurai's social standing.

One must also remember that, while *bushidō* was generally associated with personal honour, a samurai was connected to his clan and the clan to its lands. As has been seen many times throughout Japanese history, a fall from grace for one family member could lead to disgrace for the whole clan and the loss of its lands. The idea of chivalry was propped up on the backs of farmers working in the fields to produce a surplus for the samurai to convert into military might.

WOMEN

If [a wife] has a bad attitude all along and seems to be no good, [a samurai] can simply divorce her and send her back to her parents.
Bushidō Shoshinshū (c1700)

In the West during the Middle Ages, chivalry and courtly love went hand in hand, and women featured prominently in knightly works such as Sir Thomas Malory's *Le Morte d'Arthur*. However, women are mentioned only infrequently in Japanese texts from that era.

The characters for wife (婦人) translate literally as 'a female who sweeps', but these are Chinese in origin and do not necessarily reflect the Japanese attitude. In fact, it would appear that during certain periods of samurai history women enjoyed a relatively high status. In the sixteenth century, women were said to walk in front of men (according to accounts by European travellers). The powerful weapon known as the *naginata*, a long polearm, was once a weapon of the battlefield but later became associated with samurai women, who used it to defend the home and train their children. Women had an important role managing the day-to-day running of the household while their husbands honed their battle skills. Unlike in many other cultures, Japanese women had the right to divorce and they could own property and some became extremely powerful.

The importance of women within the clan is often underestimated, partly because most of our information comes from the Edo period when Confucian ideals of correct behaviour in society took over and women fell in status and became quite oppressed at times. Therefore, it is interesting to see the freedom that women enjoyed in earlier times by looking at Luís Froís's 1585 account of life in Japan.

Another possible reason for the downplaying of women's value is that it was considered improper for samurai to praise other members of their own family. This was because the clan was seen as a single entity, so to praise, for example, your wife or daughter was like praising yourself and therefore seen as boastful. (However, it has to be said that there are countless examples of samurai men praising themselves.)

A woman who is born in a warrior clan and is of marriageable age
would never allow herself to be hit if she were a man, but because
of her low status as a woman she has no choice but to cry and
endure it.

Bushidō Shoshinshū (c1700)

Women in samurai society

The role of samurai women in *bushidō* was small, while their role in society was large. It is difficult to understand how Japanese men felt about their women for three main reasons: the texts rarely cover the topic; European accounts are written from a Western perspective; and Japanese family life was conducted mainly behind closed doors. All we can do is infer the samurai attitude toward women from those accounts left to us. The following episodes give an overview of some of the challenges women faced in samurai society.

Concubines and ladies of the harem

As well as a wife, powerful samurai often had harems and concubines. In some cases, they also had more than one wife, as polygamy was acceptable in Japan during certain periods. The main wife was known as the *seishitsu* (正室), while the others were the *sokushitsu* (側室) – 'side wives' or 'wives in other quarters'. However, in some cases these were more like mistresses than wives. The *shōgun* in his personal residence would simply have to say, 'What is the name of that woman?' to signal that she should be in his bed that night. The women of some harems were extremely restricted socially and could not venture out. In Edo Castle there were gardens in which they could enjoy the day but they were always under watch. After 1716 these women were guarded by the *oniwaban* secret service under the title and position of 'men of Iga' (although the guards were actually from Wakayama).

To disobey is to die

According to the *Heike Monogatari* chronicle, Lord Kiyomori invited Giō, one of his favourite ladies, back to court after a prolonged absence. However, she refused, to which her mother told her, 'You cannot live in this land and safely ignore Lord Kiyomori's wishes', meaning that she would most likely be killed if she disobeyed.

The pulse of men and women

The early eighteenth-century *Hagakure* scroll makes reference to Japanese men of the day becoming more feminine in quality than their ancestors. The author backs up this assertion by noting that, whereas men and women used to have different pulse rhythms, now their pulses had synchronized into a single beat. This, he maintained, made men incapable of carrying out deeds of blood and slaughter.

The beheaded wife

The seventeenth-century French trader François Caron related a tale about a wife who was found with another man. The samurai husband instantly killed the intruding man, 'publicly ridiculed' his wife and then beheaded her.

Raped by beasts

In 1628, during a period of persecution, some 'military men' tried to force an 18-year-old man to rape his own mother. When he refused, they forced 'beasts' to have sex with her instead. This is not the only example of women forced to be raped by their own family members nor is it the only use of animals in torture against women.

SOURCES

A great lord must have sons … for what is the good of daughters?
Wife of Tokugawa Ieyasu (16th century)

In Europe, the love between relations of both sexes for one another is very great; in Japan it is very little, they act as if they hardly know each other.

In Europe it is very rare, if ever, that an infant is killed after birth; Japanese women put their foot on a baby's throat and kill all that they do not think they can raise.

In Europe, the men walk in the front and the women behind; in Japan, the men walk behind and the women in front.

In Japan, the women are often the ones to repudiate men.

In Japan, daughters go out for the whole day, or many days, wherever they want to without telling their parents.

Japanese wives are free to go wherever they please without telling their husbands.

In Japan, convents for nuns are as good as brothels.

Extracts from Luís Frois, *Tratado* (1585)

In times of siege, [the samurai] amass their treasure [in the keep] and it is here that they assemble their wives. When they can no longer hold out, they kill the women and the children to prevent them falling into the hands of the enemy; then after setting fire to the tower with gunpowder and other materials so that not even their bones or anything else may survive, the men cut open their bellies.

Writings of João Rodrigues (late 16th/early 17th century)

Any man may lie with a whore or common woman, although he be married, with impunity; but the wife may not so much as speak in private with another man without hazarding her life.

Writings of François Caron (17th century)

Piecing together evidence from primary Japanese and European sources gives us an imperfect and paradoxical picture of how the samurai viewed their women. They certainly did not idealize them as their knightly counterparts often did, but they did give them various social freedoms not available to women in other cultures at the time, such as the right to own property and to divorce. One cannot overlook the brutality displayed in some of these accounts, but then samurai treated other men brutally too. The whole system was based on powerful people controlling others, regardless of whether they were male or female.

PERSONAL HONOUR

[The samurai] regard honour as their principal god.

Writings of Cosme de Torres (16th century)

A samurai's personal reputation was founded on his individual talents and traits, whether physical, mental or emotional, as well as the way he conducted himself in society. Above all, he had to show loyalty to the lord without fail, although this was not necessarily a life-long commitment. In this part of the book, we will look at how a samurai could cultivate his personal honour and how he could end up losing it.

CHAPTER FIVE

THE QUALITIES OF A SAMURAI

Samurai should hone themselves by first disciplining their minds. Alongside mastery over the mind should be mastery over the body. 'Discipline' means preparation, and to be 'prepared in the body' means that a samurai must have a good foundation with the weapons that they carry: the katana, *the* wakizashi *and all other kinds of martial tools.*

Heika Jōdan (c1670)

The archetypal samurai was known for his skill with the sword and other weapons, but in reality there was much more to being a successful warrior than physical prowess on the battlefield. Qualities such as intelligence, self-control and preparedness were just as important, if not more so. Perhaps the most valuable attribute of all was an ability to fight without fear of death.

WHAT IS THE POINT OF A SAMURAI?

As samurai, the following is the primary principle to keep in mind during daily life: in a time of order you should prepare for war and in a time of disorder you should seek peace.

Heika Jōdan (c1670)

To understand anyone's behaviour it is important to understand their motivation, and the samurai are no different. So, we should ask the question, what did samurai actually want to achieve? To answer this question, it is useful to divide the samurai into two broad groups:

- **The pack leader.** These were the samurai whose goal was to achieve ultimate power. They wanted to be the alpha, to be in a position that was second to none in their social sphere. Depending on the extent of their ambition, this might be the head of their clan, their region or even the nation.
- **The pack.** These were samurai who did not want the responsibility of outright leadership. They showed loyalty to the pack leader in return for benefits such as prestige, office, salary and land.

The pack leader was always planning and acting to take power. They married and moved politically, built up forces and usurped or conquered others to gain more influence.

However, the majority of samurai fell into the 'pack' category. They pledged their loyalty, risked their lives and even died to keep their clan in a position of favour for the benefit of future generations.

Samurai of all levels relied on the support of others. They needed to build bonds with their group and remain at a level above the general population in their readiness for war. To maintain their position, they had to be seen as excellent in the eyes of their leaders and peers and to be feared or at least respected by those below them. In this context, *bushidō* can be seen as a mechanism to define and defend a samurai's position within the hierarchy.

Retirement from leadership

Many leaders, from the Emperor to the head of a clan, chose to retire in order to ensure a peaceful transition of power to the next generation. The term for this practice is *inkyo* (隠居). After retiring from office, former leaders often became advisers or followed a spiritual path, which was known as *nyūdo* (入道), 'to enter into the spiritual way'. Sometimes, however, these retirements were not all that they appeared to be; the leader might relinquish their title while retaining power for the rest of their life.

ACHIEVEMENT AND ABILITY

> *Warriors doing their work as* bushi *in times of warfare invariably participate in their first combat by the age of 16 or 17, so they practise martial arts from the age of 12 or 13.*
>
> *Bushidō Shoshinshū* (c1700)

Samurai had to demonstrate their worth, whether in combat, administration, politics, measuring rivers or whatever field in which they specialized. However, it was not enough to excel; you also needed your achievements to be recognized by the people who mattered. A samurai who performed a deed of merit on the battlefield had to make sure it was vouched for by a man of reputation, such as a captain or famed warrior; otherwise, the action might be deemed not only worthless but possibly even suspicious. Not having your achievements recognized was a grave affront. When the *shōgun* Minamoto no Yoritomo failed to reward his younger brother Minamoto no Yoshitsune for his great victories, it sparked a family war that raged through Japan and even involved the Emperor.

The best leaders saw beyond physical attributes. For example, when Tokugawa Ieyasu was in audience with three of his advisers, all of whom had some physical disability, the pages in attendance laughed at their appearance, to which Ieyasu is recorded as saying:

> *A disability is never a disgrace, but bravery in the heart should be held in high esteem. These three warriors are the crème de la crème; you should follow in their teaching and set them in your very bones.*
>
> *Musha Monogatari* (1654)

KNOWING YOUR LIMITS

The *Hagakure* lays out four basic levels of understanding one's own ability:

1. A person who is terrible at something knows they are terrible at it.
2. A person who is good at something knows they are good at it.
3. An expert is someone who can do something and make it look easy.
4. A true master will ignore what level they are at and just focus on improving themselves at all times.

Ability versus nobility

When weighing up your worth, the samurai would take into account both your individual ability and accomplishments and also your family history. During many periods, particularly times of peace, it would appear that breeding outweighed merit. A tendency to appoint people of pedigree rather than people of ability was a major factor in the downfall of ruling clans. This was not unique to the samurai and nor was it universal in old Japan. As we have seen, talented figures such as Toyotomi Hideyoshi were able to overcome the disadvantages of low birth and rise rapidly through the ranks. However, nepotism was instrumental in bringing the samurai era to an end.

Nepotism over the safety of the state

By the end of the thirteenth century, the powerful Hōjō family had a controlling majority within the government council, holding just over half of the seats. This meant that they were able to appoint young, inexperienced clan members to senior positions for which they were totally unsuited. The result was that a few powerful Hōjō members monopolized debate and government decision-making suffered from a lack of scrutiny.

ENTRY REQUIREMENTS

In the writings of the seventeenth-century merchant François Caron there is a description of the samurai who directly served the *shōgun*. They had to meet the following criteria to be allowed into his service:

- Pass an examination
- Have an active body
- Be ready in the use of arms
- Have studied well
- Be highly trained
- Escort the *shōgun* dressed in black
- March in formation
- Be silent

SOURCES

The nobles are proud to serve their lord, obeying his least command. And this, I fancy, is not due to any fear of punishment which the lord might inflict for disobedience, but rather on account of the loss of honour that they would suffer if they were to do otherwise.

Writings of St Francis Xavier (16th century)

In an old samurai story, Lord Hōjō Ujiyasu and his heir and son, Lord Ujimasa, were sharing a meal. Upon seeing his son eat, Lord Ujiyasu began shedding tears and said, 'The Hōjō family, our clan, will end with my life.' At this the atmosphere was ruined and not only the Lord Ujimasa but all his chief counsellors had a disheartened look about them. Then the Lord Ujiyasu said, 'Look at how my son Ujimasa is taking his meal; he has put some soup onto his rice, then he has added more. Every single person, noble or humble, eats two meals a day, so it cannot be possible that he is not well trained in this. His judgement is so poor that he cannot properly estimate the amount of soup that he should put in his bowl of rice and so he needs to take more. If he does not have the basic judgement for even a routine task such as this, one that is done every morning and evening, how could he ever evaluate someone and discover what they are really thinking, deep below the surface. If he does not have this ability, then he cannot recruit good samurai. If he does not have good samurai under his command in this time of war, it is obvious that, if I die tomorrow, the clever lords of the neighbouring domains will invade us and ruin my son Ujimasa. I am afraid this is the truth. Thus our Hōjō clan will end with my life.

Musha Monogatari (1654)

There really is no blame to be laid upon a bushi *who receives an injury in the course of being the first fighter to [enter into the fray] of a group.*

Heihō Yūkan (1645)

There are samurai who are achieved in military matters and they are called monoshi no ie *(物シノ家), meaning 'those from a clan of excellence' or alternatively they are known as* buhen no ie *(武邊ノ家), meaning 'those from a clan of military prowess'.*

Heika Jōdan (c1670)

Tales of achievement and failure

The following anecdotes highlight aspects of samurai achievement and the importance of gaining a reputation for ability and prowess. However, sometimes a preoccupation with glory on the battlefield could blind the samurai to other forms of achievement.

The pride of envoys

During the Japanese invasions of Korea in the late sixteenth century, Tachibana Yasuhiro, a high-ranking samurai of the Tachibana clan, was sent as an ambassador to Korea by the Japanese ruler of the time, Toyotomi Hideyoshi. The objective of his visit was to bring a Korean official back to Japan to negotiate a peace settlement with Hideyoshi. The ambassador met with the Korean magistrate named Song Ŭnghyŏng and all were entertained at a party. Tachibana said that he had been in many battles and wars all his life and that was what had given him grey hair. Then, in a veiled insult to his host's lack of military ability, he pointed out that the magistrate also had grey hair despite having experienced a life of luxury and peace.

Later, Tachibana was at another banquet in Seoul, during which he threw some rare and expensive food onto the floor. He thought that the Koreans would all rush forward at once to pick up the delicacy. Sure enough, this is what happened and so he was able to announce to the room that Korea would be easily conquered because its people did not have any discipline within them.

Having offended his hosts, Tachibana returned to Japan without a Korean official. When he reported to Toyotomi Hideyoshi, Hideyoshi had him beheaded and his entire family killed because he had failed in his mission. The samurai envoy valued practical military achievement and ridiculed those who did not have an impressive war record, but was then executed for having no achievement in his appointed task of ambassadorship.

METHOD BEHIND MADNESS?

Toyotomi Hideyoshi instigated two separate invasions of Korea, in 1592 and 1597. After initial successes, the campaigns ended in stalemate and the Japanese army eventually withdrew from the peninsula in 1598. It is unclear what exactly motivated Hideyoshi to order this action, but theories put forward include the following:

- Hideyoshi was trying to secure more power to maintain his family after his death.
- Hideyoshi had become a deranged megalomaniac.
- He was trying to kill off troublesome samurai veterans.
- He had run out of land to award to loyal samurai and so needed to expand his territories.
- He thought he would be able to take Korea and then go on to conquer China.
- He wanted to protect the peace in Japan by sending restless samurai to fight elsewhere.

If Hideyoshi was trying to preserve peace in Japan, it was to be in vain. Shortly after his death in 1598, the peace was broken by Tokugawa Ieyasu when he set out to take the country by force and become *shōgun*.

A shameful boar hunt

The *Hagakure* manual recounts a boar hunt that went wrong. A group of samurai managed to wound a boar, but when they went in for the kill the stricken animal suddenly got up and charged at them, scattering the group in fear. At the sight of this, the lord of the samurai lifted his sleeve to his eyes, claiming that he was trying to protect them from dust in the air, but really it was because he did not care to observe such ineptitude. Instead of reprimanding his men, the lord showed his displeasure subtly and indirectly, but no less clearly. Incidentally, one warrior stood his ground, approached the boar and cut it down, but his achievement was overshadowed by the incompetence of his comrades.

Levels of ability

The *Hagakure* continues with a method for categorizing clan retainers according to their ability:

- Quick to start but then lagging in action
- Lagging in initial action but then quick to act later on
- Quick to start and quick to finish
- Always lagging from start to finish

According to the *Hagakure*, the manner in which a samurai approached a task was more important than the degree of success. However, it must be remembered that the *Hagakure* was compiled at a time when loyalty was valued above ability.

MENTAL CONTROL

> *Do your job with your mind as taut as an iron bow strung with wire. Use your mind strongly when you walk down the street, such that you would not even blink if someone unexpectedly thrust a lance at your nose. All warriors should employ such a state of mind all the time, even in everyday life.*
>
> Writings of Suzuki Shōsan (1579–1655)

The great samurai leaders were set apart by their superior intelligence and temperament. In this section we will explore how a disciplined and capable mind was as much a part of a samurai's armoury as elite swordsmanship.

Intelligence

The sixteenth-century warrior Tsukahara Bokuden was one of the more famous samurai in history, a peerless sword-saint said to be undefeatable. One day, a reckless samurai challenged him while they were on a boat together and they agreed to fight when they had reached a nearby island. As they were about to land, the challenger jumped out of the boat and awaited Tsukahara Bokuden on the shoreline. However, the sword-saint just turned the boat around and left his would-be opponent stranded. He jokingly said that his school was called Mutekatsu Ryū (無手勝流) – the school that defeats without the use of hands. In the movie *Enter the Dragon*, Bruce Lee's character follows this story to establish himself as a martial arts thinker.

Another tale tells of a samurai swordsman who set a test for his three sons to see who should take over from him as head of the family. He propped a pillow above the door to a room and called his sons in one by one. The eldest son saw the pillow as he entered, reached up to remove it and then put it back afterwards. The second son dislodged the pillow, but caught it in mid-air and put it back in position. The youngest son also caused the pillow to fall, but he instantly drew his sword and, with lightning speed, cut the pillow in two before it hit the ground.

One might judge the youngest son to be the best candidate because of his skill with a sword. However, the head of the family declared his eldest son to be the best, because he was the only one who was fully aware of his surroundings and showed the skill of foreplanning. This scene was recreated in the classic Akira Kurosawa film *Seven Samurai*.

While these stories may be apocryphal, they highlight a key element of samurai prestige: to have intellect and wisdom as well as physical fighting prowess. In large-scale battles the great leaders needed untold calmness and foresight above all else; it was the fighters on the front line who really needed skill with a weapon.

Managing emotions

There is no doubt that the samurai made a great effort not to show their emotions. In all accounts, be they Japanese or Western, any display of hunger, anger, frustration or loss of self-control was seen to detract from a samurai's standing and honour. For this reason, contentious matters would be discussed through a third party to avoid tempers rising.

That does not mean, however, that the samurai were not emotional; in fact, there are many examples of warriors showing strong feelings such as anger, sorrow and grief, as the following episodes demonstrate.

In 1579, Tokugawa Ieyasu was forced to order his son Matsudaira Nobuyasu to commit suicide for complex political reasons (see chapter 7). Everyone knew the young man was innocent, but he had to die to preserve the honour of the clan and to maintain the alliance between Ieyasu and Oda Nobunaga. Ieyasu sent two of his retainers, the renowned Hattori 'the Devil' Hanzō and Amakata Michitsuna, to oversee the *seppuku* ritual. Hanzō was instructed to act as the *kaishaku-nin*, the person who beheads the suicide victim at the appropriate time. However, it was recorded that he was brought to tears and could not do the deed, so it fell to Amakata Michitsuna to take the head of his lord's eldest son instead. Upon hearing of his retainer's distress, Ieyasu is reported to have said, 'Even a devil like Hanzō cannot take the head of his master.'

Ieyasu himself was not immune to such displays of emotion. He was said to have been inconsolable when parting company with his loyal general and friend Torii Mototada. Both men knew they would never see each other again, because Mototada was about to defend Fushimi Castle against a force many times greater than his garrison. However, his bravery in holding out gave Ieyasu time to escape and prepare for victory in the decisive battle of Sekigahara.

There was also Kumagai Jirō Naozane, the Minamoto clansman discussed previously who wanted to spare the life of the boy-samurai who looked like his son. Kumagai was reported to have cried when he had to take the boy's head.

These are just a few of the many examples left in literature of samurai shedding tears. The term 'wetting one's *kimono* sleeves with tears' was commonly used in these instances. While such displays of emotion were not encouraged, it was accepted that they might occur, particularly in extreme situations like these.

Speaking truth to power

While the samurai clearly aspired to a high level of mental discipline, they did not always reach this ideal. Throughout this book, which aims always to demonstrate the difference between ideal and reality, there are ample examples of warriors rampaging out of control, or warlords inflicting cruelties on their subjects in anger.

The wisest leaders, recognizing their shortcomings, appointed private advisers to help steer their behaviour and attain a better level of self-control, as described in the following account by François Caron.

> *Most of the lords entertain by them some choice of persons to observe their actions and tell them of their faults, which they must exactly do without respect or flattery. For they say, no man can see his own errors so well as another, especially those who are called upon to govern. Being more subject to the transports of passion and pride, they would therefore rather hear of their faults from their true servants to be able to correct them than be ill spoken of behind their backs. For this reason, these secret monitors are always near the lord's person, observing their words and actions, especially at feasts and public meetings.*
>
> Writings of François Caron (17th century)

Some lords were more open to the use of such 'secret monitors' than others, and, as Natori Sanujūrō Masazumi states in the following extract from his manual *Heieki Yōhō*, a retainer in this position had to be careful how they reprimanded their lord. Too blunt an approach could be fatal.

> *In older times [in China] there was a position called* kangikan *(諫議官), 'counsellor of caution'. However, high-ranking retainers, even if they do not hold such a position, should admonish the lord whenever needed, but only in a way that the lord will accept. If they flatly admonish a lord who is not on the correct path, they should be aware that the lord will not only rebuke such a statement but may also make the retainer pay for it with their life. Be aware of this.*
>
> *Heieki Yōhō* (c1670)

SOURCES

For a person to be bad tempered is more disgraceful than anything. No matter how annoying the situation, at the very first feeling of irritation you should calm your mind and ask yourself whether you are right or wrong. Only if you are in the right may you get angry.

Writings of Shiba Yoshimasa (1349–1410)

If the servants bark back at the samurai like dogs, it shows that the servants are weak. A common saying goes, 'Rudeness blooms out of cowardice.' Just as the most cowardly dogs bark the loudest, so it is with people.

Zōhyō Monogatari (1657–84)

[If a warrior] cannot enter into service, they will overeat, drink too much and become addicted to sex, paying no heed to the worry that they cause their parents.

Bushidō Shoshinshū (c1700)

Dignity is a state in which a person's preparation is both determined and correct and in which he cannot be influenced at all by the opponent.

Ittōsai Sensei Kenpō no Sho (1664)

Being prepared

The *Hagakure* scroll says that before an important event samurai should take a day out to relax and prepare mentally; they should never be busy before they engaged in something that could have repercussions. Practical preparation with regards to matters such as armour, weapons, rations and funds was also essential. In short, samurai always needed to be prepared. To be caught out was considered shameful.

Good preparation can be seen as an important foundation for mental discipline. The samurai who were able to remain calm in battle were those who had planned a wide range of tactical scenarios and who had taken the time to compose themselves before fighting started. It was acceptable to charge among the dead on a battlefield, rush into danger or beat upon the doors of the enemy fortress if there was a military strategy behind such an action. To do it without reason was simply to be blood hungry and to sell your life, and those of your men, too cheaply.

SOURCES

Generally in budō *– the military way – you should hope to be regarded as honourable after your death through the preparations you have made while living.*

Gunpō Jiyōshū (c1612)

A warrior should never be unprepared or surprised, and consequently meet with disaster; this is completely shameful.

Musha Monogatari (1654)

You should keep your musket loaded at all times and not waste your bullets by shooting in 'rapid fire' without killing a single enemy. What shame such a thing is!

Zōhyō Monogatari (1657–84)

As well as samurai, even lower people should maintain discipline within. In the chapter of Great Learning in the Book of Rites it says, 'Cultivate oneself.' Therefore, samurai should hone themselves by first disciplining their minds. Alongside mastery over the mind should be mastery over the body. 'Discipline' means preparation and to

> be 'prepared in the body' means that a samurai must have a good
> foundation in the weapons that they carry, such as the katana, *the*
> wakizashi *and all other kinds of martial tools.*
>
> Heika Jōdan (c1670)
>
> *Correct preparation will encourage discretion – it is essential to*
> *remember that you are* bushi.
>
> Heika Jōdan (c1670)

KNOWING HOW AND WHEN TO DIE

> *Fate is in the hands of heaven, but a skilled fighter does not meet*
> *with death.*
>
> Japanese saying

The samurai attitude to death is an important but often misunderstood subject. The familiar statement from the *Hagakure* that 'Death is the way of the samurai' is often taken out of context to mean that samurai did not care whether they lived or died. This is not entirely true. The way of the samurai was to live well but also to recognize the correct time to die. They did not want to outstay their usefulness or pass up an opportunity to serve a higher goal by dying, but neither did they want to die needlessly.

In the following sections we will consider some aspects of the samurai relationship to death.

Nothing left to do but die

At the fall of Kamakura in 1333, Nagasaki Jirō Takashige was facing defeat, having run out of ideas to take back the advantage. In despair he approached a monk and asked him what he should do. The monk told him that he should go forward with his sword in hand. Understanding that there was truly nothing left to do but meet his fate, Takashige took up his sword and drove into the enemy. Taking as many enemy samurai with him as possible, he died a glorious death.

Likewise, when the legendary warrior-monk Benkei was defending his master, Minamoto no Yoshitsune, in a last stand, he is said to have stood in the enemy's path and fought against many opponents. Even when he was finally killed, he remained on his feet. It was not until a samurai cautiously approached him to check why he was so still that it was discovered that he was, in fact, dead. This account is probably an exaggeration of the truth, designed to present the behaviour expected of an ideal samurai.

The Japanese concept of *isagi-yoku* (潔く) is hard to translate directly, but encompasses the idea that you should die without reluctance or regret and with a clear mind, knowing that you have left nothing undone and everything correct. The *Hagakure* stated that no amount of skill and strength could protect you against someone who had a genuine willingness to die, so a suicidal burst from a less powerful warrior could devastate a stronger opponent who was not prepared to throw away their life.

The principle here is an important one in understanding *bushidō*. It is to recognize the point when there is nothing more that can be done, the moment when a samurai becomes redundant. Once a samurai realized that they would never achieve their goal, never win the war, never be useful, then they knew that it was time to die. To cling to life when there was no hope had no place in *bushidō*. That does not mean a samurai could not die of old age. If they had won their victories and the clan was flourishing, if they had not had to face an occasion to die, a samurai could lead a long and fruitful life. But if all was failing and there was nothing for them in the future, this was the ideal time to die. If they missed this chance to die well, they would face a dog's death.

A dog's death

The concept of *inujini* (犬死), a 'dog's death', features throughout samurai literature. To die like a dog was to die cowering and passive, unwanted and cast out. Dogs were badly treated in old Japan; the country was filled with starving strays and, as we have seen, they were even used as practice targets for archers in training. The character for dog (犬) was also used as a euphemism for thief. So, the idea of dying like a dog would have been abhorrent to the samurai. It was the opposite of the ideal death: when the time was right, facing your enemies in battle and for a worthwhile cause. To miss that opportunity and instead die retreating is an example of a dog's death.

An honourable death was all about timing and purpose. If it was judged that the actions of the samurai were correct in the situation he found himself, then there was no shame in his death. However, if the samurai's response to a situation was flawed and he had a chance to grasp glory but did not take it, then this could be considered as dishonourable.

Accepting death

Yagyū Munenori, a renowned swordsmanship teacher of the early Tokugawa shōgunate, was once talking to some prospective students. It is said that he came across one new student who immediately appeared to him to be a master swordsman even though he had never seen this student show his skills. Yagyū asked him in which military school he had studied to reach such an obvious level of expertise; the student said none. Master Yagyū refused to believe him. The student insisted that he had never trained in swordsmanship to a high level, but that what he had done was learn to accept death so that he was now ready to die as a samurai. Yagyū said that this was surely why he emanated such a powerful aura, for accepting death was one of the hardest skills for a warrior to master.

One of the core strategies of swordsmanship and other military arts was to enter into combat fully accepting the risk of death. Any hesitation could be fatal. The military general Uesugi Kenshin said that, 'Those who cling to life will die, while those who defy death continue to live.' This may not hold true in every case, but the point is that you were more likely to succeed and survive if you acted purposefully and without wavering. To get in, kill and be gone before the enemy could respond was often a rewarding strategy and a do-or-die attitude was a great foundation for victory.

YIN-YANG SWORDSMANSHIP

Yagyū Munenori founded the Edo branch of the Yagyū Shinkage Ryū school of swordsmanship. This was notable for stances known as *in no kamae* (陰の構え) and *yō no kamae* (陽の構え), which were based on the idea of *yin-yang*. In the stance of *in* (*yin*), the sword leaned against the right shoulder; while in the stance of *yō* (*yang*), the sword leaned on the left shoulder. This is because right is the direction associated with yin and left is associated with *yang*. *Yin* and *yang* are also associated with death and life respectively, and the school contained the idea of 'a sword of death' and 'a sword of life'. It wanted to teach swordsmanship for a new age of peace. The aim was not to kill but to incapacitate so that the victor could then show mercy.

SOURCES

There is no nation in the world that fears death less [than Japan].
Writings of Francesco Carletti (1606)

To regard your one and only life as dust and ashes and die when you should not is to acquire a worthless reputation. A valid reason to give up your life would be for the sake of a sovereign or in the service of a military general in time of need. [...] However, if you sneak past the proper time to die, you will regret it afterwards.
Writings of Shiba Yoshimasa (1349–1410)

One who claims to be a warrior must keep death in mind at all times.
Bushidō Shoshinshū (c1700)

> *If you are killed for nothing, the enemy will be encouraged and gain an advantage; while your allies will become panicked and will be put at a disadvantage. If you cannot help but be killed, try at least to cancel out your loss by taking one enemy with you. Killing two makes it an advantage for the allied side. Kill as many as 100 if you can find the strength in the sinews of your arms. It is cowardly to be killed without killing anyone. If you die for nothing, the rations you have been given will have been wasted.*
>
> *Zōhyō Monogatari* (1657–84)

Indoctrinated death

The samurai have often been likened to a death cult. While it is tempting to dismiss such claims as far-fetched, events throughout world history have shown that you can indoctrinate people into accepting death. We have to remember that there are numerous examples of samurai performing *seppuku* of their own free will. There are many possible reasons for these voluntary suicides, some of which could be seen as supporting the death cult theory. For example, some were acts of devotion by retainers who wanted to follow their lord into the afterlife, while others were inspired by bloodlust and battle emotions. Death was so big a part of the samurai experience that it is little wonder modern scholars look for evidence of indoctrination, whether it is there or not.

CHAPTER SIX

LOYALTY

Inform your wife, children and other family members on a constant basis of the position that you hold and that all are also indebted to the lord and that if the lord should order so, you must sacrifice your lives to expunge this debt. This is mononofu no michi, *the way of the warrior.*

Heika Jōdan (c1670)

The classic image of the noble samurai retainer faithfully following his lord even into death was an idealization created during the Tokugawa era to reinforce national unity. As we will see in this chapter, the true picture was much more complicated. Loyalty did exist, but it was far from unconditional and betrayal was a fact of life.

FORMS OF LOYALTY

In order to understand the samurai approach to loyalty, it is important to realize that there were various different types, including the following.

True loyalty

This normally applied to an inferior freely choosing to support a superior without coercion or indoctrination and with no care for financial gain. The inferior devoutly believed in the superior's cause and remained true even when benefits were lacking.

Paid loyalty

This was an arrangement in which a superior hired an inferior into service. There would be a contract and if one side broke the contract the arrangement came to an end. The inferior often left for a better option or fled when the situation became more troublesome than the payment was worth. While the two parties might develop a deeper bond over time, this was, above all, a transactional relationship.

> ### LOYALTY DOES NOT ALWAYS PAY
> Tokugawa Ieyasu gave some of his most loyal men the lowest salaries, but he also rewarded them with the most important strategic positions. Less trustworthy men were kept at a distance but with a higher income. On the surface, it seems unfair to have given more money to less loyal retainers, but Ieyasu evened up the score by making sure that life cost them a lot more.

Loyalty of cause

When two parties had a common goal, the inferior would follow the superior. However, their relationship was defined purely by the shared aim, and the duties of loyalty would cease once the objective was either achieved or abandoned.

Indoctrinated loyalty

When a superior browbeat an inferior into believing that their goals were correct and that the inferior must follow their orders no matter what, then this was indoctrination. The inferior was not obeying the superior out of genuine loyalty but as a result of extreme pressure.

Generational loyalty

In samurai culture, those from families that were in the first generation of service for a lord or who habitually moved between lords were known as *tozama* (外様), 'those on the outside', while members of families that had served the same lord for multiple generations were known as *fudai* (譜代), 'those in hereditary vasselage'. *Fudai* families might serve the same family for many generations; however, the other types of loyalty described in this section would still be applied to each member of the family as appropriate.

After Tokugawa Ieyasu took power in 1600, the terms *fudai* and *tozama* were used respectively to refer to those who had supported him during his victorious campaign and those who had not. This kind of labelling was also found in the Kamakura period when the term *goke'nin* (御家人) referred to housemen of the *shōgun*, *higoke'nin* (非御家人) was for retainers outside the *shōgun*'s clan, and *zatsunin* (雑人) were the common folk.

Length of service

> *Lord Daizensei Toshitane had a retainer named Kanazawa Bicchū. This retainer's family had served the Soma clan for generation after generation. By the time of Kanazawa Bicchū, as many as eleven generations of his family had been killed in battle in front of their lord's horse. Kanazawa Bicchū had a son named Kanazawa Chūbei and when the 26th lord, one Daizensei Yoshitane, was dying because of illness, the samurai retainer said, 'Some eleven generations including my father have died in front of the lord's horse, but I have done nothing to serve this lord in such a manner, as no need has arisen during my generation. If there is one thing I can do, it would be to follow my lord on his journey to the otherworld.' Then he killed himself. It is rare indeed for twelve generations of a samurai family to have died in the service of their lord.*
>
> *Musha Monogatari* (1654)

There was no stigma in a skilled samurai becoming a *rōnin* and switching between various lords during times of war, so it would be wrong to think that newcomers to a clan were frowned upon. Having said that, there was prestige in a family maintaining a long record of service – the more generations the better. Samurai from long-serving families could stand on the shoulders of their ancestors, whereas newcomers would have to rely on their own achievements to receive preferment.

According to the quote above, a record of twelve generations of service – especially twelve generations of death in service – was a rare achievement. Estimating each generation at twenty years, Kanazawa Chūbei would have had an advantage of 240 years of ancestral achievement and sacrifice over any newly established rivals in the clan.

THE *RŌNIN* MYTH

The modern idea of the *rōnin* as an outcast is half myth. They are often wrongly thought of as samurai who refused to kill themselves after the death of their lord. *Junshin* (殉死), ritual suicide after a lord's death, was only performed by a small proportion of retainers, because if they had all killed themselves when their lord died the whole clan would have come to an end. Admittedly, there was a law early in the Tokugawa period that forbade *rōnin* from gaining employment, but this did not last long. These factors, coupled with the vast number of Japanese films portraying the *rōnin* as underdogs, have led to a massive misunderstanding of this respected and necessary category of samurai.

Loyalty by force

Normally, the chains of loyalty followed the established social hierarchy, but certain powerful figures turned the status quo on its head through force of arms. One such individual was Oda Nobunaga, the first 'great unifier', who rose in the mid-sixteenth century to become more powerful than the *shōgun*. Luís Froís witnessed the highest-ranking members of Nobunaga's court facing the floor on their hands and knees in front of their leader. The mighty warlord allowed Froís to go where he liked and told him that neither the Emperor nor the *shōgun* could stop him, because he, Nobunaga, was in command. Loyalty in such a situation was a matter of self-preservation.

Freedom of choice

For loyalty to be genuine, the person giving the loyalty has to be able to choose where to place it. When all of Japan became unified under a single leader at the end of the sixteenth century, this choice was no longer available. In essence, Japan entered into a dictatorship that lasted until the final days of the samurai, and so loyalty throughout most of the later samurai period was simply enforced subordination. While, undoubtedly, some samurai did feel a true sense of loyalty to the leader, we cannot know how many because their loyalty could not be tested through free choice.

Loyalty to the people

People often talk of loyalty that goes up the hierarchy, from retainer to lord, but what of loyalty that goes down, from lord to retainer and so on? At their best, feudal clans were like extended families, with a benevolent, paternalistic lord at the head who understood the hardships that his people had to endure and did his best to alleviate them. However, during the Sengoku period, domains were frequently conquered and so bonds of commitment forged over generations between master and vassal were broken. Even under the Tokugawa shōgunate, which was supposedly a period of stability and peace, there were numerous peasant uprisings against cruel local lords.

MAN OF THE PEOPLE

Tokugawa Ieyasu mainly ate wheat porridge, a lower-class staple, although he could have had his choice of the finest foods. It is said that one day his attendant added something extra to improve the taste. At this the lord became angry. He said he wanted to eat exactly the same food as his people, who were experiencing poverty in this time of war, so that he would share in their suffering.

THE IDEALIZATION OF LOYALTY

During the turbulent Sengoku period the samurai would swap sides without compunction and the breaking and making of new alliances was common. However, when the Tokugawa clan took control of Japan, they wanted to solidify their position by instilling the idea of loyalty as a great virtue. This is when the classic image of the noble and faithful samurai we recognize today began to take shape.

During this era, historians painted Minamoto no Yoritomo, founder of the Kamakura shōgunate, in a positive light. His hunger for power was downplayed and his role in bringing order to Japan was emphasized. In contrast, they saw Ashikaga Takauji, founder of the Ashikaga shōgunate, as a negative influence, because he had changed sides and had been somewhat difficult as a commander. In truth, there was not really much difference between them, but the Tokugawa needed examples of good and bad samurai as propaganda to guide the populace into submission.

Tokugawa policies to enforce loyalty

As well as idealizing the concept of loyalty, the Tokugawa brought in various practical measures to curb the ambitions of individual *daimyō* warlords.

For example, Tokugawa Ieyasu forced the *daimyō* to contribute to the gigantic cost of building Edo Castle, a move that strengthened his physical position while weakening the financial position of his potential rivals. The Tokugawa clan also brought in the policy of 'one domain, one castle'. Each clan could have no more than a single castle, normally built on open flatland, which made it hard to defend and, therefore, reduced the chances of any warlord mounting a successful rebellion.

In 1634, Ieyasu's grandson Tokugawa Iemitsu introduced the system of *sankin-kōtai* (参勤交代), by which all the *daimyō* in the land had to spend a certain proportion of the year in the capital at Edo. Dividing their households in this way was a massive and costly undertaking. When the warlords did return to their ancestral lands, they had to leave their wives and heirs in Edo as hostages to guarantee that they would not cause trouble back home.

When the Tokugawa shōgunate finally cracked after 250 years of rule, many warlords were quick to rebel. This showed quite plainly that the clans felt no actual loyalty or love toward the *shōgun*.

MASTER BUILDERS

In popular imagination, Roman soldiers were fighters and builders, and the samurai were not dissimilar. According to the *Bushidō Shoshinshū* manual, the two main responsibilities of the samurai were military operations and construction work.

When Oda Nobunaga was building one of his castles, he had men of all ranks do the work. Everyone stripped down to their bare skin, with a kind of cushion or rug they could tie around the waist for sitting down. Until that castle was finished, it was said no one dared wear fine clothes anywhere near him.

Commanders in charge of construction projects had a high status. When Tokugawa Ieyasu was building his castles, his main architect, Toda Takatora, was the only samurai allowed to carry a pair of swords on site; everyone else had to leave their *katana* at home while they finished the work.

The oath for all warlords

One of the central measures in the Tokugawa bid to impose discipline was a new oath of allegiance, which was introduced in 1611. Warlords had to agree to all manner of instructions and limitations, including the following:

- Promote the study of letters, arms, archery and horsemanship.
- Reduce the number of drinking parties and social events.
- Refrain from hiring law-breakers, rebels and murderers.
- Do not associate with people from other provinces (after the year 1615).
- Report any social changes or new factions.
- Follow new marriage restrictions for the samurai class.
- Limit the number of retainers you bring with you to Edo.
- Obey restrictions on types of clothes that can be worn and on the use of palanquins.
- Be thrifty (Tokugawa Ieyasu was famously frugal).
- Appoint people who are suitably qualified.

This set of rules took Japan one step closer to a national dictatorship and was a far cry from the previous picture of rival clans vying for power.

The Hagakure *view of loyalty*

As a product of the Tokugawa era, the *Hagakure* scroll presents an idealized view of loyalty, epitomized in the following stories.

Staying true to your beliefs

During a council meeting, a retainer grew frustrated because his proposals kept being rejected. Eventually, he threatened to kill the head of the council if he continued to be ignored. This persuaded the head of the council to start adopting the retainer's policies. The now victorious samurai responded that the head of the council was clearly the wrong man for the job, because even a threat of death should not sway a samurai from his decisions.

Putting loyalty to the test

Some lords would call a samurai to their presence and tell them, as a ruse, that their service was to be terminated. The lord would then be able to assess how loyal the retainer really was by observing his reaction.

Servants for eternity

The famous loyalist Kusunoki Masashige and his brother Kusunoki Masasue gave their lives for the Emperor, killing each other in a suicide pact when their position was hopeless. In truth, they knew their mission was doomed from the start, but they went through with it anyway because that is what the Emperor commanded. Far from feeling any resentment, with their last words they declared that they wanted to be reborn seven times into the service of the Emperor. Echoing their wish, the author of the *Hagakure* stated that he wanted to be born seven times into the service of his clan. (Note that 'seven times' may have been an expression meaning 'for all time' rather than a specific number.)

TALES OF LOYALTY AND DISLOYALTY

As the following selection of episodes suggests, the idealized Tokugawa view of samurai loyalty was not always supported by historical events.

An offer that could not be refused

Following the Heiji Rebellion of 1159, in which his family were driven out of Kyōto and his father killed, Minamoto no Yoritomo grew up in exile. With no army to command, he had to think of a way to restore the Minamoto clan to power.

At that time in Japanese history, middle-level samurai vassals managed the estates of the upper-level samurai, collecting the taxes that enabled the high-ranking landowners to live in comfort in Kyōto alongside the aristocrats. The vassals gave service and loyalty to their lords because the lords had the power to appoint or dismiss them.

Therefore, to build an army from nothing, Minamoto no Yoritomo approached the estate managers and asked them to fight for him instead of their lords. In return, if he was victorious he promised to make their positions hereditary for all time and also increase their share of the revenue from the land. No longer would the vassals have to worry about maintaining their income or securing the future of their dependents. Obviously, many or most of the estate managers seized this offer and forgot the loyalty they had sworn to their lords. Having thus built up an army of highly motivated samurai, Yoritomo eventually became the *shōgun* of all Japan.

This took place in the twelfth century, a time all future samurai looked back to as the golden age of heroes, and yet it showed that, even then, most samurai would readily change lords in return for more money and job security. What's more, after Yoritomo's victory he repaid many of the allies who had helped him by killing them off one by one. Even his own half-brother Minamoto no Yoshitsune was not spared.

Death at dinner

The renowned fourteenth-century commander and poet Imagawa Ryōshun decided to make an example of a disloyal general called Shōni Fuyusuke by having him killed during a banquet. He intended that this would discourage other supporters from betraying him. However, his plan backfired: a number of his other generals, outraged at Fuyusuke's treatment, defected to the other side.

The overly loyal samurai

Showy displays of loyalty could be seen as currying favour. The sixteenth-century samurai Uemura Masakatsu or Shinroku annoyed his fellow retainers by always carrying his swords and being extremely deferential in the presence of the lord. His behaviour marked him out from the rest and stopped the others from feeling at ease. But when the master learned of their resentment, he commended Shinroku for showing proper military conduct and rewarded him with a fine blade made by the master swordsmith Yukimitsu. This episode shows that even within the same clan not everyone had the same view of what constituted a proper degree of loyalty.

Faith versus fealty

As was the case in Reformation-era Europe, samurai were sometimes faced with a conflict between their religious beliefs and the loyalty they owed to their lord. The Honda family broke up into two branches, each supporting a different version of Buddhism; one branch joined Tokugawa Ieyasu's forces and the other remained with the Ikkō Ikki league of clans. Some of these splits were strategic moves to enable a family to play both sides, but religion did still play a real and significant part in the politics of old Japan. However, the influence enjoyed by religious institutions was curtailed by Oda Nobunaga, who destroyed monastic military complexes.

Loyal insubordination

When Tokugawa Ieyasu was facing defeat at the battle of Mikatagahara, he refused to leave the battlefield even though staying would mean certain death. Recognizing this, Natsume Yoshinobu, one of Ieyasu's oldest and most loyal commanders, grabbed his lord's horse by the reins, smacked its rump and ordered Ieyasu off the field and back to their battle camp, accompanied by a bodyguard.

The valiant Natsume then shouted 'I am Ieyasu!' and mounted a suicide charge into the enemy. This *kagemusha* (影武者), or 'shadow double', move confused the enemy for long enough to allow the real Ieyasu time to escape.

Whose side are you on?

At the battle of Adzuki-zaka in 1563, a samurai named Naitō Masanari had to face his uncle, Ishikawa. At one point in the battle Ishikawa was directly attacking his nephew's lord, and so Masanari had to decide whether to side with his clan member or his lord. He called out so people could hear him, 'Ishikawa may be my uncle, but my lord comes first,' and then shot his uncle in the legs.

In the same battle, Tsuchiya Chōkichi, who was fighting against his own lord, saw that his lord – now his enemy – was hemmed in with only a small band to protect him. Declaring that he would not lift a spear against his lord, he turned on his own side, rejoined his lord's cause, and fought to the death.

Hachiya Hannojō was another samurai at the battle who was rebelling against his lord. A retainer of Tokugawa Ieyasu saw him retiring from the field and accused him of cowardice. Hachiya replied, 'I retire because I cannot fight against my own lord in personal combat.' When another samurai, Matsudaira Kinsuke, continued calling him a coward, Hachiya turned back and killed him, which proved that he was retreating not out of fear but because of a clash of loyalties.

As a postscript to this last story, Tokugawa Ieyasu himself charged Hachiya off the battlefield before he could claim Kinsuke's head. Many years later, Ieyasu boasted that he had forced Hachiya to flee without having fought, which was clearly not true – another example of an illustrious samurai failing to live up to the ideals of *bushidō*.

The ultimate show of loyalty

When a high-ranking samurai was told he had to die, it was common for one of his retainers to offer to take his place. For example, when Tokugawa Ieyasu was forced to order his son Matsudaira Nobuyasu to perform *seppuku*, the retainer Hiraiwa Chikayoshi volunteered to die in the young man's stead. However, the noble offer was refused because his death would not have been enough to resolve the political situation that had made Nobuyasu's death necessary (see chapter 7).

The betrayal of Oda Nobunaga

At one of the most exciting points in Japanese history, Oda Nobunaga was storming his way through Japan, conquering province after province. Just as he was about to unify all of Japan under his banner, one of his most trusted retainers, Akechi Mitsuhide, turned on him when he was staying at the temple of Honnōji. Oda Nobunaga, not having enough men to repel Akechi's army, was trapped and decided to perform *seppuku*, having first instructed his page Mori Ranmuru to set fire to the temple so that no one could take his head.

Some think that Akechi was making a power play, others that he was reacting to having been insulted or struck by Nobunaga, but, whatever his motive, this was one of the biggest betrayals in Japanese history. It led to the temporary break-up of the main samurai army at the time; Tokugawa Ieyasu had to flee in his now-famous run across the province of Iga, while Toyotomi Hideyoshi went on a hunting mission to take the head of the traitor, which he did.

Oda Nobunaga's eldest son and heir, Oda Nobutada, also performed *seppuku* in Akechi's attack on Honnōji. Next in line was Nobunaga's second son, Oda Nobukatsu, but sections of his own samurai did not want him to rule because he was considered to be a 'fool'. The powerful Oda clan stepped into the background and true power was taken up by the lower-born Toyotomi Hideyoshi.

SOURCES

Forget the following to aid loyal devotion to a lord:

- *Wives and children*
- *Treasure and properties*
- *Your body and your life*

Do not forget the following to aid loyal devotion to a lord:

- *Determination in loyalty*
- *The name of your family*
- *Your parents and ancestors*

Heika Jōdan (c1670)

The second defect of this nation is the meagre loyalty which people show toward their rulers. They rebel against them whenever they have a chance, either usurping them or joining their enemies. Then they turn about and declare themselves as friends again, only to rebel once more when the opportunity presents itself. Yet this sort of conduct does not discredit them at all.

Writings of Alessandro Valignano (16th century)

In the Warring States period much of the land was not tilled and the parts that were cultivated were destroyed at sowing time and plundered by neighbours and opposing factions, with men killing each other everywhere. And so the entire kingdom and all the nobles were left in the greatest poverty and wretchedness, and the only authority or law was military might. Men chastised and killed each other, banished people and confiscated their goods as they saw fit; treachery was rampant and nobody trusted his neighbour. Often, the most influential servants would murder their own lord and join up in league with other more powerful men in order to be confirmed in the possession of their territory, and as a precaution they would kill off the kindred of their lord. In this way, the leading noble families came to an end and were destroyed. Some people would rebel and join up with others, but a man could not trust his neighbour and always kept his weapons close at hand.

Writings of João Rodrigues (late 16th/early 17th century)

CHAPTER SEVEN

REPUTATION

Victory and defeat are temporary states brought about by circumstance. Shame is different. The only way to escape it is through death.

Hagakure (1716)

Nothing mattered as much to the samurai as their good name and that of their clan. A reputation lost was hard to regain, except by a glorious death or honourable suicide. In this chapter, we will explore how the samurai maintained their reputation, through achievement, honesty and a remorseless determination to take revenge on those who wronged them.

GOOD NAME

One time while Manbei was in the castle, some nosy young samurai came to him and said, 'I don't remember exactly what your name is. Is it Mabei or Manbei?' On hearing this, Manbei realized that he was being mocked and replied, 'It depends on the level of your morale. When your morale is high, you will call me Manbei with good pronunciation, and when you are hungry or lacking in will, you can call me Mabei.' Then the nosy samurai was embarrassed and thus retreated.

Musha Monogatari (1654)

Minamoto no Yoshitsune was held in high regard by the Minamoto clan retainers for his many and varied military achievements, including crossing mountains to invade impregnable fortresses, travelling in stormy seas when others dared not, landing his troops before others and taking victory in naval battles. However, he eventually fell out of favour and his elder brother, Minamoto no Yoritomo, the *shōgun*, started a smear campaign against him to stop him from finding support elsewhere. In contrast, when Ishikawa Kazumasa betrayed Tokugawa Ieyasu, Ieyasu said that, while his former retainer may have been disloyal, his military prowess should not be discredited.

Above all things, the samurai valued their reputation for integrity and capability. Even if they did not possess such attributes, they had to be *seen* to possess them. They knew how hard it was to gain a good reputation and keep it. Harder still was to clear a bad reputation.

Clearing a bad reputation through achievement

> *According to an old samurai story, during the Winter Siege of Osaka Castle, Suzukida Hayatonosuke, who was on the side of Lord Hideyori, was given command of a ship to defend against the central west provinces and he was stationed at Etsuda Castle. However, Hachisuka Awanokami from Ieyasu's side attacked and captured the castle so Hayatonosuke fled to Osaka to save his life.*
>
> *The next spring, when Lord Hideyori's senior counsellors met together to talk about strategies, this Suzukida was also present. Then a 12- or 13-year-old page boy went to him with a large fruit and said, 'Look at this, Sir Hayatonosuke. Do you not think it is a beautiful fruit?' To this, he agreed that it was quite beautiful. Then the boy said, 'This big fruit is just like you, Sir Hayatonosuke – if it were a human, that is. It looks so graceful, but it is not quite so on the inside; therefore, it cannot be served as food. Remember, you cannot judge things by their looks alone.' At which, the defeated samurai Hayatonosuke was terribly embarrassed.*
>
> *However, at the Summer Siege, on the sixth of the fifth month,*

he was killed magnificently at the Dōmyōji entrance to the castle and his head was cut off by Kawakami Shinpachirō, a retainer of Mizuno Hyūganokami Katsunari. It is said the page boy was told to speak as such by Ōno Shurinosuke.

Musha Monogatari (1654)

A samurai who lost his reputation could regain it through a new achievement. If that new achievement or series of achievements outweighed an old transgression, and if the newer achievements were spoken about more than the older problems, his reputation would become clear again.

Clearing a bad reputation through death

Dying was seen as a sure way to clear a bad reputation, if the death occurred in the correct way. Even if you did not fully restore your good name, you were sure at least to cancel out the negative aspects of a bad reputation by a proper suicide. When the alternative was to live out the rest of your life in shame, shunned by your peers, it is perhaps little surprise that samurai sought atonement through suicide or by a glorious death in battle. A samurai who had led a relatively negative life could achieve fame and forgiveness in a beautiful and heroic death or by taking their own life as an apology for their past misdeeds.

SOURCES

A son of Tomita said, 'Even though my father betrayed Ashina Morishige [which caused great shame to our family], we maintain our standards.' He then went deep across the enemy line, killed a samurai named Tarōmaru Kamon and brought his head to show his lord [hoping this deed would atone for his father's actions].

Musha Monogatari (1654)

> *While I was carrying a spear with silver fittings for my master samurai,*
> *I fell asleep and the silver sakawa binding clamp on the spear end was*
> *stolen. I am to blame for this and I might be killed as punishment.*
> *To atone for my mistake and regain my honour, I was hoping to do*
> *something fine such as killing an enemy.*
>
> Zōhyō Monogatari (1657–84)

Gaining a bad reputation through ignorance

> *You should never enquire about matters of warfare from someone*
> *born timid, no matter how well you know him.*
>
> Writings of Shiba Yoshimasa (1349–1410)

To be constantly unprepared or ignorant of correct samurai ways invariably created a negative reputation. In the *Chasō Kanwa* (茶窓閑話) document, Lord Sansei complained that warriors in his day only enjoyed the tea ceremony and other artistic pursuits and that they had no ability in military matters. He said that samurai should always be prepared, be ready to fight and know how to use all military arms and equipment, and that the way of a samurai lord was to demonstrate a love of military ways as an example to all the retainers below him. This would improve the clan's overall martial ability. Sansei also warned that if a lord loved only tea, then his retainers would also love only tea and they would neglect their military skills. We will explore this issue further in the next chapter.

> *In the worst case, some may even venture the opinion that warfare*
> *is not the path of a samurai. Keep in mind that, whether in times*
> *of peace or times of war, samurai should be prepared for war and*
> *should never forget* heidō, *the way of the soldier.*
>
> Heika Jōdan (c1670)

WHAT'S IN A NAME?

While the samurai were intent on establishing a good name for themselves, in the sense of building a positive reputation, confusingly, they often changed their actual name. For example, when Oda Nobunaga awarded the samurai Okudaira Sadamasa the honour of being able to use the first syllable of his own name, he thereafter became known as Okudaira Nobumasa.

It was not unusual for a samurai to change his name multiple times. Below, we trace the name changes of the samurai born Matsudaira Takechiyo and better known today as Tokugawa Ieyasu. Particularly significant is his change from Motoyasu (元康) to Ieyasu (家康), which was believed to have been done because the character for *ie* (家) was associated with past *shōgun*s. This change was made well before he himself became a *shōgun* and some historians see it as a signalling of his grand ambitions from an early age.

The name changes of Tokugawa Ieyasu were as follows:

1. Matsudaira Takechiyo (松平 竹千代) (*yōmyō* – birth name)
2. Matsudaira Motonobu (松平 元信) (*genpukuna* – coming-of-age name)
3. Jirōsaburō (次郎三郎) (*haikōmei* – nickname that represents the order of birth)
4. Matsudaira Motoyasu (松平 元康) (*kaimei* – name change, after marriage)
5. Matsudaira Ieyasu (松平　家康) (*kaimai* – name change, after the battle of Okehazama)
6. Tokugawa Ieyasu (徳川家康) (*kaisei* – name change, to make him a descendant of the Minamoto family)
7. Tōshō Dai-Gongen (東照大権現) (*shingō* – a name given through Shintō)
8. Tōshō Dai-Gongen Ankokuin den Tokuren Shasūyo Tōwa Daikoji (東照大権現安国院殿徳蓮社崇誉道和大居士) (*kaimyō* – death name, never used in life)

In addition, he was also awarded the following honorific titles:

- Taikun (大君) (title for use on official documents, meaning 'great lord')
- Ōgosho (大御所) (title after he retired, meaning 'retired *shōgun*')
- Shinkun (神君) (posthumous title, meaning 'great deity')

The samurai tactician and student of war known as Natori Sanjūrō Masazumi wrote the now-famous *Shōninki* manual on *shinobi* tactics. In the introduction to the manual, which was written by a samurai known as Katsuda, he refers to Natori as 'Masatake' and not 'Masazumi'. This was most likely a compliment, because 'take' (武) means 'military', so by changing the second syllable of Natori's name in this way, Katsuda was calling him 'Masa the military man'. This was probably an informal nickname of sorts rather than an official name change, adding a further layer of complexity to the issue of samurai names.

Sometimes the samurai moved characters around in their names to convey a certain image, or even to bring themselves good fortune following the principles of *seimei handan* (姓名判断), a name-based divination system. However, anyone who thought that by changing their name they could change their reputation was likely to be disappointed.

OATHS

Oath-giving in samurai culture is a complex subject. There were various levels of oath and vow used for different kinds of promise. Examples include a *kishōmon* pledge, which contained the phrase, 'In witness whereof I hereto set my hand and seal to this *kishōmon*.' It had a blood seal at the end and was written on a special type of paper known as *goō*. A *shinmon* pledge had a blood seal at the end and was written on normal paper, while a *seimon* oath used normal writing paper and had no blood seal.

Oaths often involved calling on the gods that the oath-giver worshipped so that the person making the oath took it seriously. Japanese archives contain many examples of oaths, declarations and the like, all signed in ink and then stamped with a thumbprint in blood.

The sixteenth-century Jesuit missionary Gaspar Vilela described witnessing the signing of a pledge of loyalty from a samurai to a lord. The samurai stood before an idol – most likely a Buddhist statue – cut his arm and used the blood to write his oath, including characters that the samurai did not understand, which may have been in Sanskrit. Afterwards, the paper oath was burned and the ash mixed into a liquid, which the samurai then drank.

This account underlines the sacred nature of a samurai oath. Created using the samurai's own blood and then reabsorbed into his body, it was a promise not only to his lord but also to the gods. And it would be the task not only of the lord but also the gods to punish any samurai who failed to keep his promise.

It should be pointed out here that samurai did not have to stay with the same lord forever. Oaths could be set for a certain time period, as is the case with a modern contract.

HOLY ABALONE

Legend says that the Chiba family were at sea and a hole was made in their ship. In response to their plight, a school of abalone fish came and plugged the hole, thereby saving the clan from drowning. From then on everyone in the Chiba family vowed not to eat abalone; if they did, they would be cursed with boils. However, one clan member broke with tradition and ate one of the fish, which brought doom upon him.

The seven-sheet oath

The *Ippei Yōkō* scroll, which contains teachings of the Natori-Ryū samurai school, explains the protocol for writing a *shichimai-gishō*, or 'seven-sheet oath'. As the following overview shows, this was a complex contract, with each sheet dedicated to a different deity or deities and requiring a blood seal from a different part of the samurai's body.

Sheet one

Shichisha kishōmon – seven oaths from seven shrines given with due respect. Though the promises made are difficult to achieve, if there is any infringement or violation, I shall receive divine punishment from the Lord of Heaven, the Four Guardians of Taishakuten and all major and minor gods from more than sixty provinces from all over Japan, especially Atago Daigongen. In witness whereof I hereto set my hand and seal to this *kishōmon*.

Apply blood from the left ring finger.

Sheet two
Shichisha kishōmon – seven oaths from seven shrines given with due respect. For this oath, which is protected by the Daigosan temple, know that punishment shall come from Sanbō in Godaidō. In witness whereof I hereto set my hand and seal to this *kishōmon*.
Apply blood from the right ring finger.

Sheet three
Shichisha kishōmon – seven oaths from seven shrines given with due respect. For this oath, I will receive punishments from Fuji Daigongen. In witness whereof I hereto set my hand and seal to this *kishōmon*.
Apply blood from the tongue.

Sheet four
Shichisha kishōmon – seven oaths from seven shrines given with due respect. For this oath, I will receive punishments from Ōmine Daigongen. In witness whereof I hereto set my hand and seal to this *kishōmon*.
Apply blood from the nape of the neck.

Sheet five
Shichisha kishōmon – seven oaths from seven shrines given with due respect. For this oath, I will receive punishments from Hachiman Daibosatsu. In witness whereof I hereto set my hand and seal to this *kishōmon*.
Apply blood from the left foot.

Sheet six
Shichisha kishōmon – seven oaths from seven shrines given with due respect. For this oath, I will receive punishments from the god representing the Jūra for that day and also the *happō-yū*. In witness whereof I hereto set my hand and seal to this *kishōmon*.
Apply blood from the right foot.

Sheet seven

Shichisha kishōmon – seven oaths from seven shrines given with due respect. For this oath, I shall receive the difficulties and agonies from Buddha of the [Konpon] Chūdō in Ōmi province, which shall last through the afterlife no matter how long. In witness whereof I hereto set my hand and seal to this *kishōmon*.
Apply blood from the left and right palms.

> **A SACRED BOND**
> A retainer of Tokugawa Ieyasu was given a piece of ginseng as a gift. Having nothing in which to wrap the gift, he attempted to pull down a piece of paper reserved for giving oaths. This greatly displeased Ieyasu, because paper used for oaths was considered sacred.

False promises

In what is becoming a familiar pattern, whereby the principles of *bushidō* appear to be somewhat elastic, there are various accounts of samurai being celebrated for having broken their promises.

For example, the *Heike Monogatari* describes what happened when Moritoshi, a powerful samurai from the Heike clan, defeated Noritsuna, a samurai of similar status from the Genji clan. The defeated warrior surrendered and asked to be spared. The victor agreed and promises were exchanged. Immediately after, Moritoshi was distracted by the approach of other horsemen, at which point the defeated Noritsuna – who had just given a binding oath – took the opportunity to kill Moritoshi, decapitate him and take his head. It is said he was honoured for this deed despite the fact that he had broken his vow.

HONESTY

> *It can be said that the words that samurai give forth can be counted*
> *as more secure than gold or iron.*
>
> *Heika Jōdan* (c1670)

One element of *bushidō* that seems to hold fast throughout samurai literature is honesty. If a samurai said something was true, it had to be true. For a samurai to speak falsely – even to make a slight exaggeration – could put an indelible stain on his honour. Deceitful actions, particularly in battle, do not seem to have been condemned – indeed, they were often celebrated – but lying to a fellow samurai was considered demeaning.

There are countless historical quotes illustrating that samurai were meant to tell the truth, of which the following are just a small selection. However, to what extent the samurai actually did tell the truth is unknown.

SOURCES

When no one is there to see you, think that the walls have eyes and do not let your guard down. In your manners toward other people, needless to say, you should not make a misstep. Even in saying a single word you should not give others the impression that you are shallow.

Writings of Shiba Yoshimasa (1349–1410)

Honesty just means a straightforward mind. If the mind is distorted all behaviour is distorted.

Writings of Ichijō Kaneyoshi (1402–81)

Lord Oda Nobunaga once gave his attendant Mori Ranmaru his sword to look after while he relieved himself. While waiting for his lord, Ranmaru counted the number of notches on the scabbard. Knowing

---

his attendant would have done this, Lord Nobunaga gathered his pages together and said, 'Try to guess how many notches there are on my scabbard. I will give this sword to the one who can guess right.' So, everyone put forward their guess, all but Ranmaru. Then Lord Nobunaga said, 'Ran, why do you not say anything?' To which he replied, 'Because I have already counted the notches and so I know the answer.' Impressed with his attendant's honesty, Lord Nobunaga gave him the sword.

Musha Monogatari (1654)

Essentially, monks and merchants do not do anything that will not pay and have little resolve in a righteous sense. One or two out of ten may be sincere, but samurai are advised not to rely on them. When you are in a weak position, ask another samurai for help. You should never feel ashamed of putting your trust in a samurai, even if your faith in him turns out to have been misguided. [...] Therefore, as a samurai, if you fall into a serious situation and have no one to ask for help, it would be more praiseworthy to leap to your death into deep water with stones in your sleeves than to rely on a monk or merchant, which would be extremely disgraceful.

Musha Monogatari (1654)

Good bushi with a number of great achievements do not talk about their feats all through their lives, no matter how much people ask them to. They do not need to talk because their reputation as extraordinary samurai of incomparable courage goes before them. On the other hand, some bushi of lesser renown and achievement – those, for example, who have got two or three retreating enemy's heads – have an avid desire for fame and talk about how great they are. If invited to, they talk more than ever, especially when in the company of young samurai. It is like when you put sake in a barrel. When the barrel is full, it makes little sound; while a barrel containing only a little sake will resound very loudly.

Musha Monogatari (1654)

VENGEANCE

Dying without achieving your long sought-after goal of avenging yourself is not only a failure for yourself but can blemish your family's name. The shame can result in scorn and contempt being directed at your family.

Heihō Yūkan (1645)

Revenge, known by the term *katakiuchi* (敵討), 'enemy striking', was an integral part of samurai honour. For one's own good name and that of the clan, insults, slights and injuries had to be answered. When the head of a clan had been murdered, his heir could not succeed him until he had killed his murderer. A younger brother could not return home until he had killed the murderer of his elder brother. This was the way of the Japanese blood feud.

The importance of vengeance in samurai culture can be seen in the fact that the scroll *Heika Jōdan* dedicates an entire chapter to the art of revenge killings, while the samurai school called Mubyōshi-Ryū can be confidently described as a school of revenge because its founder, Hagihara Jūzō, only created the school as a result of the blood feuds he had been involved in during his youth.

The issue of vengeance was at the heart of Tokugawa Ieyasu's need to order his son Matsudaira Nobuyasu to commit suicide. Nobuyasu's wife was the daughter of Oda Nobunaga. She wrote to her father to accuse her mother-in-law, with whom she did not get along, of plotting against him with the Takeda clan. Nobunaga brought this to Ieyasu's attention and, in order to appease his ally, Ieyasu had to put his own wife to death. For the same reason, he then was forced to order his son to perform *seppuku*, because otherwise Nobuyasu would have sought to kill Nobunaga to avenge his mother's death.

A notable act of revenge was carried out by an unnamed samurai who was made masterless by his superior, Ankokuji Eikei. The lower-ranked samurai, now a *rōnin*, later got his own back by telling Tokugawa Ieyasu where Ankokuji Eikei was hiding after a battle. Upon the successful capture of the target based on the *rōnin*'s information, Ieyasu attempted to reward him with a large amount of gold. At first, the *rōnin* refused, saying it was a matter of honour, but when pressed he took the gold and gave it to his village.

The legalities of revenge were vague and shifted over time. For example, the famed '47 rōnin' who in 1702 killed the man who had murdered their lord were punished for their act of vengeance by being forced to commit suicide, yet they were widely considered to have done the right thing morally. The Tokugawa government of the time were trying to phase out violent samurai traditions such as blood feuds and the practice of a retainer following his lord into death. However, even in the nineteenth century blood feud killings were still common. Western travellers reported that every morning a headless body would be laid out somewhere in Edo with a reed mat covering it, and another vendetta was settled.

It would appear that the murder of a female family member was not usually considered serious enough to trigger a feud. If a male member of the family was killed, revenge absolutely had to be taken, yet if something bad happened to a female member of the clan then the incident was forgotten. Luís Froís wrote in 1585: 'In Europe, the abduction of a female relation threatens the survival of all her family; however, in Japan, her father, mother and brothers conceal it and just let it pass over.' The episode described above involving Tokugawa Ieyasu's wife and son muddies the issue, as it was fear that his son would avenge his mother's death that motivated Ieyasu. However, what is clear is that any murder of a male clan member would provoke a blood feud that would only be settled when the offender had been tracked down and murdered.

THE *MADRE DE DEUS* INCIDENT

The 1609 incident of the *Madre de Deus* ('Mother of God'), a Portuguese trading ship, was an example of samurai revenge spilling out beyond Japan. The feud had been sparked the previous year when the samurai crew of a Tokugawa trading ship had run amok in the Portuguese colony of Macau. The authorities tried to arrest them, but they retreated to some buildings, which the locals set on fire. When the samurai ran outside, some were shot dead, others were imprisoned and strangled in their cells, and the rest were expelled.

Upon hearing of this, Tokugawa Ieyasu targeted the next Portuguese ship to arrive in Japan, which was the *Madre de Deus* (sometimes given under the name *Nossa Senhora da Graça*). There ensued a short but memorable sea battle in which the foreign ship was destroyed and its captain, who, interestingly, had also been an official involved in the Macau incident, was killed.

SOURCES

I was born a warrior, and to my house, just as to me, the sudden shame [of being murdered] would be a bitter blow.

Heike Monogatari (14th century)

If you are going to kill someone, you should first be determined to die and think nothing of yourself but only of the enemy.

Mizukagami (c1670)

When [Hagihara Jūzō] Shigetatsu was young he unexpectedly had to kill someone and because of this he was targeted, day and night, for nine years. In order to kill the enemy, he devoted himself to training in the martial ways and sought various schools and asked for many teachers to instruct him.

Bishamonden (c1698)

Poisoning

Poisoning was a particular danger at times of war or feuding. Upper-class families would employ testers to ensure that their food was safe, because samurai often attempted to poison their rivals at meals. There seems to have been little shame in using such an underhand method, but neither does there appear to have been any honour.

SOURCES

The meals for Yodo-dono were prepared by the staff in the kitchen and passed to the serving attendants. The servants in the kitchen tasted the food for poison before they passed it to the attendants. Or sometimes the attendants tasted before they offered it to the lady.

Unknown

If someone tries to give you poison, he will mix it in booze, tea, food, hot water and so on. However, it has to be in something only you consume and never in what you share with the master or others. From ancient times there have been cases where a master poisons his guests; however, it is possible to give the poison back to the master of the house. Keep in mind that there are countless ways to avoid being poisoned; for example, swapping a cake that you have been served for another one.

Shōninki (1681)

Look at the reflection of yourself in sake, tea or water. If the drink has poison in it, you will not be able to see your own reflection.

Scrolls of Sekiguchi-Ryū under Yamada Toshiyasu (Edo period)

CHAPTER EIGHT

SOCIAL CUSTOMS

The samurai were not only military men but also members of society and they had to navigate the same customs and conventions as everyone else. While social niceties such as when and how to bow, who to give a gift to and where to sit did not compare to the critical, split-second decisions that had to be made on the battlefield, they were still important. Getting them wrong could lead to embarrassment, shame or even, in extreme circumstances, death.

EDUCATION

> *A child of a samurai family should not be raised among merchants or peasants. Ideally, he should start learning reading and writing at the age of eight and become acquainted with martial arts at the age of 14 or 15. Poor parents who cannot provide their children with such an education should raise their children among samurai. No matter how highborn you are, if you are raised as a commoner, you will look and speak like a commoner.*
>
> *Musha Monogatari* (1654)

The concept of *bunbu* (文武), 'the brush and the sword', meaning a combination of literary and fighting skills, was what defined the samurai approach to education. Originally, samurai boys were taught at home, but schools of education were later established. Overall, the samurai had an education better than common folk but lower than the religious orders. In later periods, most samurai could read, even if just phonetically, and an understanding of the classics of philosophy and military strategy was considered as something to which to esteem. They were brought up to be independent military men who would serve in a conglomerate army and further the interests of their clan and they needed an education of some sort to distinguish their actions from base thuggery.

Samurai children were not protected from the harsh realities of life. They might be forced to commit suicide and even the youngest of children were executed for political reasons or for the crimes of other family members. Therefore, they learned the potential consequences of improper action and lack of respect from a young age.

They also learned about fear and bloodshed. Children were sent out at night to 'haunted' places like execution grounds, where they would have to touch the decapitated heads on display, or venture on other spine-chilling excursions. The *Hagakure* says that in the old days samurai boys trained for war by beheading dogs before graduating to criminals in execution yards. According to the scroll, when one boy was ordered to kill ten bound criminals in succession, he let the tenth one go, as an act of mercy. The author recalled his own childhood visit to an execution yard to try his hand at beheading, saying that it gave him a positive feeling.

Natori Sanjūrō Masazumi, founder of the Natori-Ryū school, recommended that young samurai should watch public executions and become used to the spilling of blood, because it was unseemly for a samurai to vomit or faint at the sight of killing. This is backed up by the assertion in the *Hagakure* that many samurai men had lost their desire to perform blood deeds and that they often tried to weasel their way out of the duty of *kaishaku* (beheading the victim during the ritual of *seppuku*).

CHILD SOLDIERS

Samurai youths were very much like the child soldiers used today in developing countries. They were indoctrinated for war from an early age, forced to kill in preparation for being warriors and brought up to maintain order by enforcing their will on the lower echelons of society. When trying to rationalize samurai behaviour, always remember the way in which they were conditioned as children.

REFINEMENT AND THE ARTS

We treasure gems and pieces of gold and silver; but for the Japanese
it is old cauldrons, broken old porcelain and clay vessels.

Luís Froís, *Tratado* (1585)

While the samurai were renowned for their military prowess, they were also devotees of the arts. The *Hagakure* states that warriors would hide poetry inside their helmet and breastplate when going to battle. The samurai were also dedicated collectors of works of beauty such as cloths and wall hangings and pots, tea sets, flower vases and trinkets.

Japanese life was full of poetry, *nō* theatre, tea ceremonies, ritual dance and comedy. When Tokugawa Ieyasu met the Hōjō clan there was a theatrical performance in which the powerful Ieyasu himself took on the role of the comic Chinese character Jinen Koji and his retainer Sakai Tadatsugu danced the 'prawn dance' to great amusement. Luís Froís described the entertainments laid on at the court of Oda Nobunaga, which included a finely dressed dwarf who was brought out of a basket to perform, much like the jesters found in European courts.

There were different kinds of theatre for different levels of society, ranging from lowly travelling street entertainers to the heights of dramatic sophistication at court in Kyōto. The samurai were particularly keen on *kōwaka* dances (幸若舞), military-based affairs in which the performers had the right to wear two swords.

Sometimes art was found in the midst of war. During the siege of Nagashino Castle by Tokugawa Ieyasu, when the besieged heard that there was a famous *nō* actor within the besiegers' camp they sent out a message to the enemy requesting that the actor sing and perform for them below the castle walls because soon they would be dead. Ieyasu granted their wish and at the end of the performance one retainer came out of the castle and gave gifts to the actor in thanks. The next day, the final assault came, the castle fell and the defenders died with honour. One samurai was allowed to live because he could recite all of the *Kin'yō Wakashū* anthology of *waka* poetry, a tremendously prestigious feat.

Great importance was attached to preserving works of art and literature even in the most dire circumstances. When trapped in a siege, the renowned poet-samurai Hosokawa Yūsai was permitted to send out a rare copy of the *Kokinshū* poetry collection so that it would not be destroyed in the impending slaughter and destruction. In a similar situation, when the Akechi samurai were besieged, they were allowed to lower down their prized collection of swords from the castle.

IN SEARCH OF SIMPLICITY

The point of the Zen approach to the tea ceremony was to replace the earlier Chinese-influenced exquisite and expensive tea sets with rough pots made of clay and simple utensils made of bamboo. However, within a short space of time, these common objects themselves became prized and, therefore, valuable and the trappings of the tea ceremony became exquisite and expensive once more.

FLOWERS

To the samurai, flowers were more than just adornments: they held important symbolic meaning. For example, the stunning but short-lived cherry blossom was seen as representing the career of a valiant warrior who falls gloriously in battle while still in his prime. In the following historical episode, a flower did not merely symbolize the death of a samurai, it actually helped to cause it.

When the powerful warlord Sasa Narimasa was awarded the province of Higo by Toyotomi Hideyoshi, he showed his gratitude by giving Hideyoshi's wife, the Lady Yae, a black lily from Kaga domain. The Lady Yae, never having seen such a bloom, was delighted with her gift and held a tea ceremony in its honour with the lily as the centrepiece. However, her rival the Lady Yodo, Hideyoshi's concubine, found out where the flower was from and ordered a great number of them to be delivered to her. She then held her own ceremony, but placed the lilies among very common flowers, which belittled both the lily and, by association, the Lady Yae.

The strife this caused between the two women fanned out into a full-blown factional dispute, which eventually, by a complex set of circumstances, resulted in Hideyoshi ordering Sasa Narimasa to commit suicide. It is recorded that he sat down on a stone and gave the man who would behead him 30 gold coins and his fine clothes. He asked that the stone he sat on be talked about in future as the place where his life had ended so that his memory would carry on. After this, he performed a cross cut to open his guts, pulled out his entrails, turned to the aide and said, 'Strike now', at which he was beheaded.

OVERINDULGENCE IN THE ARTS

> *If interest in such subjects [as the arts] expands and you become overinvolved in their meanings, negligence in* budō *will follow.*
> *Heika Jōdan* (c1670)

There was a recurring pattern in Japanese history in which one clan, having fought to gain power, would overindulge in artistic pursuits and forget military ways, and so would end up having their power usurped by another clan. In turn, this clan would be seduced by the refinements of court life and, sooner or later, be replaced by yet another clan. This rhythm continued all the way through to the end of the Sengoku period.

When the Tokugawa clan gained power at the battle of Sekigahara in 1600, they managed to stay at the top for most of the next three centuries. However, they did this as much by weakening the military and financial base of their rivals as by maintaining their own strength. The result of this prolonged period of peace was that interest in warcraft fell across the board. While there are examples of good and hardy warriors during this era, many samurai turned their attention to other pursuits.

This decline is typified by the following episode recorded in the *Chasō Kanwa* document. A young samurai asks Lord Sansai if he can become a student of the tea ceremony under him. Wanting to make sure that the youth's military studies are up to scratch, the lord asks him how he would decapitate an enemy who was still wearing a helmet (*kitsuki*). It is clear from the vagueness of the youth's answer that the only experience he has comes from watching stage dramatizations of the act. The lord teaches him the correct method and tells him he should give up his infatuation with tea and take up military arts instead.

In a contrasting story from the same manual, another young samurai cleverly refers to the strings used on Japanese tea bags during a discussion with Lord Toyotomi Hideyoshi about how to decapitate an opponent with his helmet 'strings' still in place. By drawing this comparison, the student is making it clear that warriors should concentrate on understanding the cords of their armour and not concern themselves with tea bag strings.

TEA NINJA

The *Chasō Kanwa* document, translated into English as *Stories from a Tearoom Window*, was written by Chikamatsu Shigenori, who, while being a lover of all things to do with tea, was also a skilled military tactician and a qualified ninja (*shinobi no mono*). A translation of his ninja scrolls is published in English as *Iga and Koka Ninja Skills* (History Press).

Chapter Eight

WASHING AND GROOMING

The Japanese preoccupation with cleanliness in both body and home is not a modern phenomenon. The great sixteenth-century leader Oda Nobunaga is believed to have been clinically obsessed with hygiene.

Bathing in public baths using water from hot springs was a popular custom in samurai times and remains so today. Often the baths would be unsegregated between the sexes and there was little shame in nudity, at least among the family. However, when a Western visitor to Japan during the samurai period came across a naked woman walking to the baths in a remote village, the woman was hugely embarrassed. She had not expected to be seen by a man, as all the men of the village were out working.

Originally, samurai used to pluck their hair out to form their distinctive topknot; later, they shaved their hair instead. In the *Heika Jōdan* scroll, it is said that if a samurai was urgently called away while tending to his hair, he would tie a *tenugui* cloth around his head to avoid drawing attention to his unpreparedness. According to the Florentine merchant Francesco Carletti, to touch a samurai's topknot, even by accident, was regarded as a great insult.

TOOTH BLACKENING

To modern eyes, black teeth appear unattractive, but in the samurai era it was fashionable for aristocrats, in particular, to dye their teeth with a mixture of iron filings, vinegar and tea powder. The samurai also adopted the practice in order to mark themselves out from the common folk. The teeth of fallen warriors were blackened to underline their status as the 'glorious dead'. The class distinction between those who did and did not blacken their teeth was made explicit in the term *aobamono* (青歯者) used for lower-level warriors, which literally means 'blue teeth people' but actually refers to white teeth. As well as its role as a social marker, tooth blackening is also believed to have had a practical function; the dye formed an impermeable layer over the teeth that protected them from decay.

Tooth blackening can trace its roots back a long time before the samurai period and well into prehistory. Among the early samurai clans, the Taira were said to have blackened their teeth, while the rustic and unrefined Minamoto did not. Later, the Hōjō clan also took up the practice to show their rise above common stock. Women in common society would start the process of blackening the teeth during their teenage years but would only fully blacken them when they were married; however, members of the outcast class were excluded from the practice.

It appears that tooth blackening went in and out of fashion. One Jesuit missionary reported that when he first arrived in Japan in the late sixteenth century the practice was popular, but that it had fallen out of favour by 1600. The traveller Bernardino de Avila Girón wrote that women used lip powder to colour over the stains the black dye made on their lips.

Tooth blackening officially came to an end by imperial decree in the Meiji Restoration of 1868. However, when the British diplomat A. B. Mitford met the Emperor that year, he still had blackened teeth and the Empress kept hers until 1873. It would appear that this powerful status symbol was hard to give up.

MANNERS AND ETIQUETTE

> *It is better to criticize what should be criticized. By saying what needs to be said, you will keep your mind at ease and not be considered as an ignorant, mindless person.*
>
> Writings of Shiba Yoshimasa (1349–1410)

There is a distinction between manners, the polite, considerate way to treat other people, and etiquette, the correct protocol at social events. In old Japan, as in all other cultures, there was a complex set of social customs, covering everything from bowing and seating positions to the polite way to use chopsticks or pass objects. Bear in mind that manners and etiquette were different from chivalric behaviour. Simply being polite or performing the correct social graces could not compare with the conduct required of a warrior.

Chapter Eight

Bowing

> *The people greatly venerate their ruler and it is reckoned a high honour for the sons of the greatest nobles to serve him. They kneel down, placing both hands on the ground when they receive anything or hand something over in his presence. They like to speak softly and look down on us for speaking roughly. Etiquette demands that a man receives guests of equal rank by kneeling with his hands on the floor until they are seated.*
>
> Writings of Jorge Álvares (16th century)

The widespread Japanese practice of bowing is a tradition that has been carried over from the samurai era. The type of bow depended on the person's status in relation to the status of the person to whom they were bowing. Whereas in today's Japan men typically bow with their hands at the side and women bow with their hands to the front, sixteenth-century accounts by Western visitors suggest that all Japanese tended to bow with their hands at the front when in the submissive position. Other accounts report that, when in the presence of the lord, samurai would face the floor fully or half-prone, or at least with their faces fully on the floor and hands in front.

Bowing was done reciprocally between people of all classes; the lower-status person would bow in full, while the higher-status person would return the bow in the form of a slight head incline, touching their hands to the floor or a very slight forward bend of the body.

If a samurai leader walking with his retainers flanking him stopped for a period of time, the other samurai all dropped to one knee while they were waiting. When the lord talked to them, they placed their left hand on the ground and slightly bent their heads in acknowledgement. They only stood and moved off when their lord started moving.

The basic bowing etiquette between ranks is thus:

- Senior – slight bow to those below them
- Junior – full bow to those above them
- Equal ranks – a half bow to each other

Early Western accounts tell of how even the most powerful samurai in Japan would bow like common servants to the regent or *shōgun* because of his absolute power over everyone.

Public displays of respect and subordination

There were various intricate protocols governing what should happen when two samurai came across each other in public. The principle behind these observances was to avoid samurai of lower rank taking a physically higher position than their superiors.

If a samurai on horseback came across a higher-ranking samurai who was on foot, the horseman would have to dismount. For the avoidance of doubt, important samurai would carry a spear as a sign of their office. Writing in the very early seventeenth century, the Portuguese missionary João Rodrigues gave details of the procedure. He noted that the further away the dismount took place, the more respect the lower-ranking samurai was offering; dismounting too close was an offence. The average distance was fifteen paces away. The horseman would walk on after the high-ranking samurai for a certain time, after which, as a show of courtesy, the superior would send one of his servants back to tell the inferior that he was permitted to remount. Likewise, in a military context, if a messenger arrived (with the understanding that messengers in samurai armies were high-ranking, trusted retainers) they had to dismount from their horse to deliver the message.

If a lower-ranking person met a higher-ranking person but both were walking, then the lower-ranking person slipped their feet out of their footwear (which in earlier times was like a half sandal) and stood with their toes on the back edge of the shoe. This was done to display submissiveness, but in a way that still kept their feet clean.

There were similar intricacies for many other permutations of public meeting, including, for example, how to approach a samurai who was carrying a hawk and the protocol for lowering your parasol on a sunny day (see chapter 2). Many of these are no longer practised in Japan and have been lost from the collective imagination.

THE GO-BETWEEN

In order to avoid unseemly arguments or displays of emotion, the samurai would often use a messenger to convey unwelcome information or to transact delicate business. The Italian missionary Alessandro Valignano wrote:

This method is so much in vogue that it is used between fathers and their children, masters and their servants and even between husbands and wives, for they maintain that it is prudent to conduct through a third person for such matters which may give rise to anger, objections or quarrels.

Sitting and seating

Both the pose you adopted when sitting in conversation and the location you were assigned at a formal gathering were important indicators of your status in relation to the other people present. The order in which attendees entered and left the room was also a marker of status. To fail to observe the correct etiquette would be highly disrespectful.

Sitting postures

There were two main sitting postures used in formal situations: *seiza* (正座), a kneeling position, which is well known today as a pose used in martial arts and Japanese cultural activities; and *agura* (胡座), a cross-legged position. *Seiza* was a position of submissiveness adopted by inferiors, while the superior party would sit in *agura*.

A person might have to change between the *seiza* and *agura* positions depending on who they were talking to. Imagine that there were three samurai: one of low rank, one of middle rank and one of high rank. When the low-ranking samurai sat in conversation with the middle-ranking one, the low-ranking one would sit in *seiza*, and the middle-ranking one would sit in *agura*.

However, if the middle-ranking samurai then sat in conversation with the high-ranking one, he would have to switch to a kneeling position. If both the low- and middle-ranking samurai faced the high-ranking samurai then they would both kneel in *seiza*, while the most senior would sit cross-legged in *agura*. However, if the three of them faced an altar they would all kneel, because they were all inferior to their ancestors and gods.

In 1775, Carl Peter Thunberg, the surgeon on board a visiting Dutch East India Company vessel, observed that the Japanese knelt in *seiza* for as long as they could but then shifted to a more comfortable position later on. However, women remained in the submissive kneeling position. This tradition of men sitting cross-legged and women remaining kneeling persists even today in some contexts.

Seating positions

The position in which one sat within the room at a banquet or meeting was extremely important. As in Western traditions, the lead figure sat at the head of the table, while other figures sat to the sides. The lowest-ranking people took the position closest to the door.

Japanese houses were divided in two, with one half of the floor plan dedicated to public activities and the other half being a private space. (This arrangement is still the norm in modern houses.) Gatherings took place in the public area of the house. The highest-ranking individuals sat with their back to the inner wall and facing the outside wall, a prime position as dictated by the principles of *feng shui*. The people next in prestige sat with their backs to the side walls, facing either east or west; and the lowest-ranking people had their backs to the outside wall and faced the inner wall.

The German doctor Engelbert Kaempfer described an audience he had with the *shōgun* in 1691. He said that there were multiple raised sections of different heights used for people of different ranks, with the *shōgun* himself being veiled behind a screen. Other unidentifiable people were also behind screens; they had inserted folded sheets of paper between the slats of the blinds so that they could observe proceedings without themselves being observed.

Determining the relative social standing of a group of samurai in order to assign seating positions was a complex process. It had to take into account various competing factors, such as achievement in battle, reputation, family ties and bloodline. Everyone in the room would have their own idea of where they stood in the pecking order and sometimes individuals would dispute the position they had been given.

Nō show

During preparations for a *nō* theatre production, Tokugawa Ieyasu was given a map of the audience seating plan so that he could confirm the arrangements were correct. He noticed that two clans were not represented on the plan. When Ieyasu questioned this, the organizer explained that the representatives of those clans were away from Edo at that time. Ieyasu said that not including them on the plan was a dishonour and that they should indeed be allocated seats, even if they could not attend. When the invitations went out, the two clans in question sent out different representatives to watch the performance in the stead of the officials who were away at the time, giving all clans their correct due and honour.

Eating and drinking

> And then, with her own hands, she gave us the sakana *(which is something like olives among us). This is what is done when they wish to honour a person at court.*
>
> Luís Frois, *Tratado* (1585)

At mealtimes in old Japan, some of the social boundaries were lowered. A banquet was supposed to be an enjoyable, relaxing experience. Often pages were in attendance to make sure that the wine was flowing, or possibly to restrict the flow. It was also polite for diners to pour drinks for each other; it was a great honour for a person of lower rank to be poured a drink by a high-ranking person. However, perhaps as a result of the free-flowing wine, dinners were also a common setting for disturbances such as arguments, fights and even murders – either killings in the heat of the moment or premeditated political assassinations.

> **MARK OF RESPECT**
> When a samurai wanted to show respect for something, they would hold it up to their forehead in a sign of reverence.

Chivalry versus politeness

The chivalric ideals of *bushidō* went way beyond social niceties such as bowing, dismounting, kneeling and sitting in the right place. The rules applying to these matters, though complex, could be learned and followed by any diligent student of etiquette. What set the finest samurai apart was their ability to act correctly in a state of conflict or emergency. In those situations, the normal rules did not apply and no amount of politeness could compensate for a dishonourable action.

GIFTS AND BRIBES

The giving of small, beautifully wrapped tokens is a central part of Japanese culture that is rooted in samurai traditions. Lords would reward their retainers with all manner of gifts, including hawks, clothes, land, tea utensils, fans, armour, swords, guns and so on. The recipient would treasure them all the more for having come from the lord. Sometimes they would even ask for them; for example, Tokugawa Ieyasu once asked for Toyotomi Hideyoshi's red military surcoat (*jinboari*) as a gift.

However, there was a fine line between a gift and a bribe. It reached a point where things did not get done in samurai culture unless the correct 'gifts' found their way to the correct people, even though these people were invariably government officials who already had a salary. To get the wheels of society to turn in your favour, you needed to apply a little oil.

This problem was the trigger for the famous incident of the '47 *rōnin*'. Their master, Asano Naganori, received assistance from a high-ranking government official called Kira Yoshinaka. However, when Asano did not supply sufficient 'gifts' in return for this service, Kira publicly insulted him, which provoked

Asano into trying to kill the official. As punishment, Asano was ordered to perform *seppuku*, leaving his retainers masterless and thirsty for revenge. They slaked their thirst by infiltrating Kira's mansion and assassinating him.

Of course, some gifts were genuine tokens of gratitude and recognition, but still there was always an undercurrent of obligation in samurai society. Most people accepted the need to give small, informal gift-bribes as an unwritten rule of etiquette.

Heirlooms

After a battle in which Tokugawa Ieyasu had helped Oda Nobunaga, Nobunaga presented him with a sword made by the famous smith Nagamitsu, which had previously been owned by the *shōgun* Ashikaga Yoshiteru. He was also given an arrowhead that had belonged to Minamoto no Tametomo. After the battle of Mikatagahara in 1572, Ieyasu gave his own helmet and bows to those who had helped him escape death. Such items were kept as heirlooms.

Why would a samurai want more swords, bows and helmets? You might think he would prefer gold coins or something of more practical use to him than older, often poorer-quality examples of objects that he already owned. However, such heirlooms had a value in terms of the prestige of their illustrious previous owners that outweighed their monetary worth.

In the document *Chasō Kanwa*, two lords were communicating about tea. One of them asked to see the other's family treasures, expecting to be dazzled by an array of precious tea ceremony utensils. However, when he arrived on the appointed date, he was dismayed to be shown armour, swords, bows and all kinds of other military gear. He gently pointed out to his host that he had been hoping to see some tea utensils, but his host replied that these were his clan's real treasures and that, because they were both samurai, it was only proper that he should display the family's military heirlooms.

Even seemingly insignificant items were revered if they had come from an important person or family. When I interviewed members of the Natori family of Wakayama, they told me about a thumb-ring pick used for playing a *koto* (a Japanese stringed instrument) that their ancestors had been given by the Tokugawa family. This plectrum had the Tokugawa crest on it and had been kept in the Natori clan for generations, but was lost in a B-27 air raid on Wakayama in 1945.

The treasured item did not even need to have belonged to the notable figure. Once, a lord was on parade with his retinue when he felt faint and stopped by a local shop to sit and take a drink. The mat that he sat on became an heirloom of the shop and was displayed high upon the wall, in pride of place. After this, a representative from the lord's clan would visit from time to time to make sure the mat was being treated with the appropriate respect.

All families in Japan have their heirlooms, from the three imperial regalia passed down as symbols of office within the various lines of the imperial family to humble household items handed down among the common people. Preserving such items is a valuable way to connect to and honour the past.

MONEY AND FINANCE

> When Lord Ōuchi Yoshitaka of the Suō province, also called Sir Kanewaka-maru, was a child, he saw some lower children playing with money and said, 'I want to play with it too.' His attendant, Sugi Hōki-no-kami, replied, 'Sir, that is too filthy and indecent a thing to be exposed to your view,' and then put a gold hairpin through the money and threw it into the latrine. This was done to teach him [not to lust for gold].
>
> Musha Monogatari (1654)

The samurai had a complicated relationship with money. They looked down on merchants and regarded money with disdain. Even today, Japanese martial arts teachers do not directly handle the money they are paid by the students, delegating this task to a high-ranking subordinate. However, retainers still expected to be rewarded for their service in one form or another, and they recognized that, however distasteful money was, it was also a necessity.

Why should we help?

People who think of rewards are nothing but military merchants.
Writings of Suzuki Shōsan (1579–1655)

In 1333, during the war between the Northern and Southern imperial courts, a samurai named Chikafusa wrote a letter calling the warlords to join his side. When they asked what recompense they would receive for helping him, he replied that the way of the warrior was not to seek reward, but that if they *did* join him they would at least get to keep their clans and lands if his side won. The point of note here is that the samurai expected reward, whether in terms of land, title or valuables. Chikafusa's response drew upon samurai ideals, though it was backed up with an undercurrent of threat.

Playing favourites

In the *Taiheiki* chronicle, Madenokōji Fujifusa says that samurai flocked to the imperial banner only in the hope of reward for their trouble but many were left vexed and disappointed, because only the favourites of those in power were rewarded.

From rags to riches

When the Jesuit Francis Xavier first came to Japan in the 1550s, he presented himself as 'a poor man of Christ'. However, no one took him seriously because being poor in Japanese society was not a noble or notable position; even the monks heaped riches on themselves. Therefore, the next time Xavier visited he brought letters of introduction, dressed as a wealthy man, and conducted himself in a refined manner. This time people showed him respect and he was admitted into court life.

At another point in his travels within the country, he found himself again in rags and so he was ignored once again. It was not until a wealthy Portuguese merchant called Mendes Pinto told people that Xavier was, in fact, an extremely powerful religious figure capable of commandeering any European ship he wanted that doors opened for him once more.

The castle store room

As a youth, Tokugawa Ieyasu was shown into a castle store room by the samurai Tori Tadayoshi, who was then 80 years old. He asked the young Ieyasu to look at all the rice stored there and to think of it in terms of the number of retainers it could pay for. He also pointed out the coins carefully stacked in wrapped piles so that they were easy to manage and did not fall over. The lessons Ieyasu learned about financial prudence and the connection between staple foods and power appear to have stayed with him, judging by his dismissive reaction to the rare peaches he was sent by Oda Nobunaga (see chapter 4).

Spend everything and borrow nothing

There was a samurai named Ishida Masazumi who often boasted that he spent every penny his lord gave him but never needed to borrow. At the end of each year, his books balanced perfectly – showing he had perfect control of his estates' finances. Unfortunately, he died in a vain attempt to defend his castle, which was burned down in the attack. When the flames had died down, it is said that no gold was found in the ashes, which was taken as proof that his claims were true. Whether factual or not, this episode highlights the samurai's distrustful attitude toward money. They understood that money was a necessity, but they also saw it as the cause of many problems.

Offer half but pay double

It is said that Toyotomi Hideyoshi told his samurai in advance how much land or money he would give them in return for their service. However, he always had double that figure in mind for those who performed well. When they received double the amount they had been promised, they were, of course, extremely surprised and grateful. This solidified their loyalty to Hideyoshi and made them keen to excel in their future duties. Word spread and others were inspired to do the same. Conversely, if any samurai performed poorly, he might receive only half of the agreed amount. Tokugawa Ieyasu is believed to have continued to use this system after Hideyoshi's death.

Underground money lenders

For a samurai to be seen to borrow money would have been dishonourable. However, sometimes they had no choice, so money-lending was a profitable underground operation. The lenders used *miko*, or shrine maidens, as the carriers. Because of their respected position in society, shrine maidens could call on houses without arousing suspicion and the loan repayments they collected could be disguised as donations to the shrine. This meant that prestigious families could borrow and repay money without losing face.

The meaning of money

The samurai strove to acquire productive agricultural land to finance their military life and support their clan. Land was valued more highly than money, because it was a more predictable, sustainable source of income. While it was fitting to treat money with distaste, it was also dishonourable to be financially insolvent. Therefore, the samurai knew that they needed the means to ensure a healthy cash flow, but they also had to show that they were not motivated by money for money's sake.

SAMURAI IN SOCIETY

Medieval Japanese society was highly structured. As in most other cultures of that era, there were protocols for seating, meetings, marching and all other occasions. Such traditions were built up gradually over hundreds of years. It is, of course, well understood that at certain periods in Japanese history the 'screws' of restriction were tightened, but it is important to point out that they were never released to the point where all people enjoyed social freedoms. It was up to the individual how far they pushed for a better standing in society.

CHAPTER NINE

DISHONOURABLE BEHAVIOUR

*With us treason is rare and extremely reprehensible; in Japan it is
so common that it is almost never criticized.*

Luís Froís, *Tratado* (1585)

Having now some idea of what samurai chivalry actually is and being aware
that it may differ from modern preconceptions, we now turn to examples
of behaviour that would appear to be dishonourable in any context. In this
chapter, we will highlight episodes in Japanese history where *bushidō* seems
to be lacking, although in some cases a closer examination of the perpetrator's
motives may provide some justification.

MISCELLANEOUS MISDEEDS

The city of vengeful spirits

Minamoto no Yoritomo said he would spare the town that was sheltering his
brother Minamoto no Yoshitsune if its inhabitants gave him up. The people,
according to most traditions, killed Yoshitsune and presented his head as
instructed, but Yoritomo burned the town down anyway. Recognizing later that
he had acted wrongly, he built a temple to appease the vengeful spirits.

Beheaded in the bath

Minamoto no Yoshitomo rode into Kyōto and abducted the retired Emperor, who had failed to give Yoshitomo the expected reward for supporting him in a previous conflict. Yoshitomo's aim was to bring about the downfall of his enemy Taira no Kiyomori and raise his family's status. Moving on in a rampage, he burned down the imperial palace and had any people who ran away killed. It is said that those who jumped in the wells to escape the flames were drowned by the mass of people trampling on top of them. At this point, Kiyomori came to the aid of the retired Emperor. Yoshitomo braced against the assault but, failing to withstand it, he killed his wounded son and retreated to a trusted retainer's house. However, his brutality was repaid in kind: while Yoshitomo was in the bath, the retainer killed and beheaded him.

An attack on the regent

As recorded in the *Heike Monogatari* document, the regent Fujiwara no Motofusa was travelling to his palace by carriage when he encountered a young samurai and his similarly young retainers travelling in the opposite direction. This was Taira no Sakamori, the grandson of Lord Taira no Kiyomori. The guard commander of the regent said that Sakamori and his party should all bow and drop to their knees, for the regent was about to pass by them. Sakamori decided that instead of paying homage he and his men would ride through the procession at a gallop. When they did so, the regent's bodyguard humiliated them by dragging them all from their horses and forcing them to the ground.

When Lord Kiyomori heard of this, he arranged for a group of his retainers allied with some bandits to ambush the regent on his travels. The ambushers chopped the hair off all of the regent's attendants and threatened the regent himself, cutting the straps from the oxen of his carriage. It is said that the regent's troops cried through the shame they endured.

At this, Sakamori's father, angered by all the trouble his son had caused, banished Sakamori – to the relief of the people of the city. This case clearly shows that young men armed with a sword and a sense of entitlement could easily be moved to rudeness instead of following *bushidō*. Japan was full of young men like this.

> ### ROAD RAGE
> The *Bushidō Shoshinshū* document observed that trouble often started when two different processions of samurai lords met. If the people at the front of the groups quarrelled with each other, the disturbance sometimes escalated to the point where the two lords themselves came out to fight each other, resulting in all manner of diplomatic problems.

A final prayer cut short

During the Heike conflict, a mortally wounded samurai was trying to say a last Buddhist prayer as he lay with his life ebbing away, but a member of the Taira army cut his throat before he could finish. Preventing a dying man who was no threat from preparing his soul for the next life was a shameful act.

Death of a dancer

The tale of the Minamoto archer standing on a beach and shooting a single arrow which hit a fan on the masthead of an enemy ship is well known (see chapter 10). However, this remarkable display of samurai achievement gave rise to an equally remarkable act of dishonour.

Having witnessed the fan being hit, both sides applauded this great feat. In the enemy ranks, a shamanic figure performed a dance of victory to commend the archer's skill. Instead of accepting the tribute in a chivalric way, Minamoto no Yoshitsune, the leader of the Minamoto force, ordered the same archer to shoot again and kill the dancing man. Though mortified at this request, the archer had no choice but to obey. With a shot just as accurate as the first, the dancer was felled. However, this time the enemy were in uproar; they leaped into the water and moved to fight. They attacked without tactics and some drowned as they tried to kill the archer for his heinous crime.

It is said that Yoshitsune gave this order because he knew it would enrage the enemy into abandoning the safety of their ships. Viewed in this light, it can be seen as an example of tactics outweighing honour. However, killing the dancer was still an extremely unchivalrous action.

Abuse of power

In 1285, the rival families of Adachi and Taira fought each other in the so-called Shimotsuki Incident. This led to the destruction of the Adachi clan. Taira no Yoritsuna, the victor, gained the power he craved but abused it greatly. Therefore, he was attacked by his own side so that he could not take full control of the government – an example of power held by a single person or faction leading to ill behaviour.

Insulting the Emperor

In 1341, Toki Yoritō was riding around the city of Mino at dawn when he encountered the procession of the retired Emperor. The imperial procession demanded that he and his men dismount and show respect. While most of his samurai obeyed the request, Toki Yoritō shouted back, 'Did you say retired Emperor? I thought you said dog.' The insult hinged on the similarity of the word *in*, meaning 'emperor', to the word *inu*, meaning 'dog'. Having called the retired Emperor a dog, Yoritō went on to say, 'I should shoot the beast.' He fired an arrow at the imperial carriage, causing a panic in which the vehicle overturned and left the former Emperor sprawling on the ground. The Ashikaga clan had Yoritō arrested, but he fled and tried to fight back. However, in the end he was recaptured and beheaded.

Burning a temple for maple leaves

In the 1340s, a notorious samurai named Sasaki Dōyo sent his men to gather maple branches from a tree inside Myōhō-in Temple. The temple was headed by an abbot of imperial blood (known as a *monzeki*), who ordered the trespassing samurai to be expelled from his grounds. Dōyo retaliated by having the temple burned down; he was later sent into exile.

4444

Duped out of a castle

The sixteenth-century samurai Matsudaira Nobutaka lost his castle in a plot
hatched by his own allies. Having been lured away to a ceremony of honour, he
returned to his fortress to find that it had been given to someone else. When he
went to his superiors, his complaints fell on deaf ears and so he simply switched
sides and joined the Oda clan. This shows that lies and deception were not a
problem for the samurai but also that the response was simply to change sides.

A twisted family

The warlord Saitō Toshimasa burned and boiled alive those who displeased
him. His son, Saitō Yoshitatsu, was no better. A leper who measured over six-
and-a-half feet tall, he tricked his brothers and murdered them, then went to
war with his father, killed him as well and took the clan by force.

The broken idols

According to the sixteenth-century traveller Luís Froís, Oda Nobunaga built
castles with massive stone ramparts. To the horror of the population, Nobunaga
raided nearby temples for stone idols and smashed them to pieces to help
construct his fortresses.

Assault on Mount Hiei

In 1570, Oda Nobunaga warned the monks of Mount Hiei that if they helped
the enemy army that was retreating to their mountain he would burn down
every one of their buildings and kill every monk inside. However, if they did
not help the enemy, he would reward them greatly.

The monks ignored Nobunaga and helped his enemy and so he marched on
the holy site. Even the Emperor and his generals implored him not to destroy the
temple complex, but after a prolonged campaign he destroyed the whole place
and put thousands to the sword. Many works of art were lost in the destruction
and some high-ranking scholars were killed. Nobunaga replied that they had
lost their way and forgotten what it meant to be monks.

Froís wrote an account of the destruction. He said that Nobunaga 'slaked
his thirst for vengeance and fame' and that he had people hunting in the hills

for monks to kill and destroyed every building possible. Women and children were put into a temple with holy statues for protection, on the assumption that Nobunaga would not dare to damage those relics, but Nobunaga burned the whole place down, destroying everything and everyone inside.

KILLING THE INNOCENT

Killing was samurai business and therefore killing in itself cannot be seen as unchivalrous behaviour. A distinction needs to be drawn between the killing of an enemy and the killing of an innocent. The following episodes highlight some examples of samurai killing what can be considered, to varying degrees, as innocent people to satisfy their own desires and objectives.

KILLING CHILDREN

To what extent was it acceptable in samurai culture to kill children? We have learned of the absolute power that samurai held over their own children, which included the lawful right to kill them, but what about killing other people's children? When slaying an enemy, it was seen as a wise precaution to kill their sons as well, regardless of their age. Those boys not killed by a conquering samurai would soon grow into armed and vengeful men – as was the case with Minamoto no Yoritomo and Minamoto no Yoshitsune, who took revenge for the killing of their father. Therefore, it could be argued that only the killing of children unconnected to a conflict and for no good reason was considered as a negative action.

Blood wedding

The marriage of Taira no Masakado to one of his cousins, the daughter of Taira no Yoshikane, sparked a clan war that led to the killing of many innocent people. The problem was not the marriage itself, which was all considered correct. The issue arose from the difference in status between the two branches involved.

The Taira clan descended from the imperial line, but Yoshikane's side was considered as closer to royalty than Masakado's. Therefore, Yoshikane insisted that Masakado come to live with his clan instead of his daughter moving in with her husband. Masakado refused, because he could not accept being relegated to subservience in this way. And so clan war broke out.

There were, of course, many samurai casualties in this dispute, but more controversial was Masakado's decision to burn down over 500 enemy buildings, from rich mansions to poor people's dwellings; anyone who tried to escape was shot with arrows. The massacre was deemed worthy of being reported to the imperial court.

After Masakado and Yoshikane had entered battle more than once, the matter was eventually settled politically. The atrocity of the burnings and murder was 'brushed under the carpet' by a powerful Fujiwara ally and no charges were brought against Masakado. However, his wife was seized back by her original family and the dispute started again. Yoshikane died of natural causes, but by this point the conflict had escalated beyond anyone's control and hatred was fuelling widespread destruction.

During the war there was a famine, and a powerful samurai of the Fujiwara clan started to burn down other people's food stores and withhold grain from the local people. Masakado was ordered by the court to relieve the suffering of the starving people; instead, he joined with the local power elite and took control of the area, setting himself up as an authority outside of the government.

Masakado was following what he considered to be the samurai ethic of rule by power in the name of the Emperor (or to become the Emperor because he was of royal blood), but the fact remains that many innocent people died because he did not want to move in with his father-in-law.

GRUESOME REMEDY

There have been many apocryphal stories about Masakado since his death in 940. He was reputed to have murdered a pregnant woman to get her male foetus and powder it down as a remedy for a battle wound.

The pirate samurai

Around the same time as Taira no Masakado was burning down villages and, allegedly, powdering down foetuses, another issue was emerging. Fujiwara no Sumitomo (893–941) was from a powerful family but had found himself isolated in the provinces. Having been accused by another samurai of starting a rebellion, Sumitomo intercepted his accuser, who was on his way to the capital, and cut off his ears and nose, stole his wife and had his children killed.

Sumitomo was also the leader of a local pirate fleet large enough to attract the attention of central government. After attempts to neutralize the pirate menace failed, Sumitomo was betrayed by one of his close followers for a reward and was captured and beheaded.

JAPANESE PIRATES

The classic image of the pirate as an outlaw operating at sea for himself and his crew and no one else does not always stand up to close examination. In truth, some 'pirate' ships were officially sanctioned by one nation or clan to attack ships of another nation or clan. True pirates had no affiliation to any form of government. The Japanese had a mixture of true piracy and attack fleets sanctioned by various clans, making the distinction between navy and pirates hard to draw.

Misjudged mercy

Earlier we spoke of the death of Minamoto no Yoshitomo at the hands of a trusted retainer when he was fleeing from Taira no Kiyomori. After this, Yoshitomo's wife fled with her sons, knowing that they would be next to be targeted. Having spent some time out in the wild with no means to survive in the long term, she presented herself to the Taira clan and threw herself on the mercy of her husband's enemy. It is said that Yoshitomo had chosen her to be his wife ahead of a thousand other beautiful women and Taira no Kiyomori was equally susceptible to her beauty. He made her his wife and sent her children off to monasteries, ignoring the advice of his councillors who said that he should kill the children so that they could not rise up and overthrow him, which eventually they did. This is clearly one of those situations where killing innocent children would have been a prudent strategy.

Murderous uncle

The concubine of Minamoto no Yoshitsune was called Shizuka. After he died, she fell into the hands of Yoshitsune's half-brother Yoritomo, who had ordered his killing. It soon became apparent that Shizuka was pregnant, to which her new master, rather than celebrating his impending unclehood, said that the unborn child should be cut out of her immediately, which would kill both mother and baby. Yoritomo was persuaded not to do this. Instead, Shizuka was forced to dance for him while heavily pregnant, and it was determined that if the baby was a girl it would be taken away from her mother, while if it was a boy it would have to die. The child was born and it was a boy, so he was drowned in water nearby to eliminate any risk of his being raised to take revenge against his uncle.

Death or freedom?

When Minamoto no Yoriyoshi captured the fort of Kuriyagawa, he found the 13-year-old son of his enemy among the survivors. Praising the boy for his valour, Yoriyoshi was about to set him free when a samurai named Kiyohara persuaded him that if he did this the boy would later seek him out for revenge. So, the brave son of an enemy was killed to prevent future problems.

Family affair

The eighteenth-century *shōgun* Tokugawa Ietsugu had a concubine called Ejima, who served as the point of contact for the giving of gifts and goods to people in the castle. In this capacity she became acquainted with all types and was invited to the Nakamura theatre where she had relations with an actor called Ikushima Shingorō. The relationship was discovered and the theatre closed down permanently. One might have expected Ejima to have been executed, but instead she was exiled and her brother – who had had nothing to do with the affair – was ordered to perform *seppuku*. According to Japanese ways, the affair was the fault of Ejima's family as a whole and so it was considered correct to make a leading member of her family pay for her mistake.

Heir today, gone tomorrow

Until 1593, Toyotomi Hideyoshi's heir had been his nephew Toyotomi Hidetsugu. However, in that year Hideyoshi became father to a son, Toyotomi Hideyori, who immediately replaced Hidetsugu as heir. To prevent Hidetsugu mounting a challenge for the leadership, Hideyoshi sent his nephew into exile and forced him to kill himself. However, all Hideyoshi's succession planning was in vain as Tokugawa Ieyasu took over instead and wiped out the whole Toyotomi family line. This episode shows how quickly a fall from favour can become a death sentence, even for the second-most powerful man in Japan at the time.

Great fighter, bad man

As an 11-year-old, Hosokawa Tadaoki was said to have displayed considerable ability in battle; by the age of 15, he had become a truly great warrior. However, it seems he was more vicious killer than noble knight. As an adult, he drove his eldest son away and had his second son killed, threatened to kill his wife if she did not renounce Christianity, and cut off the noses and ears of some of his foster mother's ladies in waiting for trifling matters.

Slaughter at Hara
The brutal suppression of the Shimabara Uprising in 1638 (see chapter 3) left an indelible stain on the samurai reputation. Particularly shameful was the way in which the Siege of Hara Castle was carried out. Tens of thousands of rebel *rōnin*, peasants, women and children were first starved and then butchered in what can only be called an atrocity. The samurai commander Matsudaira Nobutsuna ensured that the final attack was not launched until the rebels' provisions had run out. Some of the other samurai wanted to move in more quickly and gain fame; sections of the Hosokawa clan made tunnels below the castle walls in preparation, as well as rounding up innocent relatives of the besieged rebels and using them as threats to those inside the castle. The killing of people inside a besieged castle after they had run out of food was not uncommon in warfare, but the slaughter at Hara was on a massive scale.

Breach of promise
When the Tokugawa laid siege to the Toyotomi stronghold of Osaka in 1614–15, Tokugawa Ieyasu was keen to rescue his granddaughter, who, as the wife of Toyotomi Hideyori, was trapped inside Osaka Castle. Ieyasu declared that any man who could bring her out safely could have her hand in marriage. Lord Sakazaki Dewa no Kami Takachika rose to this challenge. However, when he delivered the young woman to Ieyasu, he did not receive the reward he was expecting. Breaking his word, Ieyasu married the girl off to a different family for a greater political gain. To the consternation of his clansmen, Sakazaki threatened to move against the mighty Tokugawa. In order to avert a war they knew they could not win, the clansmen got their lord drunk and beheaded him. The saviour of the woman may not have been an exemplar of chivalry, but to be lied to by Ieyasu and then assassinated by his own men was a poor reward for his enterprise.

The murder of women on the run
Just before Takeda Katsuyori made his last stand during the fall of the Takeda clan, the women fleeing with him were captured by the enemy and put to death. They had done nothing wrong and were not armed, yet still they had to die.

A convenient solution?

Matsudaira Nobuyasu is best remembered as the son of Tokugawa Ieyasu forced by his father to commit suicide to appease Oda Nobunaga (see chapter 7). Although Nobuyasu cannot be blamed for the circumstances surrounding his death, he was guilty of great cruelty during his life. For example, when he found out that his wife's lady-in-waiting had told his wife that he was lusting after another woman, he forced his way into his wife's chamber and stabbed the maid. As she lay dying, he carved open her mouth with a knife and said that this was the fate of those who caused discord between a man and his wife.

Nobuyasu is also said to have shot and killed a dancer with an arrow because their dancing was not good enough. On another occasion, after a fruitless day's hawking, he blamed a passing priest for his lack of success. He tied the priest to his horse and dragged him along the ground until he was dead. Furthermore, he is said to have almost shot one of his father's retainers who criticized his bad conduct, but decided it would be better not to incur his father's wrath.

As eldest son of one of the most powerful men in Japan, Nobuyasu was expected to take over the clan. Perhaps Ieyasu calculated that it would be better for the Tokugawa if Nobuyasu did not succeed him. Therefore, when Nobunaga called for Nobuyasu's death, it might not have been such a terrible a dilemma for Ieyasu. It might, in fact, have been a convenient solution to an awkward family situation.

The wife and the hawk

The 1692 diary of a samurai in Nagoya tells of a woman who killed a stray hawk that had landed in her kitchen. The woman's husband reported the incident to the local authority and the issue went up the chain of command. When it transpired that the hawk belonged to a local warlord, the wife and husband were bound, led away and presented to the lord. As a point of justice, the lord had the wife crucified while the husband went free because he was not at home at the time the bird was killed. Some reports say that the woman survived the crucifixion and was allowed to live on. Either way, it is clear that the life of a bird owned by a lord was considered more valuable than that of a lowly human.

Summary justice

Luís Froís describes an incident that took place while Oda Nobunaga was building his great castle. Samurai of all ranks stripped down and acted as workmen and Nobunaga himself walked around supervising. One day a samurai workman lifted the cowl of a woman to look at her face. Seeing this, Nobunaga decapitated the man himself without any trial or questions asked. He simply deemed it rude to approach a woman in such a manner.

Executed for asking for a holiday

When the senior American naval officer Commodore Matthew Perry visited Japan in the 1850s on a mission to force the country to open back up to the rest of the world, a young samurai intellectual named Yoshida Shōin saw an opportunity. He petitioned Perry to take him back to America so that he could observe foreign culture. Travel outside of Japan was prohibited at this time. Perry declined his request and so Shōin submitted himself to the courts for judgement. He was placed under arrest and moved to various locations. However, at such a delicate point in Japan's history, the authorities were particularly determined to avoid alien ideas corrupting the nation's mind and so in 1859 Shōin was beheaded in Edo just for *wanting* to travel to foreign lands. Not long after, the country did open up and the Japanese were free to travel the world.

MILITARY HONOUR

Above all, the samurai were warriors and so their conduct in battle was at the heart of their sense of self-worth and honour. However, as we will discover, there was more to the samurai than the popular image of the *katana*-wielding master of hand-to-hand combat. Other weapons and other, more devious forms of warfare were valued just as highly. What mattered most of all was winning.

CHAPTER TEN

MILITARY GEAR

The Japanese think that no other nation can compare with them with regard to weapons and valour and so they look down on all foreigners. They greatly prize their arms, and prefer to have good weapons decorated with gold and silver.

Writings of St Francis Xavier (16th century)

The samurai were public figures and their armour, clothing and weapons were important markers of their status, as well as providing coded information about their military achievements. In this chapter we will look at how these items helped to create the samurai identity and the contribution they made to the story of samurai chivalry.

ARMOUR

Armour is an integral part of samurai identity, and a subject worthy of detailed study in its own right. This short summary focuses on armour in the context of chivalry and the relationship between the samurai and his military equipment. Overall, armour went hand in hand with honour and reputation. A suit of armour was a decipherable expression of its owner's military prowess.

Helmets

Helmets were rich in meaning. The most symbolic part was the *hachimanza*, the vent hole at the very top. As well as allowing trapped air to escape, it represented the 'seat of the god Hachiman', the place where the gods entered the samurai and imbued him with a warlike spirit. This air vent should never be touched unless a samurai was about to commit suicide, in which case he might remove the helmet by placing his fingers in the hole and lifting the helmet from his head.

Also on the helmet were the side wings known as *fukikaeshi*, which normally carried the samurai's family crest or, if not, they might have a representation of a Shintō *torii* gate. (The gloves also carried the family crest.) As the following quote indicates, the shape of the side wings was also significant.

> Fukikaeshi *helmet wings are meant to enhance one's spirits. Generally, anything jutting outward is considered to be positive and, although there is no superiority given to larger over smaller helmet wings, larger ones may be considered as more positive as they show higher levels of spirit.*
>
> Heigu Yōkō (c1670)

The length of the helmet peak was also something to be considered. Too short a peak would cause the wearer to tilt his head forward to protect himself, which might be perceived as cowardly; but if it was too long then the samurai would have to tilt his head back to be able to see, which would make his face vulnerable to a stray arrow. The ideal peak length was such that a samurai did not need to tilt his head either back or forward. A samurai wearing such a helmet would be called an *ikubimusha*, or 'boar-necked warrior'.

Sometimes fur was used on a helmet, but never in two colours, because the term for this, *nige*, sounded too similar to the word meaning 'to flee', *nigeru*. A leader's helmet typically bore either a dragon or garden hoe, or both combined. The dragon represented the power of a rising force (because they rose out of rivers in Japanese culture) and the hoe represented earth, which, in ancient Chinese Five Element theory, is the element at the centre controlling the other four elements. For the same reason, leaders also wore yellow or gold, the colour associated with the earth element.

THE 98,000 GODS OF WAR

The god of war is the deity Miwa Daimyōjin (三輪大明神), who is also known as Ōnamuchi-no-mikoto (大己貴命). The manifestation of this god is a snake that has 98,000 scales, which is the origin of the phrase '98,000 gods of war'.

Heigu Yōhō (c1670)

Through their armour, samurai called on the power of Miwa Daimyōjin, the giant serpent god of war. It was often thought of as a multitude of gods – 98,000, to be exact. However, as this quote from the Heigu Yōhō explains, it was actually a single deity with 98,000 facets.

Body armour

The Japanese when they wear armour are as naked as the day their mothers bore them.

Luís Froís, *Tratado* (1585)

Having been accustomed to seeing knights from their homelands in full-body plate armour, European visitors like Froís were surprised to find the samurai entering battle comparatively 'naked'. They would sometimes have a chest plate, but their arms and legs were often unprotected. Foot soldiers would wear even less armour.

Early forms of armour had a backplate to cover the seam. This was known colloquially as 'the coward's plate', because if that part of a samurai's armour was visible to the enemy it meant he had turned his back on them. Conversely, the most courageous warriors were permitted to wear special back banners to mark them out from the rest.

The lacing of the various plates held particular symbolic significance. The colours of the laces and the patterns in which they were tied had meaning, and even the names of the cords were associated with aspects of warrior prowess. As explained in the Heigu Yōhō:

> The term odoshige (威毛) is used to describe the lacing in armour. This word and its characters are used with the intention to conjure the image of an animal such as a boar with its hair standing on end when it is in a state of anger. Thus, people wear these lacings to stir dauntless courage within themselves and to intimidate the enemy, just as an animal does with its bristling hair.
>
> Heigu Yōhō (c1670)

Red armour lacing was considered as brave and 'fiery', and was used by the famed Ii clan. Many of the different lace colour combinations referred to other aspects of samurai life, such as clan ancestry.

A single suit of ancient-style armour known as an ōyoroi was sometimes carried into battle and erected in a special mobile 'temple' – most likely behind war curtains – where it was worshipped as an embodiment of the war god.

Horo – the cape of honour

The horo was a form of cape worn by high-ranking samurai known as horomusha (母衣武者). It attached to the rear of the armour and originally served as a kind of arrow-catching device. The horo could be free flowing or stretched over a bamboo frame. Toyotomi Hideyoshi gave yellow horo capes to his closest men and called the group kiboro-shū (黄母衣衆), 'the yellow cape squad'.

As we have seen, measures designed to defend a retreating warrior were often associated with cowardice. However, the horo was held in high esteem, most likely because it was originally worn by samurai archers on mounted hit-and-run attacks. They would bravely charge in, fire their arrows and then gallop off, with the cape protecting them. Therefore, the horo represented the nerve to charge deep and close to the enemy. In terms of chivalry, we start to understand that it was totally acceptable for samurai to extract themselves from danger in these circumstances, as long as they did so in a controlled manner.

*At the siege of Odawara, the warrior Kawada had a huge flag
and with him another samurai called Narasaki had a* horo
arrow-cape 18 tan *in size. Both were walking from town to town
on their way to battle. Lord Taikō Hideyoshi, who was then
staying in Numazu of Izu province, saw them passing by with
their huge flag and* horo *cape. The lord said, 'Look what strong
warriors they are! Go and ask them for their names.' A mounted
samurai attending him immediately went and said to them, from
horseback, 'Listen to this humbly, this is from Lord Hideyoshi.
The lord admired your spectacular* horo *and flag and told me
to find out your names.' However, they did not answer and the
messenger came back in vain. Hearing this, Lord Hideyoshi said,
'Did you ask them without dismounting from your horse? That
is a very rude thing to do. Those warriors carrying such a huge
flag and* horo *could not be mounted, as no horse could bear
them, no matter what rank of warriors they are. If that is the
case, why should they give you their names if you ask them from
horseback?' He then ordered another man to ask them, this time
not from horseback, and they replied.*

Musha Monogatari (1654)

The *horo* cape is a good illustration of how proper retreat was correct for a
samurai and also how their equipment and uniform was a signal of their social
status. Originally, this item may have been a functional tool used by many levels
of warrior, but in later years it definitely became a symbol of office for higher-
ranking samurai.

CLOTHES AND ACCESSORIES

*We have new designs of clothing almost every year; in Japan the
fashions are always the same.*

Luís Froís, *Tratado* (1585)

The *Heike Monogatari* scroll tells of Iesada, a retainer of Tadamori, the head of the Taira clan. Upon hearing of an assassination attempt against his master, Iesada arrived at court in green-laced armour and a green cloak, but his appearance caused uproar, for these were the clothes of a warrior not a courtier.

As a samurai, Iesada had a right to attend court, but he was just wearing the wrong attire. There were strict rules as to what you could and could not wear in different settings. The regulation of clothes, hairstyles and even the gates of houses was established throughout all social classes. While rules changed from period to period, there was without doubt an idea that certain items belonged to certain social levels.

Some seasoned warriors saw court dress as too lavish and not fitting for battle-hardened fighters, even though the clothes represented a higher social standing. When Tokugawa Ieyasu asked for a *haori* surcoat to be brought to him because the weather was getting cold, a retainer brought him an exquisite one he had been given by Toyotomi Hideyoshi, but he refused it, declaring that such a jacket was fit only for the ostentatious ways of the capital and that out in the wilds it would not do for a warrior to wear such luxurious costume.

Conversely, when a samurai boy who was being used as a political hostage arrived at the capital from the so-called 'wilds', his minders observed that, while he spoke very well and his manners were impeccable, his clothes were too rustic. Therefore, they attired him in dress that was more fitting for life at court.

In the following sections, we will focus on certain items of clothing and accoutrements that held particular significance for the samurai in terms of the way in which they were viewed by their peers.

Crests on clothes

Samurai often wore clothes with crests on them to show the world which clan they belonged to. The positioning of the crests followed social convention; they were often found on the front of jackets and tops, one on the left and one on the right, and also on the rear. In certain circumstances, samurai were given permission to wear the crest of their master or the senior clan they served,

as a badge of honour. According to the *Bushidō Shoshinshū* document, those samurai who wore their master's crest also had to display their own crest so that they could not be mistaken for members of the higher clan. For example, they could wear their own crest on their jacket but the lord's crest on their overcoat, or vice versa. When worn-out clothes were replaced, the crests were removed from them and burned so that they could not be misused.

Footwear

> We show courtesy by removing our hats; the Japanese show it by removing their footwear.
>
> Luís Frois, *Tratado* (1585)

In Japan, shoes and other footwear continue to hold a high place in the realm of manners and customs. It is commonly known that you should never walk inside a Japanese building with shoes on, and once you are indoors you may even have to change footwear when you go into a toilet area or step into an inner courtyard garden. What is less well known is that, at least up until the end of the Sengoku period, those of a lower rank had to take off their footwear when attending or talking to a superior, even if this was outdoors.

There was also a hierarchy in terms of the footwear itself. The Heigu Yōhō manual states that, especially at court, high-ranking people should be attended by someone wearing bear-fur shoes rather than the more typical straw sandals. These ankle boots made of bear fur were part of a samurai's 'best' dress uniform, which he would wear when attending an important occasion.

As an expression of social position and respect, footwear can be seen as a starting point for correct action in society. To have bad 'shoe etiquette' was to get off on the wrong foot.

STATUS SYMBOLS

In Edo-period Japan, it would have been easy to identify a samurai, as they were the only people who had the right to wear two swords. However, before Toyotomi Hideyoshi disarmed the public in 1588, even farmers wore two swords. Western accounts of the time report that the farmers were most upset at this change. Therefore, before this, clothes, styles and speech were the only visible differences between the samurai and the rest of society. The nuances would have simply been a part of the social fabric of that time.

SOURCES

In the streets, they all bow low with their shoes in their hands until he [Oda Nobunaga] passes. Inferiors do the same for superiors, and if they meet noble and honourable people, they take off their shoes and bow very low with their hands between their thighs.

Writings of Jorge Álvares (16th century)

As I crossed over the bridge near him [the shōgun*] without my sandals on – for such is the custom here – he called after me several times in a loud voice not to worry but to put on my shoes back on.*

Luís Frois, Tratado (1585)

In the presence of those which they salute they do take off their shoes (as for stockings, they wear none) and then, clapping their right hand in their left, they put them down to their knees, and so wagging and moving their hands to and fro, they stoop and step and move with sliding steps and cry out 'augh, augh'.

Writings of John Saris (early 17th century)

Fans

There were two main types of fan used by samurai: folding fans called *sensu* (扇子) and rigid war fans called *gunbai* (軍配), which were carried by generals.

Folding fans

> *In Japan, a man always has a fan in his belt and would be considered as vulgar and wretched otherwise.*
>
> Luís Froís, *Tratado* (1585)

As the quote above suggests, it was considered improper for a samurai to be without his *sensu* folding fan. Fans had many uses other than to combat hot weather. These included the following:

- Signalling military orders on the battlefield
- Presenting a decapitated head to a superior
- Receiving rewards or gifts upon
- Writing notes on with an ink and brush
- Writing a death poem on before suicide

An inferior person was not permitted to use a fan for cooling purposes if there was a social superior in the room; however, superiors could do this in front of inferiors. It is said that priests giving sermons would slap the fan into their open hand or hit it on the 'pulpit' to emphasize their words.

Fans were as much of an emblem for the samurai as their swords were. The lower classes also used fans, but only the samurai would feel underdressed without one.

War fans and batons

War fans (*gunbai*) and war batons (*saihai*) were ceremonial symbols of office. A *gunbai* was a rod with two large wings attached to the top; it was often decorated with such motifs as the Ursa Major constellation or the blazing sun. A *saihai* was a rod with a 'mop' of paper tassels at the end. In the main, the *gunbai* was reserved for generals or other very high-ranking military personnel, while the *saihai* was for troop captains. This meant that on the field of battle, all samurai would be able to instantly identify a superior by means of the baton or fan they carried.

WEAPONS

Bows

> *In olden times, they considered archery and horsemanship the highest of martial arts.*
>
> Bushidō Shoshinshū (c1700)

The first samurai warriors were mounted cavalry archers, and so, before the sword became the symbol of the samurai, it was the bow that was the weapon of choice. Indeed, throughout the samurai period the bow remained exalted, and proficiency in archery was considered a mark of prestige for all warriors. According to the early eighteenth-century scroll the *Bushidō Shoshinshū*, archery was still one of the core martial arts that a young samurai should learn from the age of 15 or 16.

The status of the bow was reflected in the language of war: one word for warfare in Japanese was *yumiya* (弓矢), which literally means 'bows and arrows'; and there was a form of military tax called *yumiya hanjo*, 'a signed document for bows and arrows', or *yasen*, 'arrow money'.

The Minamoto clan was renowned for the quality of its archers. There was one who was said to be able to shoot two out of three birds in flight, and another who, in the middle of a battle, rose to the challenge of hitting a fan that had been fixed to the top of a ship's mast. Standing on the shore, the archer loosed an arrow that knocked the fan from its position. This he did to the cheers of both allied and enemy samurai, who all understood the huge skill involved. If the archer had missed, it would have brought great shame upon him; in fact, he is said to have declared that if he had not hit the target, he would have committed suicide.

In the same conflict, when Minamoto no Yoshitsune dropped his bow he risked everything to retrieve it. He did this not because it was particularly valuable to him, but because it was less powerful than most and so he feared that if the enemy found his bow and tried it they would know that he was not physically strong. However, in the texts of Natori-Ryū, written in the seventeenth century, it stated that a bow should, above all, be easy to draw, because combat could last a long time. This reveals a difference in tactics between eras. In the early days of the samurai, when the Minamoto were a dominant force, it was considered superb to shoot a strong bow, because fighting was done on horseback and in a skirmish style; whereas for the Natori, it was better to have troops of footed archers unleashing many arrows on a packed battlefield in support of their comrades.

Bows were also used by shamanic figures to clear the air of unwanted spirits. This was done by 'twanging' a bow over a sick person or in a specific direction. However, the *Ippei Yōkō* scroll tells us that it was bad luck to twang the bow three times. This was because the term *miuchi*, meaning 'three strikes', was similar to the term *mi wo utsu*, meaning 'to be struck on the body'.

GLOVES
Early Western visitors to Japan observed that the Japanese wore gloves only for archery and not to keep their hands warm. They warmed their hands by putting them inside their sleeves, although even this was not permitted when in the presence of a superior.

Archery and Zen
Published in 1948, the influential work *Zen in the Art of Archery* by German philosopher Eugen Herrigel has made Japanese archery (*kyūdō*) synonymous with spiritual training and ritual. However, this view has been brought into question in recent decades. In his 2001 article 'The Myth of *Zen in the Art of*

Archery', Japanese cultural historian Yamada Shōji dismantles the idea of an overriding connection between Zen and the bow. While accepting that ritual archery was one part of the picture, Yamada points out that there were various other forms of the discipline, each of which differed in style and focus. These included competition archery, which was held in temples and had a long history, and, of course, military archery upon the battlefield. Yamada dismisses the idea that archery within a military context contained Zen teachings. He maintains that in the Middle Ages archery on the battlefield was a purely practical skill and did not have any ceremonial aspect.

A 1993 article, 'Valorous Butchers: The Art of War during the Golden Age of Samurai', by American historian Karl Friday emphasizes the brutality of samurai warfare. He traces an evolution from orderly showdowns between armies agreeing to meet at a certain time and place, to surprise attacks on three sides in which one side would burn the enemy out of their camp and then massacre all those who escaped by the fourth side with hails of arrows. This was a far cry from Herrigel's image of the Japanese bowman as Zen master.

ORIGINS OF THE BOW

The Japanese bow predates the samurai by many centuries. A bronze *dōtaku* bell dating from the fourth century BC depicts an archer who is using a bow not dissimilar to the classic style. Based on descriptions in the Weishu chronicle (compiled before AD 297), it is believed that the classic Japanese bow was used for military purposes from the third century. There was also the lost technology of the *ōyumi* ('great bow'), believed to have been an ancient mounted Chinese-style crossbow used in siege warfare.

Spears and other pole arms

> *He had his men (yariwaki) back him up with the sword. By the*
> *time the third person joined the fray, all the spears from both sides*
> *of the enemy and our allies were crossed together at once, where so*
> *many spears were tangled together like bracken.*
>
> Zōhyō Monogatari (1657–84)

The *Ōgiden* document says that the spear is 'the king of weapons' and it is true that when the use of mounted archers fell out of favour and armies were modernizing and expanding in size, the spear took on a much more prominent role. In early times the *naginata*, a pole arm similar to a glaive, was also a popular weapon, but as battle formations became denser single combat gave way to group tactics and the *yari* spear became the preferred weapon because it could be used more easily alongside other warriors.

Spears could be used as a mark of valour or office. Weapons such as the 'white spear' were used only by commanders. Men of glory or those with a clan member who had been a hero in the past sometimes carried a spear with a red line painted in the groove of the blade.

The first spear

> *Among the front spearmen, be aware that the first to attack should*
> *be samurai, so do not attack until they do.*
>
> Zōhyō Monogatari (1657–84)

The most prestigious achievement of all in samurai battle was that of *ichibanyari* (一番槍), the 'first spear'. This was awarded to the first samurai to enter combat and win. Those who assisted them were also recognized, as *yarishita no kōmyō*; however, the first spear was the greatest distinction.

The two achievements could also be expressed as *uwayari*, 'upper spear' (the person who thrusts first) and *shitayari*, 'lower spear' (the person who thrusts second). Confusingly, the 'upper spear' usually ended up physically lower than the 'lower spear'. This is because the person defending the first strike would block the attacking spear downward and then they would be felled by the second striker, who would take advantage of the defender's lowered spear. In this case, 'upper' and 'lower' should be understood in terms of honour, not physical position.

SOURCES

This stage is called the yari-ba – *the field of spears. This will start when both sides are approximately 30* ken *apart, but this is not an absolute rule. When the first pair, one from each side, meet then this is called* ichibanyari – *the first spear.*

Ippei Yōkō (c1670)

When both sides take the formation of hōshi, *the arrowhead formation, and the two lead men meet, this is* ichibanyari – *the first spear. Whether to enter into a duel or not depends on the situation. It should be determined who achieved* uwayari, *upper spear, and* shitayari, *lower spear, and whether there was an announcement of the names or not.*

Ippei Yōkō (c1670)

The second spear

Nibanyari, *the second spear, is the fight following* ichibanyari, *the first spear. If the participants declare their names before engaging in combat, then* nibanyari *is considered more prestigious than* ichibanyari *combat in which participants did not declare their names.*

Ippei Yōkō (c1670)

The second most prestigious achievement in samurai battle was *nibanyari*, which translates as the 'second spear'. The principles are the same as those for *ichibanyari* except that they relate to the second fight of the battle, not the first.

The third spear

> *It is said from ancient times that the first and second person to*
> *enter battle are great and that third is of no importance.*
> Zōhyō Monogatari (1657–84)

The numbering of spear achievements did not go on indefinitely; by the end of the second spear combat, most troops had clashed and the general melee had begun. However, as explained in the following quote from the *Ippei Yōkō*, on a particularly large battlefield *sanbanyari*, 'third spear', was sometimes added as a further position of merit.

> *In most cases* sanbanyari, *the third spear, does not exist. Sometimes*
> *in larger battles, the third spear happens spontaneously. Normally,*
> *just as the second spears have joined, the rest of the forces will collide*
> *together. If the duelling area is relatively large then the third spear*
> *may be recognized as an achievement, but it is not very prestigious.*
> Ippei Yōkō (c1670)

The spear as a mark of office

The spear also served as a mark of office for important officials such as *bugyō* magistrates or commanders and *daimyō* warlords. These were honorific weapons carried by the official's servant in a parade. Generally, the servant of a particularly high-ranking official would carry the spear in front of their master, whereas a normal samurai's spear-bearer would walk on the master's right.

There were detailed specifications for the spear itself depending on rank, which varied from region to region. The following extract from the Heigu Yōhō document gives an outline of the type of spear to be used by a commander.

From ancient times, a taimai no yari *(タイマイノ鑓), turtle-shell-patterned spear, has been called a* shirae no naginata *(白柄ノ長刀), white-handled halberd, and is only carried by the commander. It has the following characteristics:*

- *The handle should be of the* nashiji *style, which is lacquering with gold and silver powder.*
- *It should be 7* shaku, 5 sun *long.*
- *The length of the blade should be 1* shaku, 7 sun.
- *The* hamon *hardening line on the blade should be in the* komidare *(小乱) style.*
- *The point of the blade (*kissaki*) should have lines in the style of* hakikake *(ハキカケ).*
- *The groove (*大樋*) in the blade should start from the* mitsugashira *(三ツ頭) section, which is below the tip of the spear blade, and the inside of the groove should be coloured in red.*
- *The style of* saba-no-o, *which means like the split fin tail of a mackerel, should be used for the spear butt.*
- *The handle should also have a guiding mark to help identify the blade edge side.*

These ways are from koryū *– old schools.*

Heigu Yōhō (c1670)

As the following quote demonstrates, for a servant the position of spear-bearer carried great responsibility and prestige.

Concerning the omochiyari katsugi, *spear-carrying servant: normally in Edo they get quite a stipend and walk at the front of a daimyō's parade, as they are carrying the most important weapon for a samurai.*

Zōhyō Monogatari (1657–84)

The red badge of courage

The Japanese spear blade had either a triangular or diamond-shaped cross-section and often had a groove down the centre. Warriors who achieved an outstanding feat in battle were permitted to have the groove of their spear blade painted red. This mark could also be carried by the descendants of heroic samurai. It is not clear from available sources quite how common this practice was, but it is referred to in this extract from the Heigu Yōhō.

> *While staying in Suruga province, the lord [Tokugawa Ieyasu] prohibited everyone from carrying a spear with a red groove. However, when the warrior Hosokawa Ecchū-no-kami was assigned to the construction of the castle one* bugyō *commander under him carried such a red spear and everyone who saw this reported it to the lord. The lord said that this warrior, whose name was Sawamura Daigaku, had attained an excellent achievement the previous year at the battle of Nagakute. He explained that when he had prohibited carrying red spears he had excluded achieved men from the rule, and so he ordered them to leave this achieved man be.*
>
> Heigu Yōhō (c1670)

Famous spears

The samurai celebrated the following notable weapons as the *tenka san meisō* (天下三名槍), 'the three greatest spears in all the world':

* Tonbokiri (蜻蛉切), the 'Dragonfly Cutter' – used by Honda Tadakatsu
* Nihon-gō (日本号), title not fully translatable without context – used by Fukushima Masanori and Mori Tahei
* Otegine (御手杵), the 'Smasher' or 'Pestle' – used by Uki Harutomo and passed to Tokugawa Ieyasu

The Nihon-gō spear has an interesting back story, which is told in the famous samurai drinking song 'Kuroda Bushi'. The sixteenth-century emperor

Ōgimachi gave Nihon-gō to his *shōgun* Ashikaga Yoshiaki. After that, it came to Oda Nobunaga, then Toyotomi Hideyoshi, and then Fukushima Masanori. Mori Tahei, a samurai with a renowned ability to drink alcohol, brought a message from his lord, Kuroda Yoshitaka, to Masanori's mansion. Masanori tried to get him to drink *sake* to test this reputation, but Tahei refused to rise to the challenge because he was there on official business.

Masanori became irritated and said, 'It seems there are no great men in the Kuroda clan!' He then filled a large jug with *sake* and said, 'If you drink this, I will give you anything you want.' Tahei took the jug, gulped down its contents and said, 'I want the famous spear Nihon-gō', and that is how he became the owner of one of the three great spears of Japan. It was a costly error by Masanori to value a samurai's ability to drink over his prowess as a warrior.

The *naginata*

The *yari* was a straight-bladed spear, while the *naginata* had a curved blade similar to that of a glaive or halberd. The *naginata* is often considered to be a woman's weapon. However, many of the European visitors to Japan in the sixteenth and seventeenth centuries witnessed it being used by men. According to Luís Froís, Oda Nobunaga defended himself with a *naginata* in the attack that resulted in his death, and Rodrigo de Vivero y Velasco reported having seen a troop of 300 castle guards all of whom were carrying *naginata*. Bernardino de Ávila Girón wrote about the *naginata*, describing it as a blade mounted upon a shaft and used by samurai in the manner of a Western great sword. He also stated that the *naginata* was a weapon of office and that there were rules as to the type and style of *naginata* that samurai of different ranks could carry during peacetime.

The symbolic spear

From a sharpened piece of bamboo held by the lowest foot soldier, to the highly prized 'white spear' of the samurai commander, spears and other pole arms symbolized the way of the warrior. Pole arms came to prominence after the bow but before the sword. At the time that the spear was considered the weapon of the samurai even average farmers were wearing two swords, so a good pole arm made the samurai stand out as a person of substance – particularly when it was paraded before him by his spear-bearer. Therefore, while the bow represented the concept of war, the pole arm symbolized the office and identity of the samurai.

Guns

> *There are no rules for guns in traditional military science.*
> *Nevertheless, in view of their function as instruments of killing and*
> *wounding, samurai have no business ignoring them.*
>
> Heihō Ōgisho (17th century)

The samurai and the gun: a combination that brought about a dramatic change in Japanese warfare. Gunpowder had come to Japan soon after its invention by the Chinese in the ninth century and primitive cannons known as *teppō* were believed to have been introduced during the Mongol invasions of 1274 and 1281. However, the use of artillery in Japan appears to have been limited until the sixteenth century. While there is some evidence for basic guns from the start of that century, it was the arrival of European weaponry in the 1540s that sparked the explosion of the Japanese firearms industry. By the end of the century, even the *shōgun*, Tokugawa Ieyasu, was well versed in the handling of a gun.

A brief history of the gun in Japan

In 1543 three Portuguese adventurers inadvertently became the first Europeans to arrive in Japan. They were travelling aboard a Chinese ship that was forced to take shelter from a storm on the island of Tanegashima off the southern tip of Kyūshū. There they engaged with the local ruler, Lord Tanegashima Tokitaka, who bought two arquebuses from them. He asked his swordsmith Yatsuita to replicate them, but the trigger mechanism proved to be beyond him, and so it is said that the lord gave his daughter to the Portuguese captain in return for the necessary technical knowledge.

After one year, ten guns had been made; within ten years, they were being manufactured all over Japan. Firearms became a common sight, even if they had not yet been exploited to their full potential. Samurai retainers were trained in shooting these new weapons and used them in military manoeuvres, becoming proficient marksmen.

OPEN FOR BUSINESS

For considerable periods of its history, Japan was largely closed off from the rest of the world, but this was certainly not the case during the fifteenth and sixteenth centuries. Even before relations with Europe took off in the 1540s, there was a huge amount of trade with China and south-east Asia. It is estimated that 67,000 swords were shipped to China in 1483 alone. Soon Japan was sending copper to Amsterdam and undercutting England in iron and steel.

Guns were first used in battle at Uedahara in 1548. Takeda Shingen had with him some musketeers, but following the traditional pre-battle rituals such as the exchange of names, the gunmen were not in the correct frame of mind to use the guns to the best effect and could not gain any advantage with them.

However, as times progressed and the old ways gave way to the new, clans reduced their spearmen and increased their gunmen. In 1560, a fully armoured samurai general was shot and killed for the first time – a sign that guns had hit the samurai battlefield in a major way. At the battle of Nagashino in 1575, Oda Nobunaga used the tactic of shooting in successive volleys to destroy the army of Shingen's son Katsuyori. He set up multiple rows of gunmen in a defensive position and had each row take turns to shoot and reload. Guns were also used to great effect during the invasions of Korea from 1592 to 1598. One lord wrote back to Japan from Korea saying, 'Forget the spears, send us guns, powder and ammunition.'

Firearms were used extensively during what remained of the Sengoku period. However, with the dawning of the Tokugawa period, when the emphasis was on centralizing power and weakening regional warlords, guns started to be regulated. From 1607, orders for new firearms had to be put through government offices, the intention being to restrict the ownership and production of this devastating weapon. With the number of legal commissions having dropped significantly, some gunsmiths returned to swordsmithing and others left the official government firearms industry and went back to the provinces to produce unregulated weapons. However, Tokugawa Ieyasu ordered them to return and gave them a subsidy from central funding, so that soon the government had almost total control over Japanese gun production. By the early 1700s an average of just a few hundred guns a year were being made for a samurai population of about 1 million.

The last bastion of Japan's 100-year romance with the gun was the city of Sakai, which had the only factory that had the legal right to manufacture firearms. However, bit by bit, the edicts and laws filtered through, closing even that centre of production. In 1776, the Swedish surgeon and botanist Carl Peter Thunberg, who got to see Japan in its closed days, reported that the shore defence batteries were tested once every seven years and were equipped with antiquated cannon. However, guns were still used by samurai clans, notably to suppress an Ainu tribal rebellion in the second half of the seventeenth century and a peasant uprising in the eighteenth century.

This sporadic use of guns sputtered on throughout the rest of the Tokugawa period, but they were so far out of date that they had no real effect. By the time Commodore Perry arrived in 1853 to reopen Japan to the world, shore batteries were often simply painted screens with a few extremely aged cannons, and were no match for the power of the West.

Samurai use of guns

> *[My master] only uses [a musket] when the enemy is at a distance*
> *but not when the enemy is too far for a shot. He also prefers to take*
> *his spear instead at times and have me hold the gun for him.*
>
> Zōhyō Monogatari (1657–84)

Did the samurai use guns? The simple answer is yes. However, high-ranking samurai would tend not to use guns in battle, although they did often carry lavishly decorated pistols. It was not that they considered guns to be an unchivalrous weapon, but it was beneath them to engage in any form of hand-to-hand combat, no matter what the weapon. Samurai commanders were discouraged from fighting on the front line; their role was to provide leadership and strategic thinking.

Guns were most effective when used by large numbers of men arranged in ranks rather than by individuals. Gunmen tended to be lower-class soldiers who had basic training in a single weapon and fought as a unit and so were quite distinct from samurai forces comprising multi-talented and independent warriors.

However, guns were adopted by lower-ranking samurai and helped them move their way up the ranks. When Toyotomi Hideyoshi was being pressed in battle with the Asakura, the men of Mikawa pushed forward to help him and Tokugawa Ieyasu himself used a matchlock gun. After the battle, a priest fired twice at Ieyasu but the shots did not penetrate his armour.

In another example of samurai gunmanship, two of Ieyasu's retainers, Okubo Tadayo and Amano Yasukage, took sixteen matchlock men at night to flank the Takeda forces and cause panic in the camp. Furthermore, at the battle of Komaki in 1584, a samurai from the Mori clan tried to rally his men. Being dressed in white, he stood out as a target and, sure enough, one of the samurai of the prestigious troop under Ii Naomasa took aim and shot him in the head.

Even considering all of this positive evidence, there are contradictory reports to show that in the Sengoku period some samurai disdained guns. The following quote is from a missionary who was in Japan during this time. However, he died in 1570 and so he did not live to see the rise of the gun to prominence at the end of the Sengoku period.

> *They do not have any kind of gun because they declare that they are for cowards alone. They are the best archers I have seen in the world and they look down on all other nations.*
>
> Writings of Cosme de Torres (16th century)

AN EXPERT PERSPECTIVE

Former British soldier Matthew Okuhara now resides in Japan and has been adopted into an ex-samurai family and serves as part of the Matsumoto Castle gun team. Their aim is to preserve the practical understanding of the Japanese gun and promote the history of the gun within Japan. The following is an overview of his understanding of the relationship between the samurai and the gun.

The history of guns in Japan does not start in 1543 as most people would believe. It is only the history of Western guns in Japan that starts in that year. Gunpowder itself had been in Asia for much longer and Chinese cannon are believed to have been in Japan from the fifteenth century.

Guns ranged from ones of low quality such as the banzutsu *(番筒), which were numbered and stocked up as military equipment under a quartermaster, all the way to much more prestigious examples like the* ōzutsu *(大筒) and the* bajōzutsu *(馬上筒). The type of gun called a* tanzutsu *(短筒) was most likely an expensive showing-off piece not intended for practical use.*

It is commonly heard within the samurai enthusiast community today that the samurai would not use guns. This is simply not true – there is overwhelming evidence for the use of guns by both samurai and ashigaru *foot soldiers and great samurai lords such as Oda Nobunaga and Toyotomi Hideyoshi were more than fond of them. Guns were generally bought by samurai lords, emblazoned with the family crest and then distributed into the hands of both samurai proper and foot soldiers. They were used for both warfare and hunting.*

The simple fact is that the gun changed the face of samurai warfare in the sixteenth century and it was only afterwards, during the time of peace, that the love of the gun diminished in the face of the romantic return to the sword. When Japan was opened back up to the world in the nineteenth century and Westerners returned with their modern firearms, the Japanese were still using guns that were 300 years old. The Japanese gun is a treasured part of samurai history, yet it remains in the shadow of the katana *as the weapon of the warrior.*

Weapons of capture

When surveying the samurai armoury, rakes (*kumade*) and other 'grabbing' tools are often overlooked. At times, samurai had a choice to make: to kill the enemy there and then, or capture them. Sometimes they took off their swords and replaced them with tools of capture so that their side assistants could perform the decapitation. At the battle of Sekigahara, a samurai known as Kinshichirō used a rake-style pole arm to drag in ten enemies so that his assistants could decapitate them, before he himself was killed. Samurai guards patrolling a city often used a rake or pole arm to restrain a target instead of going straight for the sword. Proficiency with capturing tools was a staple of the samurai arts.

SOURCES

As for capturing farmers, craftsmen and merchants, that presents no problems at all. However, there are multiple teachings on the capture of samurai and others if they defend themselves with bladed weapons or projectile weapons, such as bows or muskets. Know that various plans and measures need be taken, such as:

- *Throwing hot water or fire*
- *Putting ash into a musket and shooting it at them*

- *Protecting the body with equipment*
- *Using the* tsukubo, sasumata *and* kumade *grabbing tools along with the tradition of grappling hook*

You should be flexible according to the situation.

Heika Jōdan (c1670)

The six tools for guard duty:

1. Hayanawa *(早縄) – quick-rope for binding*
2. Kumade *(熊手) – the bear-claw staff*
3. Tsukubō *(突棒) – spiked T-bar staff*
4. Hyōshigi *(拍子木) – wooden warning clappers*
5. Bō *(棒) – quarterstaff*
6. Sasumata *(指胯) – U-shaped pronged staff*

Heigu Yōhō (c1670)

Hidden weapons

One common and quite drastic misconception is that concealed weapons were considered to be dishonourable, that they were used by the *shinobi* for their dark deeds but shunned by the samurai. This is an outright myth and actually the opposite is true.

In all the *shinobi* literature and primary evidence left to us today, there is scant description of hidden weapons. The *shinobi* used a combination of infiltration tools and conventional, overt weapons such as *tachi* and *katana* swords, hand grenades, landmines and fire tools. In contrast, the samurai used all kinds of deceptive weapons and tricks to help them in combat and to defend themselves at other times.

There are entire books dedicated to the subject of samurai secret weapons, and there appears to have been no dishonour at all in fighting with covert weaponry. It is a fundamental aspect of Japanese culture that samurai carried hidden blades or tools, commonly known as *hibuki* (秘武器) or *kakushibuki* (隠し武器), for self-defence. Examples include prepared weapons (*shikomibuki*) such as spikes within truncheons (*shikomi-jutte*), faux fans with hidden blades (*shikomi-sensu*), and sword canes (*shikomijō*). There was also the ritualistic Buddhist 'thunderbolt' (*kongōsho*). This was originally used in India, where it was known as a *vajra*. Similar to this were a short wooden bar (*yawara-bō*) and its iron counterpart (*suntetsu*), which were concealed in the palm and used to strike an enemy. Chain weapons included the 'ten thousand power chain' (*manriki-kusari*) and the ball and chain (*chigiriki* and *tobigane*). Then there was, of course, the famed *shuriken*, a weapon used by swordsmen to distract an opponent before striking; a spiked ring (*hojokuwa*) for gripping people; blinding powders (*metsubushi*) used before an arrest or attack; mini-arrow flingers (*tsutsu-uchiya*); bullet hand-launchers (*tsustu-uchidama*); and a metal weight to finish all things off and aptly named 'the beginning and the end' (*a-un*).

This list is not exhaustive, but is a good summary of the types of hidden weapons used by the samurai in addition to the more conventional weapons for which they were better known.

SOURCES

The five virtues of the hidden dagger (shinobi-zashi):
1. *It can be used in combat.*
2. *It can be used for decapitating.*
3. *It can be used in a place where swords are forbidden.*
4. *It can be used for the teaching of* santō issho.
5. *It has a smaller hilt.*

There are various types of the above.

Heika Jōdan (c1670)

If someone is approaching you in a relaxed manner with his left hand inside his kimono *and his sword in an informal position, do not let your guard down, be it day or night. If this happens at night, it is possible his sword is in a scabbard that is made of black paper and that he may immediately strike you with the sword without unsheathing it.*

Mizukagami (c1670)

The 'rod of mist' is a cane or rod that has a tip embedded with poison made from:
- *Flowers of a thistle*
- *Powdered whitewash (calcium carbonate)*
- *Iron filings*
- *Unslaked lime*

Mix the above, powder it and insert it into a rod. Swing and flick the rod toward the enemy while considering the 'wind and the wave'. Use this in war or in street combat.

Scrolls of Sekiguchi-Ryū under Yamada Toshiyasu (Edo period)

Remove the contents of an egg, clean [the inside] with shochu *liquor and fill with the poison [shown below]. Twist paper [into a string] with gunpowder wrapped within it [and put it into the hole of the egg], then ignite. The recipe of the powder is as below.*
Mix equal amounts of:
- *Saltpetre*
- *Lime*
- *Pine resin*
- *Sulphur*

Mix the above and powder. Put it into the egg and throw the egg at the enemy after igniting the fuse. This will shoot out poison and all

> *your enemies will be killed [or fall unconscious] for a while. To protect*
> *yourself from this, keep 3 bu of crystal sugar in your month and apply*
> *the oil of the Japanese anise tree onto the nine openings of the body.*
> Scrolls of Sekiguchi-Ryū under Yamada Toshiyasu (Edo period)

> *Char the livers of boars and moles and powder them down. Mix these*
> *two ingredients and powder them finely. Wrap with silk cloth or paper*
> *and carry it in your kimono at all times. [When needs arise], blow it*
> *over the enemy or throw it. Make sure to do it very quickly.*
> Scrolls of Sekiguchi-Ryū under Yamada Toshiyasu (Edo period)

SHIELDS

> *The Japanese use a piece of board flat like a door [as a shield].*
> Luís Frois, *Tratado* (1585)

Early Japanese warfare was modelled upon the Chinese style in which shields *were* used. However, as mounted combat took precedence shields became less of a requirement but did not fade away entirely, and in fact made a resurgence with the advent of the gun in the sixteenth century. There was an abundance of shields in medieval Japan, including the three types described below, and there is ample literature on the subject.

The ōsode (大袖)

When Japanese armour developed after Chinese-influenced warfare declined, oversized shield-like shoulder protectors called *ōsode* were created to stop arrows from hitting the face and chest area. While these were not shields proper, they constituted a shielding panel on the armour and performed the same function as a shield.

The tedate (手立)

The *tedate* was a hand-held shield made either of solid wood or wooden panels set in metal. Some examples had a viewing panel, and sometimes a chainmail skirt at the bottom. It was akin to the modern 'riot shield' but considerably smaller. The *tedate* was used by massed ranks of soldiers to push in on an opponent or approach an armed target, or it could be used on horseback with either a pistol or a single-handed sword. Examples of combat with these shields can be seen in martial arts scrolls up until the early seventeenth century, after which it appears to have become less prominent.

The tate (楯)

These were free-standing shields used to create a wall for massed troops to defend themselves against projectiles and were often deployed in front of *ashigaru* musketeers and archers when battle lines were formed. They are the most common Japanese shield used in samurai times.

There was no shame in a samurai hiding behind shields when it was appropriate to do so, just as long as he was also prepared to move out from behind them. There is an old story of two samurai who were delivering a message. One of them decided to ride along the front line of allied shields, open to enemy fire; the other decided to ride behind the shield wall. Both messengers reached their destination, but, when preparing to return, the samurai who had ridden outside the shield wall said he had barely escaped with his life and that it would have been better to have ridden behind the wall. The warrior who had ridden behind the wall said that he did so because the message was of vital importance and that to have died before delivering it would have been foolish. However, as he had now delivered the message he could afford to take more risks, so he rode on the outside of the shield wall this time while the other man rode on the inside. This story encapsulates the samurai attitude to personal safety.

HORSES

> *We fight on horseback; the Japanese dismount when they have to fight.*

Luís Froís, Tratado (1585)

Horses were prized and honoured and to own one marked you out as belonging to a certain social level. They were expensive to buy and also to maintain, as they required at least two grooms as attendants: one to lead at the front and the other to follow at the rear. These were trusted roles. When Minamoto no Yoritomo asked his half-brother Minamoto no Yoshitsune to lead his horse in a ceremony dedicated to Hachiman, Yoshitsune declared that it was a menial task beneath a man of his standing, but Yoritomo replied that it was a position of honour.

Horses had an impact on *bushidō* in various ways. For example, to be unable to control a horse was deemed an embarrassment (although, looking at this issue in practical terms, it was good to identify unruly horses before they caused chaos in parade lines and on the march).

Also, when a junior samurai reported to a senior samurai, if the senior was mounted then the junior could remain mounted, but if the senior was on foot, the junior samurai had to dismount and make his report on foot and bow. Such was the protocol of reporting from a horse.

Ill omens

In early times in samurai history, certain characteristics of a horse were deemed to be inauspicious. These included a single block of colour in a column from the nose to the forehead, which was said to resemble a Japanese death tablet (*ihai*); hair containing whorls; membranes on the eyes; and weak breath.

Horses of ill omen were often run across battle lines before fighting started, in order to transfer the bad luck to the enemy. They would respond by cutting its hair, making offerings to the gods and performing returning spells before sending it back.

A horse that had a base colour and then patches of another colour was associated with cowardice. This superstition was based on the similarity between the terms *nige* (二毛), 'dual-coloured', and *nigeru* (逃げる), 'to flee', which we encountered earlier in relation to fur on helmets.

A HIERARCHY OF HORSES

Not all horses were equal; like the most exquisite swords and spears, some particularly fine horses were prized above the rest. This was not always a good thing: the horses from Kyōto were said to have been protected from the cold and insects, but such pampering was a poor preparation for the hardships they would endure on the march or in battle so they tended not to be very useful to the samurai. Then there were certain individual horses that went down in history, like Ikezuki (池月), the bad-tempered beast owned by Sasaki Takatsuna, and Tayūguro (太夫黒), Minamoto no Yoshitsune's handsome black mount.

Trained for excellence

The image of the horse and its trainer, or the hawk and its handler, was used to represent how important it was to have both talented warriors and a talented leader.

A horse is powerful and can run far and fast, a hawk is naturally in command of the skies; but even the most naturally gifted horse or hawk cannot reach its full potential without a skilled trainer or handler to bring out its talents, and it is the same in samurai and military matters.

This idea, which persisted throughout samurai times, was memorably expressed when Tokugawa Ieyasu praised one of his sons, Matsudaira Tadakatsu, to which his retainer Ii Naomasa said, 'Fine hawks only come from great stock.' Ieyasu returned the compliment by countering, 'Only if they have great trainers.'

SOURCES

[The samurai under Kakihanji] would gallop all over the plains, seeming to fall off only to make a flying mount, to be mounted only to make a flying dismount, manoeuvring so freely that they were known as expert riders.

Bushidō Shoshinshū (c1700)

According to our standards, their horses are not good at all; the very best one in all Japan is only fit to carry firewood.

Writings of Bernardino de Ávila Girón (late 16th/early 17th century)

[In Japan] the mane of a horse is cut back and straw rice woven in to increase their presence, while their tail is bound up in a knot.

Luís Frois, Tratado (1585)

Kurokawa used to tell his horse in advance of combat, 'I treasure you so much and I totally trust you to be of true value. Therefore, if things turn out against my wish we will die together. Please do not think ill of me for this.' True to his word, he stabbed his horse twice at the side of the neck while they were both in the water. That is what was found after their bodies were raised from the deep.

Musha Monogatari (1654)

FLAGS AND STANDARDS

They, together with a servant named Oacha and one more, found the standard of golden gourds left behind, and considering it would be shameful if it was left, they broke it and threw it away.

Okiku Monogatari (17th century)

A samurai without a banner was not properly rigged for war. Flags were emblems of pride, identity and accomplishment. When imagining the samurai on his horse, picture his livery, including helmet crest, banners and horse marker.

The horse marker

The *umajirushi* (馬印), 'horse marker', was a special standard designed to identify the position of a samurai's horse on the field of battle. Rather than a traditional cloth flag, it generally consisted of a three-dimensional object secured to a long pole. It would normally be carried by a servant. Most of the time a samurai would be with his horse, but the horse marker allowed him to find his way back to his own men if he had separated from them.

In battle camps, each samurai would hoist his horse marker alongside his heraldic crest outside his tent. This meant that even if two samurai had the same heraldic crest, their tents could be distinguished from each other by their respective horse markers.

Individual flags

While the horse standard indicated the samurai's position, the samurai themselves had a battle flag to mark them out from the crowd. Followers sometimes incorporated the emblem of their master into their individual flag. Most samurai would wear the flag on the back of their armour, except when they went on a night raid (in which case the flag would not be visible) or if they asked permission to go into battle without it, which they might do for various reasons. For example, they might not wear the flag if they were taking an inexperienced member of the clan into battle to make their first kill.

There was also the concept of 'permitted banners', which were banners that had special meaning and were only allowed to be carried by samurai of particular achievement. For example, a flag showing 100 stalks of straw represented the accomplishment of 100 great deeds; one showing a boar denoted an ability to charge and fight ferociously.

SOURCES

Yamaguchi Mozaemon was given amour but did not have a standard, so he asked his daughter Kiku to make one for him. She sewed red and white silk together to make a standard; with this, he was very pleased.

Okiku Monogatari (17th century)

According to an ancient samurai story, there were twelve messengers within Lord Takeda Shingen's army. Each of them was supposed to carry a square flag of white cloth with a black centipede upon it. However, one of them, Hajikano Den'emon, had a white square flag without a centipede upon it. Lord Shingen, seeing this, asked who of the twelve messengers had only a white flag. Someone replied that it was Hajikano Den'emon. The lord became angry and asked him why he did not obey this rule. To this Den'emon said, 'I would never break the rules. I have a 1 sun [3 cm] centipede just next to a side loop of the flag.' And showed it to the lord. The lord asked him why it was thus. Den'emon replied, 'If I had a centipede the same as everyone else's, no one would be able to tell what I had achieved on the battlefield.' Lord Shingen laughed to hear this.

Musha Monogatari (1654)

Hōjō Saemon-dayū, a retainer of Lord Hōjō Ujiyasu of Odawara in Soshu province, had a flag of tawny silk with just two characters written in ink upon it (八幡). These characters meant, 'I am a direct follower of Hachiman Daibosatsu.' Therefore, it was called the flag of Jiki Hachiman. During the assault on Fukasawa Castle in Soshu, the flag fell into the hands of Lord Takeda Shingen. He gave it to Sanada Genjirō Nobukimi, who later entered the Katsuno family and changed his name to Katsuno Ichiemon. He was the youngest child of Sanada Ittokusai. I hear that this flag is still kept within the family.

Musha Monogatari (1654)

CHAPTER ELEVEN

SWORDS

No other weapon is as closely associated with the samurai as the sword. In the modern imagination, we picture a samurai displaying awe-inspiring sword-fighting skills with a dazzling *katana* blade. In this chapter we will explore the complex protocols and symbolism relating to the sword, as well as questioning its status in the samurai tradition. Was the *katana* really such a pivotal part of samurai identity, or is this another element of the *bushidō* myth?

THE SOUL OF THE SAMURAI

> *There is nothing between heaven and earth that a man has to fear*
> *if he carries a sword at his waist.*
>
> Japanese saying

There is an old story that says a swordsmith made the perfect sword, which he tested on a local street seller. The street seller, not aware he had been cut because of the extreme sharpness of the sword, carried on walking until his body fell apart. This obvious fiction conveyed the samurai's growing love of the sword. The *Hagakure* viewed the weapon as a reflection of a samurai's inner identity: a samurai's mind was as dull or as sharp as the blade of his sword.

This idea grew into the belief that a samurai's sword was his soul, an idea that became fixed in the modern consciousness with the publication of Nitobe Inazō's *Bushidō: The Soul of the Samurai* in the early twentieth century. Nitobe had converted to Christianity and his use of the Christian term 'soul' is somewhat problematic; the samurai and monks of the mid-sixteenth century would argue with Jesuit missionaries about the concept of the soul, which clashed with the Shintō idea that the dead became *kami*. One monk threatened to cut a Jesuit's head off to see if he could find this so-called 'soul'. Nevertheless, the saying that a samurai's sword was his soul ('*katana wa bushi no tamashii*') is recorded as early as 1750 or thereabouts. Either way, by the Edo period the sword had started to become closely associated with the idea of samurai spirit. The *Hagakure* also stated that those who never used their swords were cowards, whereas those who overused them were prone to brashness.

Although the sword's association with the samurai grew more powerful during the Edo period, the power of the samurai themselves faded during this time. By the late nineteenth century, the merchant class had risen to the top and global trade was expanding fast; metal was no longer used for swords and suits of armour but for railways and steamships. As Japan started to wield her influence in the modern world, the sword became no more than an emblem of the past.

The katana *in context*

The history of Japanese swords is complex, but a single point that stands out is the fact that the *tachi* or great sword was an earlier sword used by the samurai and it was only later that the *katana* was developed. The term *katana* can represent blades as a whole, but here we use it to refer to a sword that is shorter and straighter than a *tachi*.

As warfare moved from open and mounted to close combat, the *uchigatana* (打刀) 'striking sword' was created. This was a shorter weapon which could be used effectively for cutting from the ground. Sometimes two *uchigatana* were used together; at other times, a samurai could have three blades: a primary, a secondary and a reserve dagger. Later, the carrying of two swords was a privilege that set the samurai apart, but in earlier times this was nothing special. In fact, according to the *Heike Monogatari* (compiled before 1330) there was almost no difference in appearance between fighting monks in samurai-style armour and the samurai themselves, apart from the cowls the monks wore to show their devotion to a sect or religion.

The fact that the *katana* did not exist for the first half of the samurai period undermines the concept of the sword as the 'soul of the samurai'. In those earlier, turbulent times, it was the bow and the spear that commanded the most respect. Swords were viewed as extremely useful tools, but not considered to be more special than any other weapon in the samurai arsenal. It was only after the warring had died down, and heroic battle tales became shrouded in nostalgia, that the sword gained its spiritual significance.

AN AFFORDABLE NECESSITY

The popular idea that a samurai sword was expensive is a misconception; new swords were costly, particularly those made by a renowned swordsmith, but the average second-hand sword would have been affordable enough to be owned by farmers and foot soldiers. It becomes obvious quickly that samurai owned more than one sword. In fact, it seems they often had multiple spares. They were not the treasured possessions we might imagine them to be; manuals such as the *Heika Jōdan* and *Bushidō Shoshinshū* both mention samurai pawning their spare swords and even giving them away as victory gifts.

The *Bushidō Shoshinshū* also states that any warrior who equipped his servants with bamboo blades or wooden substitutes – presumably to save money – was lacking in honour, because it was the samurai's responsibility to arm their men with proper weapons.

Sidearms

A samurai always had to have a blade at his side to protect himself or to commit suicide with. Originally, the *tachi* was the name of the samurai's main weapon and the shorter sidearm was called the *uchigatana* or just *katana*. Later, the *katana* became the main sword, while the sidearm was referred to as the *wakizashi* (脇差), literally 'to wear at the side'. Regardless of terminology, to be without a sidearm unless asked to be so by a higher-ranking person was a dishonour and against the way of the samurai.

Hidden blades

Hidden blades were called *shinobi-zashi* (忍指), but they had nothing to do with the *shinobi* (ninja). The word '*shinobi*' here refers to hidden or secret, so these weapons were 'secret sidearms'. Samurai, knowing that they may at times be asked to remove both their main sword and their sidearm, would often hide a blade on their person in case of emergencies.

Sword hunts

> Even low-class people such as farmers, merchants and artisans all treasure a rusty sword [...] in warrior clans even the lower people and squires always wear a short sword as a rule.
>
> Bushidō Shoshinshū (c1700)

Before the mid-sixteenth century, most people could carry a sword and there was no special association with carrying two swords. In fact, documents show that samurai sometimes carried three swords instead of two: normally a primary sword, a sidearm and a concealed dagger. Common folk and religious figures, individuals and groups could all arm themselves with swords, pole arms and other weapons. Some religious orders were so well armed and manned that they threatened samurai rule.

However, as Japan became more and more centralized in the mid-to-late sixteenth century, the government increased its control over public weapons, passing edicts banning the possession and carrying of swords in public by the general population. These were known as 'sword hunts', because the swords (and other weapons) were hunted down by the authorities and confiscated. The most famous was the 1586 edict by Toyotomi Hideyoshi declaring that all blades should be collected up to make a great Buddha statue. The basic idea was to disarm the general population and allow only the samurai class to bear arms. (Commoners could still carry short swords for protection when travelling, although as time went on the restrictions were tightened and only daggers were allowed.)

From this point, the samurai's relationship with the sword – particularly *daishō* (matching swords worn in pairs) – became fixed in the public mind. The samurai would continue to be the only members of society to freely exercise their right to bear arms in full (except for guns) until the abolition of carrying weapons in public in the 1870s. With the loss of this privilege, it no longer became possible to maintain the pretence of samurai power.

> *They do not gamble; just as theft is punishable by death, so also is gambling. As a pastime they practise with their weapons, at which they are extremely adept, or write couplets, just as the Romans composed poetry, and most of the gentry [samurai] occupy themselves in this way.*
>
> Writings of Cosme de Torres (16th century)

Miyamoto Musashi and the Nitō Ichi-Ryū school

The famous swordsman Miyamoto Musashi was the head of various schools at different times. His main school was known as Nitō Ichi-Ryū (二刀一流), which is often translated as 'the school of two swords used together' or 'the school of two swords as one'. However, this is probably not the best translation. Miyamoto Musashi himself explained why he used that name in his 'earth scroll' (*chi no maki*) from his treatise *Gorin no Sho* (五輪書), 'The Universal Book [of Swordsmanship]'. Below are two translations of the same passage so that there can be no error in understanding. Other translations have also been used to cross check the passage:

> *The point of talking about two swords is that it is the duty of all warriors, commanders and soldiers alike, to wear two swords. In olden times they were called* tachi *and* katana; *nowadays they are called* katana *and* wakizashi. *There is no need for a detailed description of the business of warriors wearing these two swords.*

In Japan, the way of the warrior is to wear them at their sides whether they know anything about them or not. It is in order to convey the advantages of these two that I call my school [Nitō Ichi-Ryū].

Gorin no Sho (1643–6), translated by Thomas Cleary

We talk about the two swords: the position of members of the warrior class, from generals to foot soldiers, is one in which two swords are worn at the belt from the outset. In old days they were called tachi *and* katana, *now they are called* katana *and* wakizashi. *There is no need for the particulars about wearing of these two swords. Here in our country, no matter whether one understands it or not, wearing them is the way of a member of the warrior class. In order to indicate the fundamental principle of these two I call [this school] the Nitō Ichi-Ryū.*

Gorin no Sho (1643–6), translated by David K. Groff

It is better to break the name into the two parts *nitō* (二刀), meaning 'two swords', and *ichi-ryū* (一流), meaning 'premier school'. People often think that *nitō* (二刀) and *ichi* (一) go together as one term meaning 'two swords as one', or 'two swords used together to fight with at one time', but it is possibly not so. As seen in the parallel translations above, the 'two swords' in the name refers to the two swords carried as a symbol of samurai status. This would make the first part of the name, *'nito'*, a way of referring to a 'warrior'. The term *ichi-ryū* actually means 'the premier school or tradition', 'one' in this case meaning 'the best' and 'school' referring to the way or tradition or flow of a lineage. This is made evident by Musashi's calling the article 'On naming this style of two swords' (*kono ichi-ryū nitō to nazukeru koto*) in the earth scroll (*chi no maki*) where he clearly states *ichi-ryū* (一流) to be the suffix of the school name.

Therefore, the following might be more accurate translations of the school name Nitō Ichi-Ryū:

- The premier school of the warrior
- The school of the supreme warrior
- The school of warrior supremacy

Musashi's school is sometimes also called Niten Ichi-Ryū (二天一流), which literally means the 'premier school of two heavens'. Many people think this means 'two swords from heaven'. However, it is probably a reference to Musashi's Buddhist name, Niten Dōraku (二天道楽), which would make the translation of the school name 'the premier school of Miyamoto Musashi'. Musashi himself switches between the two school names of Nitō and Niten within his own writings.

TWO SWORDS OR ONE?

Musashi recommended holding a sword in each hand during training, not so that a samurai could learn to fight with two swords but to build strength in the dominant arm. The idea was that, by holding a sword in his other hand, the pupil would learn to resist the temptation to use both hands to wield his main sword. Musashi went on to say that the long sword used singlehanded was for open spaces and that the short sword was for enclosed spaces, implying that actually most fighting was done with only one sword. However, there were situations, such as in group fighting, where he advised using two swords.

Musashi was born at a time when the population of Japan was being disarmed, and when the sword was becoming the emblem of the samurai. He also, rightly or wrongly, considered that the samurai were fast becoming redundant. He believed that his school represented the correct way of the sword, harking back to a time when efficiency in battle was the goal of the military class. Therefore, for him, Nitō Ichi-Ryū taught the ultimate in samurai swordsmanship.

A badge of office

> *If the master holds the bridle and takes command of the horse, we*
> *grooms have our hands free and nothing to do, so it is a shame if*
> *we do not kill the enemy, as we are wearing a sword.*
>
> *Zōhyō Monogatari* (1657–84)

Walking the streets of Edo in the Tokugawa period (1603–1868), you would have seen lowly figures such as peasants and grooms wearing short swords or daggers, lower-ranking officials and what are commonly termed as 'half-samurai' wearing a single *katana*, and full-blown samurai (including *rōnin*) wearing *daishō*, the pair of swords that denoted samurai status.

With all these blades in circulation, from billhooks and knives to pole arms and daggers, it would be wrong to think that the samurai's special right to wear two swords was what enabled them to hold down the populace. What gave the samurai their power was their status as a warrior class with infrastructure and supplies enough to wage war against the masses when they rose up against their overlords, which happened more often than most people realize.

FROM BLADES TO SPADES

When new castles were being built in the late Sengoku and early Edo periods, samurai had to get stuck in and dig and build. However, they could only carry their *wakizashi* on site; they had to leave their longer swords behind. Only the construction supervisor and high-ranking dignitaries or lords were allowed to wear two swords during construction.

Chapter Eleven

Rites of passage

> *Both nobles and commoners carry a sword and dagger from the*
> *age of fourteen.*
>
> Writings of St Francis Xavier (16th century)

The samurai were initiated in the way of the sword at an early age. At around five years old, samurai boys would stand on a kind of chess board and be given a blunt sword as a symbol of their rank. By the age of fifteen a boy had become a man and was given the right to wear the sharp swords of a warrior.

Interestingly, the *Hagakure* scroll says that at the age of five boys should behead dogs to get a feel for killing and by the age of fifteen they should kill criminals so they understand the nature of taking human life. However, the ages given do not correspond exactly to Western ages. In Japan, a baby is considered to be one year old on the day of its birth and becomes one year older each New Year. Therefore, someone described as being 'fifteen' is actually only fourteen, or possibly even as young as thirteen, in Western terms.

Portuguese travellers of the sixteenth century gave different ages for these rites of passage. According to Jorge Alvarez, who was writing in 1547, samurai boys came of age when they were eight, while Baltasar Gago, writing in 1555, said that the age was ten. Luís Froís, writing in the 1580s, reported that they performed the first ritual at 'a very young age' but that they received both swords between the ages of twelve and thirteen. Taking these discrepancies into account, we can say that a samurai boy was given the blunt sword between the ages of four and ten, and the pair of sharp swords between the ages of twelve and fifteen.

BOYS' DAY

The fifth day of the fifth month was known as Boys' Day. Originally, armour would have been set in front of samurai gates on this day as a mark of family prowess, and the lower classes would have displayed mock armour to show that their own male children were also coming of age. Today, in Japan this day is still celebrated with small models of armour being displayed and boys being dressed in samurai costume. You often see banners and flags in the shape of carp, because the carp is a fish that fights to get upstream, just as young warriors must fight against the tide of battle.

PRACTICALITIES AND PROTOCOLS

Wearing a sword

What most people consider as the correct way to wear a samurai sword, with the curve of the blade pointing up and the handle and the tip pointing down, is a later adoption. There were actually various ways to carry a sword. Originally this was done 'tachi-style', which means that the blade was hung from a belt with the curve of the blade facing edge downward and the hilt and the end of the scabbard facing upward. This method was adopted both in armour and in normal clothes: there are ample images of samurai dressed in civilian clothes with their sword worn tachi-style.

Many people believe that with the coming of the straighter and shorter katana, sword blades were reversed and the blade edge was worn edge up instead. However, there are also numerous images of samurai wearing katana through a sash with the blade edge pointing down. According to sources such as the seventeenth-century Heigu Yōhō document, the distinction between wearing the sword blade edge up and blade edge down is grounded in yin–yang theory. A sword worn blade edge up was in the yang style associated with life (i.e. no killing), whereas one worn blade edge down was in the yin style of death. Therefore, the direction in which a samurai's blade faced was dependent on the situation and the intent. The Heigu Yōhō states that the *wakizashi* was always carried in a *yang* position, whereas a *katana* or *tachi* was placed in a *yin* state. There are many depictions in early seventeenth-century Japanese art of this blade up, blade down combination. After this point, most images show both swords blade up in a position of life – most likely because this was a period of peace.

There was another, more casual way of carrying a sword. Hagihara Jūzō in his seventeenth-century manuscript *Mizukagami* (水鏡) and Luís Froís both observed that the sword was carried over the shoulder in its scabbard, with one hand on the hilt and the scabbard leaning backwards, tip in the air. Hagihara Jūzō observes that the sword can be drawn from this position very quickly (see *The Lost Samurai School*). The sword could also be carried on the back in a style known as *wassoku* (輪束).

Note that all styles of carrying a sword conveyed a social message to other people. For example, the more the hilt angled upwards (making it harder to draw the sword quickly), the more elevated the rank of the samurai (higher-ranking samurai being less likely to need to fight). A more horizontal sword position implied readiness to fight and lower social status.

Sitting down with a sword

There is a debate as to whether a samurai was permitted to sit down with a sword in his belt or not. The protocol around when a sword could be placed in the sash and when it should be removed is not clear cut. There are various historical images of samurai kneeling down in *seiza* with swords in the belt, but there are also accounts that mention a requirement to take swords off before entering a building. One old reference comes from the Spanish traveller Rodrigo de Vivero y Velasco, who says that he visited Tokugawa Ieyasu in his court and that Ieyasu himself was seated on a cushion, dressed in green and wearing two swords in his belt.

Removing a sword

> *[The samurai] carry a sword and dagger both inside and outside*
> *the house and they lay them down at their pillows when they sleep.*
>
> Writings of St Francis Xavier (16th century)

A samurai was never without a blade of some description. It was seen as improper for a samurai not to have at least a *wakizashi* sidearm indoors and it was also incorrect for a samurai to be seen outdoors without a pair of swords. However, on some occasions, such as at the tea ceremony, in the presence of high-ranking people, during castle construction and so on, samurai were requested to take off either their longer sword or both swords. The sword was sometimes carried by an aide: Oda Nobunaga had a boy hold his when he went to the toilet (see chapter 7); Luís Froís reported that Toyotomi Hideyoshi had a 'girl' carry his sword over her shoulder (unless Froís had mistaken a boy for a girl, which is doubtful because he was well acquainted with Japan). Natori Sanjūrō Masazumi explains that the method of carrying the sword on behalf of a lord had social connotations. Observing etiquette even between master and servant was essential.

SAMURAI ASSISTANTS

Knights had their squires and pages, and the samurai also had trusted assistants. However, it is difficult to apply the Western terms to their Japanese counterparts. The word squire is incorrect, because the men who aided senior samurai were not waiting to become samurai, as squires were waiting to be knighted; they were already samurai by birth. Similarly, it would be misleading to refer to these samurai helpers as pages or page boys, as some of them were older men.

Acceptable places to leave a sword

When a samurai was not wearing his sword, it had to be kept in the appropriate place. The following are the positions in which swords were left in different circumstances.

- **In their own house:** within the main living room and set on a stand to the left of where the head samurai sat so he could draw it with ease (a high-ranking samurai would have an aide to carry his sword in castles and mansions)
- **At night:** by their futon
- **At lengthy social gatherings:** in a form of 'cloakroom' together with their outdoor gear
- **Visiting a house:** left with a servant
- **At the tea ceremony:** in a form of cupboard or closet
- **At an inn:** by their futon, but with the cords tied together
- **When bathing:** held by a servant

It was considered impolite to wear a sword indoors, especially in later times. However, when arresting someone the arresting officer could keep his sword in his sash; in later times, he would carry the sword and place it by his side but not leave it at the door. This does not account for the Western report that Tokugawa Ieyasu wore both of his swords while seated. While there were exceptions, what is evident is that in general there were socially acceptable places where swords should be positioned when they were not at the waist.

Minding the end of the scabbard

The scabbard end protruded behind a samurai so that when he turned, it swung around quickly. It was extremely important that a samurai never hit a person or an object with his scabbard. The Japanese term for this extremely rude action is *saya-atte* (鞘当). To hit an object such as a wall or post would be embarrassing; hitting a person was far worse. If a samurai accidently hit another samurai with the tip of their scabbard or if they touched the other samurai's sword by mistake, they would bow their head low and touch their forehead. Failure to do so would often result in a fight to the death. In the Edo period, samurai or *rōnin* spoiling for a fight would purposely hit another samurai with their scabbard and not apologize. This meant that the other samurai had to fight them in a duel or lose face.

It was also important to avoid collisions with other people's swords. To bang, knock, touch or step over a samurai's sword was a serious breach of protocol, again requiring an immediate apology. This would generally take the form of bowing while lifting your hands above your head as if you were raising the other person's sword in reverence. Sometimes the other person would lift up their actual sword and then you would just bow to it in apology.

> If your leg touches another's sidearm, then the rule is to hold [your hands] above your head [as you bow]; also, it is acceptable [if the owner] lifts up the sword, then just make your bow.
>
> Heika Jōdan (c1670)

Dropping a sword from its scabbard

The *Bushidō Shoshinshū* notes that it was improper for a samurai to allow his sword to fall out of its scabbard. For this reason, when riding a horse, samurai, especially lower samurai, would often tie the handle of their sword to its scabbard (they would also attach their spear haft to the spear sheath). The document stipulates that the securing should not be done with towels or cloth, so it must be assumed that there was a more discreet way.

Losing a sword

A samurai should never be seen in public without a sword. The following examples illustrate how dishonourable – not to say dangerous – it was for a samurai not to have his primary weapon by his side.

The document *Buke Giri Monogatari* (1688) tells of two samurai travelling on a boat among other passengers. One of them, named Takeshima, insulted the other, Takitsu, multiple times, which led to an argument and then a duel. When Takeshima looked for his sword, he saw it was gone; disgusted at himself for not taking proper care of his weapon, he tried to commit suicide. However, a third samurai passenger became suspicious when he noticed that a monk who was on the boat was missing the gourd that he had been carrying. The samurai spotted the gourd floating and anchored down by a cord. When they pulled it up, they found the sword tied to the end. The monk had stolen it and used the gourd as a float so he could retrieve the sword later.

In the next account, the samurai Manbei argues against the need to kill himself when his sword has been taken while he was asleep.

> *During the battle with Akai Akuemon, the lord of Hotsuzu Castle of Tamba, Sir Akechi encamped within the area of Mount Yahata. While inspecting his men, he found a hut where Manbei and an older and newly recruited samurai were sleeping deeply. The lord snuck in and took away their swords. The two samurai were surprised to find their weapons gone when they awoke and the older samurai said, 'All this will be revealed when the day breaks. We should stab each other to death before dawn.' Manbei contemplated this for a while then said, 'There would be no benefit from us dying in vain. It would have been a deep disgrace if our swords had been taken while we were awake, but as it happened while we were asleep it should not be considered as our fault at all. If you really want to kill yourself, I must stress that I am not of the same opinion.' When the day was nearly breaking, Manbei, wearing a red pennant, went over to the enemy camp and successfully put the pennant on a height and was there killed at the foot of the pennant. Both the sides were amazed at his magnificent deed. It is thought that Sir Akechi's actions were a mistake.*
>
> Musha Monogatari (1564)

The next extract describes one scenario in which a samurai could relinquish his sword in public with honour, although the author points out that this is a rare situation.

> *If you observe a duel in which combat is so intense that the samurai taking revenge breaks his* katana *and he asks to borrow*

your katana, *state that this is indeed not an issue, draw your sword
and pass it to him. Say to him, 'I have noticed that you are fighting
with earnest and I am impressed. If you become exhausted then I
will be your* sukedachi – *assistant to the killing.' After assuring him
in this way, you should remain in position. When the combat has
finished and the samurai returns your sword, say, 'Please keep it
and wear it, even though it may be a humble [blade], as I see that
you do not have a replacement.' In this case, do not take back [your
sword]. This situation is unusual, but it is mentioned here so that
you may be aware of it.*

Heika Jōdan (c1670)

The *Heika Jōdan* document continues with its lectures on not having swords
and shines a bright light on the popular understanding of samurai–commoner
relationships. It warns that a samurai travelling alone at night may be set
upon by common folk who hang around in gangs and whose purpose was to
embarrass and rob samurai. These robbers lay in wait and then leaped out,
pinned the samurai down and removed his sword from his belt. In such a case,
the advice was to take a submissive stance, obey the robbers' instructions, and
then do all that was necessary to get the sword back. If the gang returned the
sword there and then, the samurai should kill them all; if not, he should follow
them back to their home and make a note of its location. Then, he should return
to his own home and, in colloquial terms, get 'tooled up' before going back
to the thieves' den, murdering everyone and retrieving his sword. The most
important thing in either scenario was to leave no witnesses who could spread
the shameful story that the samurai had been caught unawares and forced to
submit to common folk.

Maintaining a sword

Today it is considered proper sword etiquette to not only clean and polish the
blade of a sword but also to avoid breathing on it. However, in older times
this may not have been the case. Remember that a sword was a functioning
weapon, so it was more important to keep it sharp than shiny. The practical

katana of an active samurai may not have had the gleaming blade and exposed hardening line (*hamon*) that is expected today. In fact, swords may have had a dull appearance, with small scratch lines from personal sharpening methods as described in the quotes below. Sword care may have consisted of 'on the street' maintenance combined with the samurai's own careful hand or even that of a page. Rust and blemishes had to be taken out and on occasion a sword may have needed professional treatment.

Swords worn at court or for religious ceremonies were, of course, a different matter. According to Bernardino de Ávila Girón, writing in the late sixteenth and early seventeenth century, *togi* (砥ぎ) 'sword polishers' were held in high esteem and samurai blades were 'like mirrors' such that you could see your face in them. As a European visitor, Ávila Girón would have been mainly in contact with high-ranking samurai and palace guards, so it is likely that his description refers to officials in court dress.

AN UNBREAKABLE BOND

The scholar Arai Hakuseki (1657–1725) recounts the story of an old friend, a former samurai who had fallen on hard times and was now living in a mountain hut. He had been forced to sell all of his equipment, but he could not let go of his swords. These he kept highly polished in bamboo tubes, following the way of the samurai even though he no longer served anyone.

SOURCES

Hayanetaba no koto – *quick sharpening*
Skin a toad in the hour of the cockerel on the fifteenth day of the eighth month and dry it in the shade. Carry this with you and when you wipe your sword with it, you will find that it can cut through even iron or stone.

Shoka no Hyōjō (1621)

Nori wo otosu kusuri no koto – *to wipe a sword blade clean of coagulated blood*
Skin a mole and dry the pelt in the shade. Sprinkle powdered 'boseki' stone on the fur side and carry this to wipe the blade after you have killed someone. This will remove the blood extremely well. There is more on this in oral traditions.

Shoka no Hyōjō (1621)

There is something called hayanetaba, *'quick sharpening'. This is to wipe the blade with the skin of a mole, which will make the blade cut well and is also good for wiping away blood. This way is good because both a* katana *and* wakizashi *require oil and if you do not use this method, you will see the difference in cutting.*

Heika Jōdan (c1670)

In a duel, your sword may get damaged when it strikes your opponent's armour or helmet, so it is essential to have a spare. [...] Have your aide carry your replacement sword, and the aide's sword should be carried by the sandal bearer or groom.

Bushidō Shoshinshū (c1700)

Chapter Eleven

Drawing a sword in a secure area

Most people have heard of the revenge of the '47 *rōnin*' (or *shijūshichi-shi* in Japanese) and will know that the events of that story were set in motion when their lord, Asano Naganori, was forced to perform *seppuku* as punishment for drawing his sword in a restricted place within Edo Castle. The English merchant John Saris reported that anyone who drew their sword in a restricted area would be cut to pieces and their family killed as well.

In contrast, the *Hagakure* tells of a man who, having been ridiculed by another samurai, drew his sword and cut down his enemy. The buzz around court was that he should now commit suicide. To which the lord said, 'What would a samurai be if he did not defend his honour?' and thus pardoned him.

Blooding a sword

According to tradition, a samurai should not use a sword until it had 'tasted' blood. A new blade had to be battle tested to make sure it was worthy. However, the person who most often received new blades was the commander, and he was not supposed to engage directly in combat. His task was to correctly control his troops who were the actual fighting force, yet if that fighting force was successful then it would be the commander who would be given a gift in recognition and in many cases that gift was a sword. He could not test his new sword because it meant entering into combat, something a good leader should avoid – so what should he do?

This dilemma is outlined below in the writings of the Natori-Ryū school.

If a tachi *great sword is given by the lord, those who are in a position of command should decline this gift – this is an oral tradition.*

[The first recorded oral tradition:]
Once you are given a tachi *[by the lord], you should not carry it without bathing it in blood [by killing an enemy]. However, if you are in a position of command over a number of people, you cannot fight for yourself, which means that you cannot bathe the sword in blood. Therefore, you should decline this* tachi *by saying, 'If I am to take this, I shall have to be excused the burden of*

command.' Alternatively, you can request that the sword is entrusted to the lord's squire.

[The second recorded oral tradition:]
'Until a victory has been won in this battle, I would like to entrust [this sword] to the lord's squire.'
There are other examples of how the lord might respond:
'You should entrust your group to someone else and concentrate on your own fighting.'
'[This sword] does not have to be baptized with blood.'
'Entrust the sword [to my squire].'
This is called tachi no kokoroe – *points to be kept in mind about the* tachi.

Ippei Yōkō (c1670)

This problem raises an interesting question. Was it more prestigious to receive a sword from a lord or to be the captain of men? We know that swords were not so special in old Japan; even farmers had a pair. However, a sword of pedigree from a noble lord might become a treasured heirloom to be passed down the generations, whereas command of a troop was a temporary honour. Considerations like this would have influenced a samurai's decision to give up the command of a force in return for a new sword.

THE SYMBOLISM OF THE SWORD

Drawing and sheathing

To sheathe a katana *after acquiring a full understanding of the situation is the proper way to correct a mistake.*

Heika Jōdan (c1670)

In samurai society, a naked blade symbolized violence and death, while the returning of a sword to its scabbard represented peace and restraint. There was a story of a *rōnin* who liked to provoke fights and enter into duels. One day he forced a tea master into an altercation; a date was set for the match where the unfortunate and quite helpless tea master was sure to meet his doom.

To try to gain at least some advantage, the tea master sought instruction from a sword master. The sword master asked the tea master to prepare him some tea, and on observing the ritual said that there was no need for him to study the way of the sword. He just needed to approach the fight with the same action and mental strength as the way of tea and consider the drawing of his sword with the same attitude.

At the beginning of the duel, the *rōnin* whipped out his sword, whereas the tea master gracefully took out his sword with the attitude of pouring tea and set himself ready in a fighting stance. The *rōnin* immediately put his sword back in its scabbard, got on his knees and begged forgiveness.

While this story may be apocryphal, it conveys the idea that replacing your sword in the scabbard was an act of apology or acceptance that the disputed matter was closed, at least for the moment. It was the gesture of a powerful yet level-headed warrior in full command of his own skill and strength.

SOURCES

If swords have been drawn between two samurai and a fight is about to commence, sometimes they simply cannot just sheath them. Basically, if samurai draw their katana, it means they have the intention to kill.

Heika Jōdan (c1670)

Drawing the sword is weak while not drawing is strong. Those who have a courageous mind will not draw without care; this is what should be kept in mind about confrontations.

Heika Jōdan (c1670)

The sword as a symbol of peace

> *In the world of fighting there has been a growing tendency toward pseudo-spiritualisim.*
>
> *Jyōseishi Kendan* (1810)

With the rise of the sword as a symbol of samurai authority came the emergence of a sophisticated sword philosophy. The sword became a poetic pen for the way of Zen and an emblem for the path to enlightenment. Swordsmanship evolved from practical brutality into a display of artistry in motion. Miyamoto Musashi was complaining about this trend as early as the 1640s. He worried that swordsmen were more concerned with ostentatious display than actual substance in battle.

A major change in swordsmanship came with the growth of the Shinkage-Ryū, which was a descendant school of sword master Kamiizumi Nobutsuna. Their scroll on swordsmanship talks about the 'sword of death' (殺人刀) and the 'sword of life' (活人劍). They propagated the idea that the sword, symbol of the samurai, was about killing one to save the many. They claimed to be fighting for the honour and protection of the people of Japan. The school took its terms from the Chinese classic the Blue Rock Collection and focused on wounding an opponent but not killing him. A samurai called Count Katsu disliked the idea of killing so much that he is said to have never killed anyone and even tied his scabbard and hilt together so that he could not even draw his sword. As the warring died down during the Edo period, the sword became more a symbol of peace than an instrument of war.

Holy swords and the philosophy of Zen

The sword is a powerful symbol in Japanese Buddhism. The bodhisattva ('Buddha to be') Monjushiri wielded a flaming sword to cut through delusions in life and dismantle failings such as duality and greed, while the deity Fudō Myō carried a sword to protect Buddhism. A Buddhist monk who had achieved a certain level was described figuratively as a 'man of the sword', and actual swordsmen aspired to achieve the dignity of monks. The pinnacle of debates on philosophy between

Zen and swordsmanship can be seen in the letters between Yagyū Munenori and Takuan Sōhō, which have been published in English elsewhere.

Overall, it should be understood that while the sword may have been a practical tool for the samurai, it always had philosophical aspects and it became a symbol of enlightenment and character refinement toward the later samurai period. Its connection to *bushidō* is found in its connection to Zen, in the development of the human character and its status as an icon of Japan.

Iconic swords

Japan has had its fair share of famous sword blades that have been named and recorded throughout history, as well as magical swords of legend. These include the following:

- Kusanagi no tsurugi (草薙剣) – the grass-mowing sword
- Higekiri (髭切) – the beard-cutting sword
- Hizamaru (膝丸) – the knee-cutting sword (used in executions by the Minamoto family)
- Inoshishikiri (猪切) the boar-cutting sword (used by Sakai Tadatsugu)

The evil blades of Muramasa

While some famous swords were glorious, others were notorious – none more so than the despised blades of Muramasa. This great swordsmith lived at the turn of the sixteenth century and created some of Japan's finest swords. According to legend, Muramasa had a fierce rivalry with another renowned smith called Masamune. One day they tested their swords by holding them in water. So fine was the blade of the Muramasa sword that it was able to cut through a leaf that was floating gently down the stream, but when Masamune put his sword in the water the leaves bobbed around it, as it was so streamlined.

At first, Muramasa's swords were celebrated as divine wonders of sword-smithing. The Tokugawa family (and their loyal samurai from Mikawa) loved them greatly and many were used within the clan. However, the following series of family misfortunes involving Muramasa blades caused them to be hated by later generations of the Tokugawa clan.

- Matsudaira Kiyoyasu (Tokugawa Ieyasu's grandfather) was killed by his own retainer Abe Yashichi with a Muramasa blade.
- Matsudaira Hirotada (Tokugawa Ieyasu's father) was also killed by a Muramasa blade.
- Tokugawa Ieyasu cut himself as a child on a Muramasa blade.
- A Muramasa blade was used to decapitate Matsudaira Nobuyasu (Tokugawa Ieyasu's son) in his forced suicide.

After four generations worth of negative experiences, the Tokugawa avoided Muramasa blades and began to circulate stories that the swords were cursed. However, such tales also caused Muramasa blades to become popular among anti-Tokugawa factions.

BLADES AND *BUSHIDŌ*

Fuelled by modern literature and cinema, the *katana* has achieved legendary status as a symbol of warrior perfection. But, as we have seen, for the samurai at war the sword was just one tool in his arsenal. Tokugawa Ieyasu is quoted as saying that it was important to be able to handle a sword but not as important as being able to handle people. The *katana* was simply not the iconic weapon we think it was today. *Bushidō* was about behaviour not blades.

CHAPTER TWELVE

HONOUR IN VIOLENCE

Warfare gave the samurai the greatest opportunity to build their reputation – or destroy it. In this chapter, we will look at the complex hierarchies of honourable and dishonourable deeds on the battlefield, different forms of combat and the correct way to approach various battle situations, including retreat, rout and surrender.

THE PURPOSE OF WAR

> *Question: There are some clans that adore those people who know much about archery, horse riding, swordsmanship, spearsmanship, and so on, and who encourage their men to practise and practise, and then there are some clans that do not. What can be said about this?*
>
> *Answer: While practising with sword and spear is not so useful, it can be an appropriate pastime for samurai. Therefore, it is called* heihō, *the way of the soldier. Matches with bamboo swords can be of some use; however, you should not think that you can escape death by practising such skills. Those arts may enable you to appear gifted and formidable when fighting, but the real goal to achieve is to injure the enemy. If you are killed, you will not have died in vain if you have injured the enemy, even if only a small amount. That being said, as you are from a samurai clan, it is important to know the ways of archery, horse riding, the sword and spear, and so on.*

> *Generally, in* budo *– the way of the warrior – you should hope to be regarded as honourable after your death through the preparations you made while living. If you were fully prepared for everything at all times, deeply determined and fought spectacularly, but died in combat owing to ill fate, know that your death will be mourned.*
>
> Gunpō Jiyōshū (c1612)

According to the seventeenth-century *Heihō Hidensho* scroll, there were three reasons to wage war:

1. To pacify the unruly
2. To correct the unjust
3. To quell the rebellious

The samurai's original purpose was actually to keep the peace, not to fight. They came into being to serve the Emperor by pacifying rebels; the term *shōgun* means 'barbarian-quelling general'. Originally, the *shōgun* was a temporary military position. He rode out to war with the army to put down rebellions and maintain central governmental control. The problem is that, for much of samurai history, the samurai were trying to overthrow other samurai in order to win power. The samurai lost sight of their responsibility to serve the imperial crown, and the position of *shōgun* lost its original meaning and purpose and became instead a de facto dictatorship.

Therefore, from this point of view most samurai warfare must be considered dishonourable and unjust. However, as we are looking to understand chivalry from the viewpoint of the samurai, we will explore the concept of honour within military conflict and individual combat, no matter whether the overall war could be considered just or not.

Victory over the enemy

A samurai was expected to prove his prowess through dominance. They should kill their opponent, take their head, capture their castle, possess their lands, loot their equipment and stores, and leave nothing unclaimed. That was predominantly what the samurai did in war. When Minamoto no Yoritomo climbed to the position of *shōgun*, he built his palace over the ruins of his defeated enemy Taira no Kiyomori's residence. Likewise, when a samurai took a head in battle, he raised it with his left hand, lifted his sword in his right and gave a cry of victory over the dead.

It is easy to see early samurai times as a golden age, during which the samurai faithfully and honourably served the aristocrats in Kyōto. But this so-called golden age, if it ever existed, soon gave way to a time of decadence. The court of Kyōto was inhabited by soft princes of the realm, and the samurai made short work of quelling barbarian tribes, which gave them ample time to fight among themselves for power.

REWARDS AND RECOGNITION

The whole system of combat was based on reward for achievement. There were two main ways to gain recognition in battle, which was necessary to climb the ranks: one was to command troops with good ability and the other was to win in personal combat and return with proof of your victory. Commanders and front-line troops knew that they relied on each other to gain achievement: the troops needed their commander to have the intelligence to devise the correct strategy and the commander needed his troops to have the ability to make the strategy work.

The rewards could be considerable. Tokugawa Ieyasu gave Okudaira Sadamasa estates and the right to audiences with himself and all other members of the Tokugawa clan – a right which passed on to his sons after him for generations to come. Likewise, Oda Nobunaga gave Tokugawa Ieyasu a famous sword for his exploits. Other rewards beyond land, money and great weapons included good political marriages and permission to take the first syllable of a warlord's name (for example, Okudaira Sadamasa gained the right to call himself Okudaira Nobumasa as a reward from Oda Nobunaga after the battle of Nagashino in 1575).

SHIFTING LOYALTIES

Okudaira Sadamasa was a man of Mikawa, a province traditionally loyal to the Tokugawa. However, the political situation forced him to pledge his allegiance to the Takeda clan. When Okudaira Sadamasa left the Takeda after the death of Takeda Shingen to rejoin the Tokugawa, his wife and brother were crucified as punishment for his disloyalty. This is yet another example of the samurai's flexible attitude to loyalty.

Honourable and dishonourable deeds in combat

At every stage of battle – from the 'wave of fear' at first seeing the enemy through to the retreat or the chasing down of the enemy retreat – a samurai was under observation by his comrades and his actions were assessed as being either positive or negative.

To help divide myth from reality, the evidence available at present shows that the following achievements were valued particularly highly.

- Being first into combat
- Taking the head of the enemy commander
- Taking the first head of the battle
- Taking the heads of socially higher enemies
- Taking the heads of enemy soldiers
- Striking deep into enemy lines
- Breaking up enemy formations
- Assisting someone to perform a great achievement
- Bringing back a captured or fallen banner
- Defending a retreat

The relative prestige of such actions depended on the situation, but all of them were considered actions of ability and courage.

The following actions were generally recognized as great deeds of selflessness and chivalry.

- Continuing to fight while wounded instead of retreating to base camp
- Helping a comrade retreat
- Giving a horse to a defeated commander who has to retreat
- Defending a commander who has to retreat
- Taking arrows to the body while shielding a superior

However, in certain circumstances such actions could be seen as insulting. For example, a warrior who defended his lord when this was not necessary might be considered to be implying that his lord was not capable of protecting himself. This was a major faux pas.

Certain deeds were dishonourable under any circumstance. Such actions included the following.

- Killing a woman or a monk and claiming them to be combatants
- Claiming a head to belong to someone it does not
- Stealing another warrior's captured head
- Kill-stealing (i.e. killing a warrior who has been defeated by someone else)
- Leading an ally into a hopeless position so that you can benefit from their death
- Running away instead of retreating in an organized manner
- Implying that the commander has lost the battle before it is evident that they have

Announcing names

Every samurai enthusiast knows that before a battle, samurai would find their equal in skill and social level, announce their name and lineage and then engage in respectable combat. Unfortunately, it did not really happen like that. It is true that samurai entering battle did announce their names, but the idea of the samurai battlefield being divided up into mini combat areas according to social class is fanciful. This notion may have come from the archaic Chinese tradition of commencing battle with a contest between a great champion from each of the two armies. Even in the golden years of the early samurai, combat was more likely to consist of night attacks, arson, siege warfare, deception, ambush, pouring boiling fluid down from fortresses and all the other brutal and underhand tactics common to warfare throughout the medieval world.

The practice of samurai crying out their own names was done so that there could be no doubt that they had taken part, which was particularly important when it was time to recognize prestigious achievements such as entering battle at the stage of first spear (*ichibanyari*) or defending a retreat. Samurai would also cry out their name in times of peace – for example, when running in to rescue the occupants of a burning house. All in all, the samurai loved to shake the ground with the roar of their names, but it was not always done in the way that the romantic war epics would have us believe.

APPETITE FOR DESTRUCTION

At the battle of Komaki in 1584, only the vanguard section of the force was engaged in the actual battle, the rest of the army had breakfast. This interesting image of soldiers sitting on the ground eating as the first samurai return with decapitated heads further undermines the myth of each samurai circling the battlefield, looking to fight an opponent equal in social rank.

This was not the only example of food coming before fighting. When the warrior Tachibana Muneshige took control of a position in Ōtsu near Kyōto, many of the city's inhabitants, rather than panicking at the prospect of battle, took picnics to a vantage point and watched the bloodshed unfold. Similarly, Tokugawa Ieyasu had a platform erected so he could oversee the battle of Kuisegawa while having a meal. Although his side was defeated, Ieyasu praised his commander Nakamura Kazuuji's skill in handling men while pointing out his tactical errors.

Reputation for ability in violence

Reputation was the cornerstone of *bushidō*. The more people knew the name of a samurai and associated it with power, ability and reliability, the further up the social scale he moved. The following sections will examine the relationship between achievements in warfare and *bushidō*.

A famous Japanese saying encapsulates the importance of a military reputation:

> *The lord Tokugawa Ieyasu has many fine men:*
> *Hattori Hanzō is known as the Devil Hanzō,*
> *Watanabe Hanzō is known as Hanzō of the Spear,*
> *While Atsumi Gengorō is known as Gengo the Head-taker.*

Attributes such as devilishness, ability with a spear and head-taking are presented here as fine warrior qualities to which any samurai would aspire. The term translated as 'devil' is *oni* (鬼) in Japanese, which was a sort of hell-troll associated with ruthlessness and brutality. Another samurai often given the epithet 'devil' was Sakuza, who shall be mentioned later. He was a samurai of Mikawa who had threatened to burn to death Toyotomi Hideyoshi's mother and all her ladies in waiting when they were political hostages. Such harsh conduct enhanced a samurai's reputation.

SOURCES

People should be employed in roles where they are suited. If the curved are made into wheels while the straight are made into axles, there will be no useless people.

Writings of Shiba Yoshimasa (1349–1410)

[In Japan] one frequently sees nonentities become powerful nobles and great men reduced to nothing with all their property confiscated.

Writings of Alessandro Valignano (16th century)

Hierarchies of achievement in combat

The four outcomes of combat are:

1. To defeat an enemy
2. To be defeated by an enemy
3. To kill each other
4. To both escape alive

The fourth outcome left the contest unresolved, which was originally seen as a dire situation. However, the Edo period swordsman Harigaya Sekiun argued that swordsmanship should be more about advancing your spiritual welfare than killing your opponent. This attitude reflects the changing emphasis during the Edo period toward peaceful resolution of disputes and a society based on harmony. Defeating your enemy still brought the best praise, but escaping without the matter having been settled was now an acceptable idea to some.

The *Ōgiden* document gives a further example of hierarchy in combat:

1. To wound the hand but take an enemy head
2. To suffer a wound but give a bigger wound to enemy
3. To have a hand cut off but cut off the leg of an enemy

The *Heika Jōdan* manual of the Natori-Ryū school lists the following three levels of sword fighting:

1. *Jō* – upper level: to strike the enemy successfully and emerge without a scratch
2. *Chū* – middle level: to strike successfully and perform *hari-kiri*
3. *Ge* – lower level: to fail in *hari-kiri*, to be seriously injured, to fall and die together with your enemy, or to be killed outright

Executing others

> *When a warrior is given the important task of an execution by his*
> *lord, he should make sure to say, 'For me to be given this task above*
> *all the men of this clan is a fitting fate for a warrior, and therefore*
> *I am grateful and do readily accept.'*
>
> *Bushidō Shoshinshū* (c1700)

There were two main forms of execution a samurai might be asked to perform: *teuchi* (手討), executing a fellow retainer at the order of the lord; and *kaishaku* (介錯), decapitating someone who is committing *seppuku*. These duties did not bring a significant amount of prestige, but failure to carry them out correctly placed a black stain on the reputation of a samurai, as it was assumed that a samurai would have no trouble taking the head from a kneeling victim.

SOURCES

Teuchi *(手討) execution is to put people to death with the sword and not to die. This can also involve the execution of people who are not fellow retainers. After you kill a retainer with your sword, never tell others what you have done. If you do, people will think that you are telling tales. Be careful: when people talk, they will use your name and the story will change the more times it is retold. Remember, what has been said cannot be unsaid. To perform* teuchi *is quite an unusual task. If you fail at it, it will bring you shame. People have said for a long time that a person who fails in* teuchi *will often be killed by the person he targeted. Therefore, your family's dignity is at risk when you receive such an order. With this in mind, make sure you do not lose your good name. Fully train yourself in the martial arts, become familiar with skilful people, abandon evil and follow good ways.*

Shinkan no Maki (transcribed 1789)

> *When acting as a second it is recommended that you decapitate the victim speedily, as they may try to fight back with the* wakizashi. *If you fail to make the cut, it is a dishonour to you.*
>
> Heika Jōdan (c1670)

Being the first to arrive

One major factor in samurai honour culture was being first to arrive in any risky situation. This was called *ichibannori* (一番乗り). When the Minamoto forces were at the Uji River, Minamoto no Yoshitsune was the first to cross his men over the fast water, an action which won him resounding praise. The scroll *Ippei Yōkō* tells us that to be first over a castle wall or even first to throw your banner over the wall brought kudos, and, as previously discussed, to be first in combat – *ichibanyari*, or the 'first spear' – was the greatest achievement a samurai could attain in warfare.

One episode that reveals the surprisingly deceitful nature of some samurai took place at the famous battle of Sekigahara, where Ii Naomasa with his 'crimson demon' or 'red devil' samurai – because they all wore a reddish scarlet – made the first strike. The problem was that his orders were to stand fast; the glorious honour of first spear had been awarded to another samurai, Fukushima Masanori, who had not been under the service of Tokugawa long. When asked to explain himself, Naomasa claimed that he had not, in fact, disobeyed orders. He said that he had scouted out the enemy, who had then attacked him and thus he had the right to defend himself. In truth, he had made a headlong rush at the enemy, which, understandably, had provoked them into engaging in combat. This is a classic example of samurai honour being manipulated to gain prestige.

SOURCES

The first person to charge in and cut a bandit achieves merit.

Heihō Yūkan (1645)

If you are first to engage and cut the criminal but do not succeed in killing him, you should be aware that allowing the merit for the kill to pass on to a person who came up later and cut him down is an act of cowardice.

Heihō Yūkan (1645)

Ichibannori *is to be the first to advance into a castle when attacking a fortress. Others are called* ainori – *those who arrive together. If you are the second to start climbing the wall but you get your* sashimono *banner on the inside first, you are classed as being the first to advance. This achievement is considered equal to the achievement of* ichibanyari *– the first spear.*

Ippei Yōkō (c1670)

Honour groups

Sometimes the best-performing warriors in a great victory would be celebrated collectively after the battle by being invested in an honour group. Each of these groups had the names of the members recorded. There were many examples, of which two have been given below.

賤ヶ岳の七本槍

Shizugatake no Shichihon yari

The seven spears of the battle of Shizugatake

1. Wakisaka Yasuharu   脇坂安治
2. Katagiri Katsumoto   片桐且元

3. Hirano Nagayasu   平野長泰
4. Fukushima Masanori 福島正則
5. Katō Kiyomasa   加藤清正
6. Kasuya Takenori   糟谷武則
7. Katō Yoshiaki   加藤嘉明

小豆坂七本槍

Azukizaka Shichihon yari

The seven spears of the battle of Azukizaka

1. Oda Nobumitsu   織田信光
2. Oda Nobufusa   織田信房
3. Okada Shigeyoshi   岡田重能
4. Sassa Masatsugu   佐々政次
5. Sassa Magosuke   佐々孫介
6. Nakano Kazuyasu   中野一安
7. Shimokata Sadakiyo 下方貞清

Being honoured in this way brought prestige to the individual, a legacy to their family and a collective pride among the members of the group. However, bear in mind that some of the groupings were formed decades or centuries after the battle in question, as people looked back to 'nobler' times.

The language of wounds

> To strike someone who is down, if he is lying face down, strike from
> the direction of his head.
>
> *Heihō Ōgisho* (17th century)

The wounds a samurai carried on his body could act as a catalogue of courageous service. However, the wrong kinds of wound could also put him under suspicion of cowardice.

Tokugawa Ieyasu had a retainer called Namikiri Magoshichirō who rebelled against him. When they were fighting on opposite sides, Ieyasu had attacked Magoshichirō and drawn blood from his back. Later, when they were reconciled, Ieyasu made fun of him saying it was improper for a samurai to have scars on the back as this signalled that he had shied away from a fight. Magoshichirō denied having retreated and claimed that he had no scars on his back, but refused to show his back to prove it.

In contrast, an old samurai named Honda described the injuries he had received in many battles. He had lost an eye and some fingers and was almost lame in one leg. By talking about his wounds, he displayed his long commitment to his lord and the tribulations they had faced together. His wounds were a symbol of his courage and loyalty.

The samurai approached the task of verifying achievements on the battlefield with forensic rigour. In the *Ippei Yōkō* scroll there is a description of the different kinds of wound made by different weapons. Such knowledge not only allowed for better treatment, but it could also be used to catch out samurai who falsely laid claim to a kill. If they claimed to have used a certain weapon in a certain way and the victim's wound told a different story, their disgrace would be considerable.

RIGHT AND WRONG WAYS TO DIE

The samurai were judged even in death. For a samurai to be mortally wounded on the back was shameful, as it suggested that he had been running away when he sustained his injury. All wounds should be on the front and samurai should fall dead either on their front with their head toward the enemy or on their back with their head away from the enemy. These are the positions of a samurai who faced up to the enemy and fought to the death.

Crippled for loyalty

When the Tokugawa took back Nagashino Castle, they found a samurai called Ōkouchi Masamoto who had been locked up in a tiny cell as punishment for refusing to renounce his loyalty to the Tokugawa. Confined in this way, he had lost the use of his legs. When he was finally released, the Tokugawa praised him for his devotion and awarded him gifts, but the crippled samurai renounced the way of the warrior and became a monk.

Cowardice versus caution

> Some say that to take care is a sign of cowardice as a samurai.
> However, this is completely wrong. If you lose your life through
> your own recklessness, then this is a dog's death and is a dishonour.
>
> Heika Jōdan (c1670)

The conduct of a samurai was paramount, and there was no place for cowardice. When faced with a choice between certain death and retreat, there was little shame in retreating, but it had to be done in an honourable manner. For example, to withdraw in haste and leave your allies in danger would be seen as cowardly.

When the imperial court sent Nitta Yoshisada to destroy the *shōgun* Ashikaga Takauji, Takauji retreated to a monastery, cut off his hair and sought to become a priest. However, his enemies declared that his priestly status would not protect him from the wrath of Nitta Yoshisada and that he would still die. In response, Takauji left the holy sanctuary and rode into battle. His men all shaved their heads bald so that their leader did not look out of place. The fact that Takauji was still able to muster an army of loyal clan members indicates that there was no shame in turning away from the warrior path to avoid battle and then returning to fight later.

A samurai walked a thin line between bravery and recklessness, caution and cowardice. His reputation depended on staying on the right side of the line.

Pretending to be ill

The *Hagakure* mentions a man called Genbei who sat down with stomach cramps, told the group to go ahead of him and said that another man should take over the command because he was ill. For this perceived act of cowardice, he was sentenced to perform *seppuku*. Stomach cramps were also known as the 'coward's pain'.

The *Bushidō Shoshinshū* tells us that samurai should never pretend to be ill, grumble about being ill or use illness as an excuse to avoid work. The fact that these failings are mentioned indicates that some samurai were guilty of them. However, the document also says that if people are genuinely ill, samurai should be quiet and respectful around them.

SOURCES

Those who feign illness just before the battle should be killed.

Heieki Yōhō (c1670)

If someone becomes ill on the march while still in your own province, leave them in a residence along the road and charge someone to take care of them. They should be encouraged to rest and recuperate. When they have recovered from the illness, they are required to regroup with the rest of the force. Anyone who does not regroup after having recovered should be convicted. If they die from their illness, the person left to care for them should see to the corpse. Even though they have not died in battle, they should be treated as if they had. The captain and his group should organize prayers for the dead as if they were a member of his own family. Not giving someone a proper burial should be considered a sin as serious as abandoning a friend.

Heieki Yōhō (c1670)

TYPES OF COMBAT

> *Oral tradition says that even if an enemy has pinned you down*
> *you can still kill them by biting the enemy's nose or wrist with your*
> *fangs. You should use any part of your body when the enemy holds*
> *you down as you cannot do anything with your sword.*
>
> Shinkan no Maki (transcribed 1789)

Whether they lived in times of intense warfare or times of peace, the samurai did not lack opportunity to exercise their capacity for violence. During the so-called times of peace – which were usually, in fact, harsh dictatorships – there were still plenty of skirmishes, street fights, revenge killings, family feuds and orders for execution. Different forms of combat, whether during war or peace, could bring a samurai either honour or disgrace.

Single combat

> *We consider sword scars on the face as ugly; the Japanese are proud*
> *of their wounds and, not taking care with their treatment, make*
> *them so much the uglier.*
>
> Luís Froís, Tratado (1585)

The samurai were outright 'dirty fighters', underhanded and no strangers to gang violence. While they admired those who fought a fair fight, not all of them would bet their lives on one. In 1562, two samurai named Ōta and Shimazu fought each other in man-to-man combat. Shimazu had gained the upper hand and was struggling to move Ōta's throat guard out of the way to decapitate him. At this point, two comrades of the soon-to-be-decapitated Ōta entered the fray and overpowered Shimazu. Then all three cut his head off, turning the once fair fight into a pile-on.

There was actually a specific term – *sukedachi* (助太刀) – for a person who helped a samurai defeat another samurai in combat and it seems not to have had any negative associations. There were certain tactics this helper could use to make sure that his comrade prevailed. However, as the following passage makes clear, the main fighter still needed to appear as if he wished to defeat the enemy unaided.

> *When there is an* uchihatashi *feud and you know one of the combatants, then it goes without saying that you should assist him. First, declare to your ally, 'I [insert name] have no part in this issue, this unexpected fight, but I will give assistance if exhaustion comes upon you.' Next, draw your sword and move to the rear of the enemy. Remember that you will not be asked for help, but your ally will make a statement to the effect that your offer is much appreciated. Most cases are like this. If your comrade is defeated, you must fight in his stead, otherwise you should let your ally strike the enemy themselves. If you do strike in assistance, then let your ally have the killing blow. While your associate is still capable, do not strike the enemy, just talk out loud to them.*
>
> Heika Jōdan (c1670)

It would be naive to think that the samurai stood proud and entered into a fair fight, duelling with honour. Samurai warfare and combat were founded not only on outdoing the enemy but also on outwitting and outnumbering them. There was no shame in being larger in number and stronger in arms, so long as you won. However, if an underdog won, or one samurai overcame many, that was seen as a particularly prestigious achievement.

The following achievements brought praise and respect:

- Killing a superior opponent alone
- Killing an equal opponent alone
- Being part of a group that kills a single target
- Dying having fought well
- Choosing to stand and die instead of fleeing

The following failings brought shame and dishonour:

- Fleeing
- Attempting to kill someone and failing
- Failing to execute a target who has been condemned to death

There were some exceptions – for example, there was no shame in retreating after making a kill or in order to lead the enemy into a trap. But the categories listed above held true in most cases.

SOURCES

If your opponent is one individual and you have an ally, you and your ally should attack from the front and behind. If you are three, attack from three sides. If you are four, attack from four sides.

Heihō Hidensho (17th century)

Whenever someone comes from behind and grabs the sword and dagger from someone in front of him [...] the one at the front can grab his hands and the one behind him can pull him up, then duck down and throw him over his shoulders.

Heihō Hidensho (17th century)

Being so numerous the enemy surrounds you. Then you should run. Even if the enemy reaches you en masse, they will not reach you all at once.

Heihō Hidensho (17th century)

When there are many enemies and you are alone, there is no shame in being defeated.

Shinkan no Maki (transcribed 1789)

> *If there are many enemies and it is a dark night, move to a fence or wall or any place that provides a barrier to one side and use it as a shield [to your rear]. However, there is no benefit to this when the enemy is positioned behind you. Also, it is effective at night to crouch down and swipe horizontally at a lower target area.*
>
> Heika Jōdan (c1670)

Unarmed and hand-to-hand combat

All samurai needed to have some ability in physical combat, but it was not actually as important as one might expect. The *Ōgiden* document states that grappling (*keisei*) was not much use on the battlefield but that it was good for limbering the body and keeping fit. Likewise, the quote from the *Gunpō Jiyōshū* that opens this chapter reinforces the idea that the study of unarmed combat was a basic requirement but not the key to success on a battlefield.

There was respect to be gained through mastery of a martial art, and all samurai coveted a reputation as a hard man, but the greatest prestige of all was reserved for leaders of men who gained victory in war and politics.

Unarmed combat

Samurai rarely engaged in unarmed combat. While skills such as Jūdō and jujutsu are heavily associated with the samurai, the warriors of early and middle periods were seldom without a blade or tool with which to defend themselves. As we have seen, a samurai slept with his sword close by and he retained his *wakizashi* sidearm at all times, unless told to remove it by a senior, in which case he often fell back on a hidden dagger or other secret weapon. Therefore, it was not really in the samurai mind to defend themselves with unarmed combat. It may have been used as a last-ditch defence on the battlefield in the final stages of fighting; terms such as *kumiuchi* ('grappling and striking') indicate that it was a form of close combat.

True unarmed combat appears to be a much later focus; even up to the mid-twentieth century, most martial arts schools concentrated on weapons training in their curriculum. Unarmed combat systems only really came to prominence in the second half of the twentieth century.

Hand-to-hand combat

The two terms 'unarmed combat' and 'hand-to-hand combat' are often considered to mean the same thing, but in this book hand-to-hand combat refers to any fighting that is close enough for opponents to strike each other with a variety of weapons, while unarmed combat is fighting without weapons – an important distinction.

Did samurai chivalry impose any restrictions on what could and could not be done in hand-to-hand combat? It would appear not. Document after document describe the various tricks samurai could use. The *Ōgiden* text clearly shows people being grabbed from behind to stop them drawing their sword. The manuals of the Mubyōshi-Ryū school include teachings on surprise attacks from behind trees or buildings, throat-cutting from the sidelines, and even leaping sword dives when chasing an enemy; Sekiguchi-Ryū teaches the use of blinding powders and hidden elements; Natori-Ryū has kill squads, and so on. The simple truth is that a samurai could attack his enemy using any methods and tools he wished. Winning was all that mattered. Though fair duels were a part of samurai culture, they have been vastly over-represented by the modern media as the standard for all samurai combat.

Use of environment

The environment around a samurai was also considered as a tool or weapon. The master swordsman Miyamoto Musashi was clearly unimpressed with the fighting styles of the more modern schools of Tokugawa-era Japan. He believed that complex leaps, jumps and stepping systems were useless in real life, where uneven or waterlogged ground would render all such elaborations redundant. It was more useful to assess the weather conditions and position yourself and time your actions accordingly. For example, it was an advantage to have the sun or the wind and rain at your back so that they would shine or blow into the face of your enemy. Similarly, during a night fight in a thunderstorm, a shrewd swordsman would make sure that his opponent was facing the lightning so that they would lose the benefit of night vision; he might also time his moves to coincide with thunder claps so that they would act as a distraction.

Even indoors, surrounding objects could be turned to a fighter's benefit. The manuals mention samurai hurling tatami mats, candlesticks and other household objects at their opponents, or using the pommel of their sword to smash out the eyes of an enemy swordsman. All of this leaves us with the distinct idea that a samurai could do just about anything to win. However, while it was acceptable in certain situations to hide behind natural features in the terrain, it was improper, according to the *Bushidō Shoshinshū*, to use an ally as a shield. The implication is that if everyone else was moving out, any samurai left taking cover was deemed as weak.

NO WAY OUT

Katō Kiyomasa built a room with reinforced iron sliding doors known as *koshi-shōji*. Anyone locked in there would not be able to break free by crashing through the doors or cutting them down.

SOURCES

In the countryside, first cut off your enemy's leg; in town, make it your priority to cut off his head. The reason for this is that in the country it does not matter if your enemy screams for help. Being far from human habitation, there will be no one to come to his aid and he will not be able to fight with a leg cut off. This is to your advantage. In town, it is more advantageous to cut off the enemy's head so that he cannot call for help.

Heihō Hidensho (17th century)

> *In a fight upon landing [from a boat], get on shore before your adversary and then strike him as he tries to climb out of the boat.*
>
> Heihō Ōgisho (17th century)

> *Walk quietly and smoothly and pay attention to the connection of your feet with the ground. Do not walk without concentration where it is dangerous. If you are filled with fear and lose heart then it is not good because it will manifest itself in your form. Anything concerning combat should be done with the above in mind.*
>
> Heika Jōdan (c1670)

Siege warfare

Siege warfare presented particularly testing challenges both to the besiegers and the besieged, and therefore the tactically minded had ample opportunity to demonstrate their ability. For example, Minamoto no Yoshitsune captured the Taira clan's fortress by having his famous warriors descend from the high mountains behind the stronghold, leading them over perilous terrain to come at the fortress from above and behind, where it was not defended. This manoeuvre won Yoshitsune his fame and is spoken about to this day.

During a siege, espionage and other clandestine operations came into their own as a means to infiltrate from the outside of a fortress or to engineer an opening from the inside. The skilful use of siege weapons, guns, traps, tricks and devilish means were also considered positive aspects of defence and attack.

For the besiegers, it was prestigious to be the first over the wall or at least the first to get their banner into the fortress after scaling the walls. It was also a great honour to be seen fighting hard in the 'tiger's mouth' (虎口), which was a euphemism for any restricted and dangerous area where the defenders had constructed kill zones or strategic defences.

For the besieged, it was considered a great achievement to hold out against the odds. Although ultimately unsuccessful, Torii Mototada's defence of Fushimi

Castle was celebrated as a crucial factor in Tokugawa Ieyasu's victory at Sekigahara. Torii knew that he would eventually succumb to the attackers, but he resisted for long enough to allow Ieyasu to regroup. When one of the castle towers was set on fire, Katō Kurōzaemon heroically extinguished the flames but died in the process.

In the end, however, it was a split among the defending warriors that brought about the fall of Fushimi. The besiegers managed to seize the wife of one of the defenders and sent a secret message inside the castle to say that she would be crucified if they did not betray Torii. Some of the men stayed loyal, but others brought the castle down from within. Most of them committed suicide, leaving their bloody handprints on the floorboards, which were later removed and are now displayed in Zenfukudera Temple.

One of the most celebrated examples of samurai achievement during a siege took place at Nagashino. When Takeda Katsuyori besieged the castle there, a low-level retainer called Torii Sune'emon volunteered to escape from the siege so as to get word to Tokugawa Ieyasu that they needed his help. With great daring, Sune'emon made his way out of the siege at night. He reached Tokugawa Ieyasu and Oda Nobunaga and told them about the dire situation at Nagashino. The army prepared to move in support of their allies, but Sune'emon decided to go ahead and try to creep back into the castle so that he could reassure those inside that help was on its way.

Unfortunately, all sides were preparing for the double siege and the besiegers had laid more traps, including tripwires with bells attached and areas of sand that could not be crossed without leaving footprints. Sune'emon was captured and taken to Takeda Katsuyori, who asked him to change sides. He wanted Sune'emon to tell the defenders that no help was coming and that they should surrender immediately.

Having agreed to do this, Sune'emon was brought within earshot of his castle and his true lord. From there he shouted to his comrades that they should hold out as help would soon be with them and the siege would be broken. For this double-cross, he was taken away and crucified, but he is held to this day in the highest regard for his loyalty. Later generations of samurai used the image of Sune'emon on a crucifix as a banner. Furthermore, his actions are recorded as a perfect demonstration of *shinobi no jutsu* – the arts of the ninja.

TOWER OF WEAKNESS

The *Bansenshūkai*, a late seventeenth-century *shinobi* manual, advised infiltrating a besieged castle from the direction of the watchtower manned by the most unruly samurai. Those who drunk and partied were likely to be the most lax in their watch. However, the manual also warned that feigned unruliness and inattention might be used as a trap. Tokugawa Ieyasu became angry at one guard house when he discovered that the guards had gone out on the town leaving only a single man to guard the gate. Other manuals recommend using a combination of old, experienced samurai and young, rowdy samurai so that the older guards can calm down the unruly youngsters and maintain a vigilant watch.

Flooding tactics

It was not always necessary to enter into combat to achieve victory. There was a great reputation awaiting those commanders who could bring about the surrender of a castle without a single shot fired simply by flooding the enemy out. Therefore, the samurai employed great teams of engineers who would look to use the landscape to do just that. With thousands of able men at a commander's disposal, entire river courses could be diverted, causing castles and fortresses to be flooded and plains that held enemy battle camps to be swamped. For example, the fortress of Takegahana was flooded by diverting the Kiso River and the besieged were forced to build platforms, but in the end they gave up and were allowed to leave freely. Likewise, the castle of Takamatsu was taken by flood tactics.

It was also important to consider water when scouting for a suitable location to set up camp. If there was not enough water nearby, the army would die; but if the ground was too swampy, the army would be vulnerable to disease and flooding by the enemy.

Aquatic warfare

In the West, we do not often associate the samurai with naval warfare. In truth, though, the Japanese have long had a reputation for being naval-minded, and Japanese freebooter pirates were once the scourge of the Asian seas. Naval warfare is known as *suisen* (水戦), *sensen* (舩戦) and *sengun* (舩軍) among other terms, while *suiren* (水練) refers to aquatic skills such as crossing rivers and military swimming for land-based warfare.

Combat at sea was a bloody and rough affair and victory on the water was as prestigious as victory on land. Generally, a ship's crew consisted of sailors, who would man the vessel, and samurai, who would serve as the fighting force. Samurai would fire weapons and throw projectiles from turrets and palisades built on the deck, and there were hinged platforms that folded out for ship-to-ship action.

There were many esoteric aspects to be aware of at sea, and the construction of Japanese warships, including *shinobi-fune* ('stealth boats'), is a specialist subject in itself.

The samurai needed to develop their *suiren* skills, which also included knowledge of submerged pitfall traps, water flows, river measurement, tides, winds and rain, and correct protocol for river combat.

NOT IN MY NAME

When Yahagi Bridge was washed away in a flood, Tokugawa Ieyasu made preparations to have it rebuilt, but his retainers advised him to leave it destroyed because this would hold up any advancing enemy armies. However, to Ieyasu the bridge was one of the most famous in all the land, sung about in heroic ballads, and he could not bear for his name to be associated with its loss, so he persisted in his plans to rebuild it.

COMBAT SITUATIONS

Levels of combat

Some forms of combat were seen as being more prestigious than others, and this was not a new thing. As early as 788, when the Japanese were fighting the northern native tribes at the Koromo River, the way they accounted for the dead revealed the way that they saw battle:

- The number who died in battle was 25.
- The number struck by arrows was 245.
- The number who drowned was 1,036.
- The number who returned with their gear was 1,257.

According to that reckoning, the total number of people who died as a result of that battle was 1,306 (25 + 245 + 1,036), yet only 25 of them were given the status of having 'died in battle'. It is assumed that drowning had no heroic value, while being killed by arrows, because it happened at a distance, had some value but was not truly heroic. The 25 warriors who died in direct combat with the enemy were singled out for particular praise.

This distinction continued to be made throughout the samurai era. It was always considered more worthy to put yourself in harm's way – to be in the first spear battle, defend a retreat, help the wounded while being overrun by the enemy. In contrast, actions such as firing a gun or a bow from the side or over a fence and chasing down defeated enemies were still valorous, but on a lower level.

Marching to and from war

There were strict protocols laid out in military manuals of the Edo period for how samurai should march: which side their spear should be on; the types of columns they should march in; how to save space within lines; and so on. The English merchant John Saris wrote that when troops marched home after their service the people in all the towns along the route need have no fear, for the soldiers were well mannered and orderly, they paid for everything they took and did not misuse the locals. That is not to say there were never any problems, but the strict regulations minimized the risk of misbehaviour.

Those manuals that do discuss marching orders tend to agree that close formations of troops would often fall to fighting between themselves. It was essential to maintain strict order to avoid other soldiers along the line mistaking an internal disturbance, such as a fracas or a commotion among the horses, for an enemy attack, which could cause the whole formation to fall into disarray.

SOURCES

Even while marching over a long distance, always keep your spear and armour close by. You can never be without these two items as any form of emergency may arise.

Ippei Yōkō (c1670)

When marching in two columns, helmet-bearers should be in the centre and spear-bearers go on the outside. If marching in a single column, the spear should be carried on the right as normal. When marching and there is a narrow path or bridge ahead, move forward and form a single file. In each row, the person on the right should go first and then the one on the left should move into line after them.

Ippei Yōkō (c1670)

If marching before a battle is not conducted in a strict manner, you will not gain victory in the battle itself. Therefore, the laws and orders given should be strictly observed.

Ippei Yōkō (c1670)

Retreat

> *On that day, a letter tied to an arrow flew into the castle. Addressed*
> *to my father, the letter said, 'You have a relative who was a teacher*
> *to Lord Ieyasu. If you want to escape from the castle, the lord will*
> *spare your life. You may flee to any province you like. All troops*
> *have been instructed to help you; therefore, you will not have*
> *trouble on your way out.' Since being told the castle would fall*
> *the next day, we had all lost heart and feared that we might be*
> *killed on the morrow. My father secretly came over to the castle*
> *tower and told my mother and us to follow him. He then dropped a*
> *ladder down the side of the north wall. We went down along a rope*
> *which hung from there and crossed over the moat in a washtub.*
>
> Oamu Monogatari (17th century)

Retreating, whether it was tactical or not, was an accepted part of samurai warfare. There are ample examples of armies withdrawing, regrouping and meeting at a rally point. The modern legend of the samurai who does not retreat can be partly attributed to the heroic deeds of Kusunoki Masashige, who, having informed his superiors that the battle they had chosen was not one they could win, stayed to fight and die while the people who had advocated for the battle retreated and lived. This elevated Kusunoki and his men to the status of samurai martyrs.

However, what is not always appreciated is that he actually did retreat. While Kusunoki stayed on the battlefield and fought, it was not the case that he never stepped backwards. Quite the opposite, in fact: he used his ability in moving troops quickly to keep the enemy from trapping him for as long as possible before retreating to a farmhouse where he and his brother committed glorious suicide.

It must be understood that Kusunoki's actions represented an ideal for the samurai and never became the norm. It was not until a wave of nationalism swept over Japan during the first part of the twentieth century that Japanese soldiers adopted a policy of no retreat or surrender under any circumstances, and some modern enthusiasts have mistakenly assumed that this mindset also applied to the samurai.

The tactics of retreat

Toward the end of the sixteenth century, Toyotomi Hideyoshi tried to force Tokugawa Ieyasu to take a more submissive position. At the time, Ieyasu was stationed within a fortress, but he knew his position was weak, so he left a force of 300 to guard his retreat while his main force left. To this, Hideyoshi said:

> *That is a leader you cannot snare with either net or line. He is both smart and stalwart, there is not another like him to be found in all the empire! However, one day I will have him in the correct dress at the Kyōto court!*

This is an example of a samurai retreating from a force more powerful than his own, even at the risk of 'losing face'.

In contrast, when Oda Nobunaga needed Ieyasu to return home so that he could carry out his plans without being observed, Ieyasu refused. He replied that someone who retreated at such a time would have no right to call himself a warrior. The difference in Ieyasu's attitude in this case suggests that generally retreat was seen in a negative light but that it was chosen as a tactic by a flexible commander when the situation called for it.

At the battle of Mikatagahara in 1572, two samurai named Takigawa and Sakuma retreated in fear and left another samurai called Hiraide in great peril. This was clearly an unacceptable form of retreat. However, in the same battle two Takeda divisions retreated, to be replaced on the front line with fresher troops. This kind of retreat and troop exchange was an organized movement within a force and did not carry any connotations of shame. Famously, this was also the battle in which Tokugawa Ieyasu's loyal retainer Natsume Yoshinobu insisted that his master leave the field so that he could continue to lead the army from a place of safety (see chapter 6).

On the whole, retreat was never considered as a wholly positive move, unless it was tactical or used to lure the enemy into a trap, in which case it was not genuine retreat but fell under the heading of deception.

Defending the retreat

When you are at war in an enemy province and confusion has spread, you may have to withdraw. Samurai who stay with the lord are considered immensely prestigious, especially if it is a situation where the lord's horse cannot retreat. In this situation, have the lord mount your horse while you attend on foot. A deed of extreme bravery is to return and retrieve a sashimono banner that has been dropped. This person is considered as an eiyū no bushi – *a heroic warrior.*

Ippei Yōkō (c1670)

While retreat was not necessarily shameful, neither did it bring any prestige. However, those samurai who stood firm and held back the enemy while their comrades escaped were praised greatly. To volunteer for this duty, a samurai had to appear before the command team and declare their desire to stand as *shingari* retreat defence. As well as fighting the enemy in front of everyone else who was retreating, *shingari* duties included helping to bring back the wounded and picking up any banners and that had been left on the ground. Anyone who survived this ordeal would gain a great reputation for bravery and honour. The *shingari* protocol shows that tactical withdrawal was often a necessary part of warfare and directly contradicts the modern myth that samurai could never retreat.

SHAME AS A MOTIVATOR

> Tsumi *(crime) belongs to the body, while* haji *(shame) is attached to the soul.*
>
> Yoshida Shōin (1830–59)

Although the samurai did not consider shame itself to be a good thing, it was seen as having a positive aspect: the ever-present prospect of disgrace inspired people to act in accordance with social expectations. The main terms for shame are *haji* and *chijyoku*; other related ideas include *na* ('name'), *meiyo* ('honour'), *iji* ('pride') and *menboku* ('face'). These concepts combine to create a samurai identity based on shame culture.

Rout

To divide the enemy and force them to retreat in a disorderly manner was a high honour in samurai culture, as it was the ultimate way to demonstrate your superiority over the opposition. Occupying space that the enemy had once controlled was another praiseworthy achievement.

Sometimes it was possible to scatter the enemy by ingenuity rather than force of arms. The Taira army fooled their enemy into fleeing without doing battle by having scouts scare birds along a river bank so that they flew up in a flock. Observing this, the enemy mistook it as a sign that the opposing army was arriving and a panic flew through their troops because they were unprepared to fight at that time.

SOURCES

If the enemy have been cornered while they are trying to cross a fence, ditch or earth embankment or while they are withdrawing in a group after they have been routed, they may reform, set their spears and engage in combat. This should not be classed as honyari *– true spear. In addition to this there is* oikakeyari, *the chased spear. If this happens when mounted this is not considered as* yariawase, *combat with spears, but is instead called* hanyari *– half spear.*

Ippei Yōkō (c1670)

For a head taken when the enemy have been put to rout and chased down: when they are running, [if the enemy] is prestigious, take their katana, wakizashi *or banner as proof [of the kill] and as a way to discover their name.*

Ippei Yōkō (c1670)

Rallying

If your allies fall into confusion, hold the banners and flags firmly in their positions. By finding such flags again, people who had collapsed will be able to regroup. [There is a flag called] ryū *– the dragon. Dragons have the energy of* yō (yang) *and perform the greatest of feats. Also, the flags are positioned at a height where the gods of war like to reside. However, I would like to offer the idea that they are used in this way because something at a height can be seen easily by everyone, rather than because that is where the gods reside.*

Heieki Yōhō (c1670)

To rally an army is to stop it fleeing and get it to regroup, stand firm and change its movement to an advance, if possible. In samurai times, troops rallied around a large, easily identifiable standard, sometimes known as the 'great dragon banner'. The central command (*hatamoto*) would get to a rise in the landscape and fly the banner to attract fleeing troops. According to samurai tradition, the gods of war resided in higher places; therefore, placing the banner up high was to use the power of the gods (although, as the quote above points out, flying it at a height also served the practical purpose of making the banner visible). However, rather than relying entirely on the rallying banner, the command group would also brief the lead captains before combat on the best places to regroup if the army broke up.

Refreshing

Many successful commanders throughout world history have recognized the need to relieve their frontline troops and replace them with fresh warriors and this appears to have been the way with the samurai. However, when Tokugawa Ieyasu ordered a commander of the Uesugi family to fall back and allow fresher troops to take the place of his men he did not receive the response he was expecting. The commander replied:

> *It may be the order of Ōgosho-sama [Tokugawa Ieyasu] for us to pull back, but as I was born in a warrior house it is our tradition not to retreat once combat has started.*

CHANGING OF THE GUARD

John Saris, writing in the early seventeenth century, described the changing of the garrison at Fushimi Castle, which took place every three years. The soldiers left in lines of five and after ten lines had passed there would be a captain of fifty men who kept them in check at the rear. The men coming in would follow the same pattern and in this way the garrison was refreshed. There was a hierarchy in the marching order, which was apparent from the different types of weapon the different types of samurai were carrying. There were soldiers carrying *katana*, archers, and even troops carrying only a short sword. Within each category, the higher-ranked samurai carried finer weapons (for example, swords with gold fittings) and went at the rear of their group.

Surrender

There were three options for the samurai when their forces had been totally defeated:

1. To die
2. To flee
3. To be absorbed into the enemy

In certain cases, death was the only realistic option. Exile was possible if the opposite army did not accept a switch of sides. Some samurai fled to other provinces in Japan, but other samurai went as far as other countries in east Asia and formed mercenary bands, became pirates or settled in Japanese communities.

As for changing sides, it must be stressed here that, in his *Art of War*, Sun Tzu advocated absorbing enemy retainers to bolster the allied forces and the samurai were known to set much store by Sun Tzu's teachings. There are countless examples of samurai being absorbed into or surrendering to superior forces. For example, the Ogasawara clan surrendered to the Takeda clan, but in turn the Takeda surrendered to the Tokugawa.

The fall of the Takeda, one of the most significant clans in Japan, took place after the death of its greatest figure, the master strategist Takeda Shingen. Control of the clan passed to his son Takeda Katsuyori, who was thought of as a fool, although it was probably just that he did not measure up to the high standard set by Shingen. A combination of misfortune, betrayal and poor decision-making and youthful hot-headedness on the part of Katsuyori led to the collapse and defeat of the Takeda. One contemporary poem of the time says:

> *Takeda Katsuyori the worthless has lost his homeland,*
> *being so low he lost his battles.*

The fall of a castle

The *Heieki Yōhō* scroll describes a surprisingly ritualistic protocol for the surrender of a castle. The defeated troops leaving the fortress and the victorious force moving in faced each other in two orderly lines. Officials from each side bowed to their counterparts and the exchange of control was sealed.

Rather less genteel were the events leading up to the fall of Kanie Castle, which was besieged by the Tokugawa forces. On the brink of collapse, the defenders sent word to the Tokugawa that they wanted to surrender and leave the castle; the Tokugawa side agreed to this on condition that they deliver the head of Maeda Tanetoshi, who was within the castle. Maeda Tanetoshi, not wanting to lose his head, tried to flee, but his own cousin and – until that point – ally, captured him and decapitated him, an act that allowed all the other people inside the castle to walk free.

Living to fight another day

The simple fact is that the samurai could endure defeat. In many cases, the loss was not by any means crippling and there are numerous examples of samurai commanders being defeated before bouncing back with a stronger force to engage in battle all over again. The image of the vanquished general killing himself in shame is a gross exaggeration. While some samurai did commit ritual suicide when all was lost, it was much more common for them to regroup and find new troops.

THE SUBTLE ARTS OF WAR

Using the correct language

> Ensure that you do not use terms which will make people uncomfortable or will be considered as ill-fated. The words to use are ikusakotoba – *military terms.*

Ippei Yōkō (c1670)

When discussing war, the samurai took care to use the correct terminology. This gave a chivalric aspect to their violence. The term *ikusakotoba* (戦言葉), which means 'words of war' or 'bellicose language', was used to refer to the correct language for a warrior. For example, they might suggest 'withdrawing' rather than 'fleeing' in order not to cast the action in a negative light. It was important to use words that struck a balance between confidence and arrogance. Expressing a belief in your own abilities or your side's superiority over the enemy was acceptable as long as this did not tip over into brashness and vulgarity. There were also words to avoid because they were seen as ill omens, sometimes because they sounded similar to spiritually negative terms.

The following extract, adapted from the *Ippei Yōkō* scroll, shows how important it was for a samurai to use the correct terms.

> In war [during the 'ceremony of resounding bowstrings'] strike the bowstring only once. Striking three times should be avoided because miuchi, 'three strikes', is similar to mi wo utsu, 'to be struck'. The term hitotsu, 'once', is preferred because it can also be read as katsu, 'victory'. The term susumu, 'to advance', should be used to indicate the movement of flags when an army departs for war and shiboru *should be used to describe the rolling of a flag around a pole.* Hata wo maku, 'to roll flags', *means to surrender*

[so it should be avoided]. Hipparu *is used to indicate that the enemy have raised their flags while* uchitateru *should be used for your own flags. Avoid the term* kiru, *'to cut', when discussing [the making of] banner poles and use* karu, *'to hunt', instead. The term* horu, *'to dig', can also be used.*

As can be seen, there were very delicate subtleties in the way in which a samurai should speak and the above list of examples is by no means exhaustive. Samurai should not sound like commoners and nor should they use vocabulary that causes embarrassment. They should deploy their words with the same precision as their weapons.

When there is a civil disturbance, they set aside normal ways for the present and adopt military terminology for their superiors, allies and subordinates. They don formal wear, put on armour and take up weapons.

Bushidō Shoshinshū (c1700)

Poems of honour

世の中は常にもがもな渚漕ぐ海人の小舟の綱手かなしも
Will this world of ours ever be the same again? Along the seashore, sailors scull their small vessels while the mooring ropes bring tears to the eyes.

Writings of Minamoto no Sanetomo (13th century)

Poetry was an important aspect of Japanese military life. One way that samurai families passed down their military teachings was in the form of poems. Even the skills of the ninja were passed on in the '100 poems of Yoshimori' (see *The Secret Traditions of the Shinobi* by Antony Cummins and Yoshie Minami).

To be a good commander and a good poet was seen as an ideal. However, the greatest commanders were not always the greatest poets. The thirteenth-century samurai Minamoto no Sanetomo is often considered to be the finest *waka* poet and the fourteenth-century *shōgun* Ashikaga Takauji left 700 *waka* poems of a quality assessed as raw but solid. In contrast, Tokugawa Ieyasu's poetry fell a long way short of his military ability.

The following are examples of military poems taken from various sources.

夜軍は功のゆかねばしかけても味方討して損となるべし
In a night raid, if you do not send the correct people you will fight among yourselves and sustain damage.

敗軍の敵かゝらば対の鑓対の道具はよはものとしれ
When chasing down a retreating enemy, be aware that their spears and other weapons, which are normally equivalent to yours, will be of no match.

人は城人は石がき人は堀なさけはみかたあだはてきなり
Our people are the castle, our people are the castle walls, our people are the moat. Compassion makes allies, while grudges make enemies.

軍兵は小鷹のざいにつくごとくかゝるも引もさうさうとせよ
Soldiers should be quick both in attacking and withdrawing, just as a falcon attacks his prey.

幾度も主の命に替るべしふた心こそながき恥なれ
You should never cease risking your life for your lord's life; banish second thoughts for all time.

君をあふぎ親を思ひて仮初もたかき賤礼義みだすな
Look up to your lord and think much of your parents, so that, high or humble, you always keep to the morals of order.

世の中能人の心の偽耳死ぬる斗そ誠なりけり
Among all the lies that flow from people's minds, the only real truth is to enter into death.

Esoteric knowledge

Certain samurai, known as *gunbaisha* (軍配者), were masters of esoteric knowledge and ritual. The characters that make up the term *gunbaisha* literally mean 'military positioning person'. This referred to metaphysical positioning based on *yin–yang* theory, the cycles of creation and destruction and ill or auspicious omens. Although the *Ōgiden* and *Bansenshūkai* documents both warn not to put too much faith in lucky or unlucky days and directions, nonetheless the samurai followed complex systems of divination and omen reading taking their lead from the *gunbaisha*.

This focus on auspicious and inauspicious directions and positions within the landscape even extended to a special status for the direction and position of the lord's house. According to the *Bushidō Shoshinshū*, samurai would never sleep with their feet pointing toward their lord's house, nor would they ever launch an arrow in that direction. The same manual says that when talking about their lord or receiving a message from them, a samurai should sit up correctly. Even if the messenger was lower in status than the samurai, they should face them as they would face their lord. This section of the document describes the embarrassment felt by a samurai who was lying down when he received a message from his lord.

Observing *chi*

One of the core tasks of the *gunbaisha* was to observe *chi*, the subtle energy that flows through all things. They would tend to focus on the *chi* in the environment – for example, in the enemy or allied army or encampment – rather than the *chi* of individual people. Conclusions could be drawn from different formations and colours of *chi* occurring at different times of the day. A *gunbaisha* claimed to be able to sense or predict such events as a death, an infiltration, a disaster, a reconciliation and so on simply by observing the *chi* patterns that others could not see. (Translations and illustrations of specific *chi* patterns can be found in *The Dark Side of Japan*.)

The luck of flags

As we have seen, flags and markers were a significant feature of the samurai army. On one level, they identified individual samurai and acted as a rallying point when the army's formation was breaking down. However, they were also associated with a more subtle level of communication. *Gunbaisha* could read omens in the direction a flag fluttered, whether or not a flag rode up the pole, a certain flag being struck by an arrow, and other such examples. Some flags carried religious slogans while others were treasures. Emblems and symbols adorned them and there was ritual significance in both the placement of flags and how a flag was moved and even stored. A samurai had to understand flags, and to maintain his reputation he had to fly the correct flag and understand both its esoteric and military connotations, for it was believed that a single transgression of flag etiquette could bring misfortune to the whole army.

Lucky days, directions and hours

The Japanese used the old Chinese system of time and dates and this included the concept that the hours of the day, the days themselves and the directions interacted to make certain days either lucky or unlucky for certain activities. When a samurai marched out to war, he had to do so at the correct time of the correct day and in the correct direction. To get this wrong was to cloak the campaign in ill omen before it had even started. Even though some documents state that this was all nonsense, the majority of samurai still acted according to these principles. While only casually related to chivalry, the idea of special days for departure and battle adds another layer to our understanding of how the samurai behaved.

War rituals

For the samurai, battle was mainly a practical affair, in which the focus was to find the right strategy and tactics to defeat the enemy. However, there were also certain ceremonial preparations to be made. First, they needed to pray to the war gods Hachiman and Bishamonten and give them offerings at the correct times and places. Then each samurai also had his own pre-battle ceremonies. These included arranging flowers and performing the *henbai* battle dance or magical seven steps. There was also a pre-battle meal with symbolic foods, chants and gestures designed to bring about the defeat of the enemy and protect the samurai. For his meal, the commander was attended by three companions and drunk sake in nine sips (each sip representing a samurai attribute – courage, loyalty, wisdom and so on). Samurai also had to sit in the correct position so that they could stand back up with the left leg, which was the leg of victory and masculinity. Adopted from mainland Asia, the daily ritual of *kuji* was another staple of protection. A samurai should move out of the gate correctly, be in their procession correctly, be armed with talismans and be prepared to use magical and esoteric methods to gain victory over the enemy.

CHAPTER THIRTEEN

DECEPTION, DARK DEEDS AND THE DEAD

To the samurai, almost any dark, disloyal or devious deed could be excused as long as there was an honourable intention behind it. Even in so-called times of peace, this was a dangerous world where you risked being beheaded at the banqueting table, betrayed by your allies, or held hostage and crucified for someone else's treachery. In battle, warriors not only fought the enemy but vied with their comrades to take the heads of high-status targets. While there were detailed protocols for dealing with the samurai dead, only a few received this respectful treatment. In this chapter, we will hold up *bushidō* to scrutiny against this shady backdrop.

DECEPTION

> *The essence of warfare is deception.*
>
> Sun Tzu (c500 BC)

The idea of *bushidō* that we get from scrolls like the *Hagakure* is based on direct, honest action. Samurai, we are told, should leave everything to fate and kill the enemy before the enemy can kill them. Deception is dishonourable. However, deception has been a staple of Japanese warfare from the most ancient times. Originally, Japanese military strategy was based on the Chinese standing army system, which was based on teachings from the ancient military classics. Works such as Sun Tzu's *Art of War* leaned heavily on deception as a valuable tactic. However, as large standing armies became too expensive to maintain and smaller personal armies became the norm, warfare teachings began to diverge and, in some cases, deception seems to have been seen as something to avoid. For example, the fourteenth-century general Shiba Yoshimasa is recorded as having declared, 'Deceptive behaviour is very bad in warfare.'

Even in the golden age of the samurai, viewed so nostalgically in the *Hagakure*, deception was not only still used but was celebrated for its ingenuity. Kusunoki Masashige is considered one of the most honourable warriors of all Japanese history, yet he is also famous for guerrilla warfare and exemplary feats of deception. On one occasion Masashige intercepted supplies that were on their way to a castle he was targeting. He and his men then entered the fortress on the pretext of making the delivery and instead launched a surprise attack on the enemy.

In a conflict at sea, the Taira clan fooled the Minamoto clan into thinking the Emperor was aboard an impressive Chinese-style ship when he was actually being kept on a much smaller and more unremarkable vessel.

The obvious conclusion is that deception was a major part of samurai life, both in war and at home. People were lured to banquets to be assassinated, ambushes were a fact of life, and deceptive tactics in general were widely admired. It appears that only a handful of texts mention any need to avoid using deception. The following exploits involving some of the most celebrated figures in Japanese history illustrate the fundamental role of deception in samurai thinking.

The unanswered blow

When Minamoto no Yoshitsune was fleeing from his elder brother, the *shōgun* Yoritomo, he had to find a way to avoid detection, so he and his men dressed up as wandering monks and pretended to be collecting tribute for their temple back home.

At one check point, the troop made the sound of a cock crowing before dawn to fool the guards into thinking it was the right time to open the gate. Yoshitsune's retainer Benkei, a noted warrior-monk and strongman, read aloud from a fake donations register to convince the guards of their authenticity. Having received the signal to proceed, they started to make their way through the gate. However, an astute guardsman recognized Yoshitsune, who was disguised as a servant, and stopped the band from advancing any further. They were about to be identified when Benkei had the idea of slapping Yoshitsune across the face and shouting at the 'servant' for holding them up. The guardsman, convinced that a high-ranking samurai lord such as Minamoto no Yoshitsune would never allow anyone to strike him, believed he had made a mistake and allowed them through.

This story was considered as a great tale among the samurai, but Yoshitsune and his group certainly did not behave in the way the *Hagakure* recommends. Their whole plan was based on deception. They told lies, disguised themselves, mimicked animals, and Yoshitsune even allowed his honour to be affronted by a strike to the face. However, Benkei's quick-thinking deception and Yoshitsune's restrained response were considered as outstanding examples of samurai fortitude and ingenuity even at the time the *Hagakure* was written and had been admired for many centuries before that.

To be struck in the face by someone lower in rank was seen as an intolerable slight. There are even accounts of lower-ranking samurai taking revenge on a superior who had struck them by killing their assailant (although they then had to kill themselves immediately afterwards). Therefore, the fact that Yoshitsune allowed Benkei's blow to go unpunished and the way that their deception was celebrated by generations of samurai turns what we think we know about *bushidō* on its head.

History in the balance

At the battle of Mikatagahara in 1573, Tokugawa Ieyasu suffered a heavy defeat. He was outmatched by the forces of Takeda Shingen, including the elite Takeda cavalry known as the 'demon horsemen of Kai'. Given no option but to retreat, Ieyasu had to fight 'tooth and nail' just to get back to the safety of his camp. However, he was still able to keep his wits about him and made several important moves that meant this defeat did not wipe out the Tokugawa cause entirely.

Takeda Shingen wore a monk's white cowl on his head instead of a helmet, so when one of Ieyasu's men took the head of a warrior-monk, Ieyasu saw an opportunity to turn the situation back in his favour. He proclaimed that this was actually Shingen's head and ordered that the gates of the battle camp be left open for the victorious Tokugawa army to march through to the beat of war drums. Then he had his fallen warriors repositioned on the ground so that they were facing away from the fortress and toward the enemy. This made it look like they had not died fleeing.

When the Takeda forces arrived to complete the rout, they saw the open gates, heard the war drums banging and beheld all the samurai who appeared to have died bravely defending their camp. Fearing a trap, they paused and decided to withdraw. If they had gone through the gates, they would have ended the Tokugawa there and then, changing all Japanese history. As it was, Ieyasu was able to regroup and come back stronger.

Ieyasu's acts of deception were celebrated just as much as those of Yoshisune and Benkei. All in all, it gives a very different image of the samurai from the one we see in popular culture.

Using doppelgängers

> *Because the arts of warfare make deliberate use of change and transformation, secrecy is paramount.*
>
> *Heihō Ōgisho* (17th century)

The tactic known as *kagemono* (影者), meaning 'shadow person', is mentioned in the Kōyōgunkan epic and in the teachings of Natori-Ryū and is also sure to be found in many other Japanese military manuals. It involved passing off a more expendable doppelgänger as the leader by having the impostor dress like the leader and take the normal position of the leader in both processions and on the field of battle. The real commander would adopt a less conspicuous costume and position, making them a less obvious target.

This kind of deception was also used to protect important women. When Omandokoro, the mother of Toyotomi Hideyoshi, was on the move in a political exchange, one of Tokugawa Ieyasu's retainers thought that Hideyoshi would have swapped her out with another elderly woman. The fact that he made this assumption shows how common *kagemono* must have been. However, it appears that Hideyoshi was honest on this occasion and presented his real mother.

THE *SHINOBI*

> As *a* bushi *warrior you should make great efforts to avoid falling into evil-mindedness. This applies especially to those who have mastered* shinobi *ways. These tactics are all justifiable, as long as they are used for loyal purposes. If you act out of loyalty, luck will follow and you will gain honour. Alternatively, if you plot with evil intent and have a mind to your own desires, then you will ruin yourself and become a notorious enemy. Therefore, study the correct way of* bu – *the path of the samurai.*
>
> *Generally, it is more than fair for a samurai to learn any kind of art. Mastering the art of the* shinobi *is in no way a bad thing. Knowledge of* shinobi *ways can be used as a defence against* shinobi *or at times it has to be used in tactics to fulfil loyalty. Military skills should not be turned to* majutsu – *skills of evil magic. Those who are known to have mastered the* shinobi *arts will be punished severely if they use them for their own desires. If a common person uses the skills of the* shinobi *for evil intent then their sins will be tenfold over those who exclusively perform* shinobi *skills as a profession. Therefore, restrain yourself.*
>
> *Shoka no Hyōjō* (1621)

As specialists in 'cloak and dagger' missions, including sabotage, infiltration and espionage, the *shinobi* were the true masters of deception within a samurai force. The *shinobi* role crossed all social boundaries and the term was used to refer to a wide variety of functions, ranging from a thief hired to harass the enemy, or a local farmer reporting on enemy troop movements, to a professional samurai infiltration agent or a spy-master at the heart of a force's intelligence service. Therefore, it would be wrong to fall into the trap of thinking, as some do, that the *shinobi* were totally distinct from the samurai. Although not all *shinobi* came from the samurai class, a significant proportion did.

The samurai saw nothing wrong in hatching plots involving breaking and entering, murder, assassination, arson, infiltration, sabotage and so on. So long as they were successful and brought benefit to the clan, such schemes were considered praiseworthy not shameful. However, certain aspects of *shinobi no jutsu*, such as lying, cheating, extortion, gambling, bribery and dark magic, were viewed with distaste. What they found particularly hard to stomach was pretending to be a servant to another warrior, disguising themselves as a lowly common soldier, walking the breadth of the land as a merchant or entertainer, living as an ordinary member of the population. This was a step too far for many. Any samurai who crossed the line into this unchivalrous world would have to quell their inner shame by reassuring themselves that their motives were pure even if their deeds were not. A samurai could justify almost any action as long as he could prove that he was acting out of loyalty.

SHINOBI, NINJA AND KANJA

Most people are more familiar with the term ninja than *shinobi*. However, 'ninja' only appears to have been in use from about the mid-twentieth century. Originally, the characters used for *ninja* (忍者) would have been said as *shinobi no mono*. The term *ninjutsu* (忍術), again modern, would most likely have been read originally as *shinobi no jutsu*. Both *shinobi* and ninja are also closely connected to, if not interchangeable with, the term *kanja* (間者), the classic spy.

Spying

All governments rely on sophisticated intelligence-gathering networks and the Japanese shōgunates were no different. As well as the *shinobi* and *kanja*, there were other officers dedicated to espionage, including the *metsuke* ('overseers') and *yokome* ('hidden informers'). The eighteenth-century *shōgun* Tokugawa Yoshimune established a secret service known as the Oniwaban, which was recruited from the families of Wakayama. Similarly, the robber-swordsman Tobisawa Jinai was captured but then pardoned on the condition that he would infiltrate the criminal underworld and become an informer for the government.

SOURCES

The role of the shinobi *involves performing many humiliating tasks. Although a* bushi *warrior should prioritize loyalty over their own dignity, it is often the case that people who are not exclusively hired for this job really do not like to accept such tasks [...] but if they harbour no evil intentions then the lord's tactics will unfold positively and they will fulfil a complete victory. If they are lacking in the power of observation and their minds are not righteous, then these tactics will fail and ruin will immediately follow.*

Shoka no Hyōjō (1621)

Basically, the bushi *should involve themselves in the art of the* shinobi, *as it is not akin to* yatō *(夜盗), thievery. People in ancient times instead referred to the art as* yatō *(夜頭), leadership in the night. Good* shinobi *were respected as they acted as guiding lights and were appointed as commanders, leading a squad of men. At critical moments, the leading* shinobi *took charge of the situation by himself.*

Shōninki (1681)

> Shinobi no mono *do not only use* myō, *wondrous magic. Before they resort to* myō, *they first utilize the five constant factors as well as wisdom, benevolence and bravery to carry out their tactics. If they try to obtain results with [only] wondrous skills, then they will become trapped in their own fabrication and lose* honshin - *original mind. Thus, in* shinobi no jutsu *it is correct to obtain results through righteousness.*
>
> *Fukushima-Ryū Shin'i Kufū no Maki* (17th century, transcribed 1797)

MURDER AND ASSASSINATION

The line between murder and assassination is thin and revolves around intent. Here, we will consider the killing of someone in anger or hatred or out of macabre compulsion as murder, whereas the killing of someone for political or financial gain will be considered as assassination.

Either way, it is clear that in old Japan there was a need for constant vigilance against attack. The Yagyū school of swordsmanship taught its students that when they were sitting indoors they should look up and to each side to check the area for obstacles; when sitting by a door or screen, they should take note of whether it might fall (or be pushed) over; and they should try to anticipate any other dangers. If they happened to be in attendance near nobles of the court, they should be aware that something unexpected might happen and even when they were going through a door, they should always be alert.

Similar teachings on caution in what would normally be considered as a safe environment are also found in other schools, giving the distinct idea that people might jump out at you at any moment and that danger lurked in dark corners. Murder and assassination were accepted facts of samurai life. There was no shame in killing someone in this way; what was shameful was not avenging such a deed.

Murder

> [The Japanese] are very cruel and easily kill their subjects for slight things and think nothing of cutting a man's head off or cutting him in half as they would a dog. If they can do it without danger to themselves, encountering a poor man they may slice him through the middle just to see how their katana cuts.
>
> Writings of Alessandro Valignano (16th century)

The samurai are often viewed in two opposing ways that do not fit together well: first as the noble knight par excellence; second as the brutal killing machine represented in Valignano's description above. To add to the confusion, Valignano later revisited this statement by saying:

> Except for killing in time of war or at the command of their lord, they live very peacefully with few killings and duels. Thus, they are not naturally cruel. While there are cases where someone kills a poor man to test a sword, it is very rare, because in Japan the punishment for murder or even fighting is great. They mainly test their swords on those condemned by justice.

The fact is, warriors of all times and all cultures have a tendency to steep themselves in blood, to ritualize and glorify murder, and the samurai were no different. Beneath their polished manner lurked a ruthlessness that was hard to conceal, as the following examples illustrate.

- In 1219, the unpopular *shōgun* Minamoto no Sanetomo, often known as the 'poet *shōgun*' because of his accomplished *waka* poetry, was beheaded by his own nephew, who may have been mentally ill and tricked into the murder by a female relative.
- When Tokugawa Ieyasu was held hostage as a boy, one of his captors, Haramiishi Mondo, was very rude to him. Years later, when Ieyasu took

Nagashino Castle he found this man stationed there and had him put to death because of his childhood experience.

- The *Hagakure* scroll relates the story of a samurai who was journeying by boat. Among the other passengers was one repugnant idiot who was causing trouble. The samurai waited for him to urinate over the side so that he could cut off his head from behind without warning. He then made the boatman take them to a remote place so that they could discard the body. Just before they left, the samurai ordered the boatman to make cuts with his sword on the headless corpse so that they would both be party to the murder.

- In the 1860s, attacks on foreign visitors to Japan were rife. When the young French military officer Lieutenant Camus was slain in 1863, his murderers photographed his badly mutilated body. This served as a graphic warning to all Western people in Japan at the time to be on their guard against racist assaults. Diplomatic immunity was no protection against murder.

Assassination

The two samurai were pleased and held a boisterous party filled with booze and revelry. In the middle of the party Yahachirō, the new travelling samurai who had just arrived, drew his sword, killed Lord Sōbeinojō, and tried to kill Lord Tatewaki as well. However, Tatewaki drew his sword and after a hard fight killed the traitorous samurai in the end. When Sōbeinojō's men came and saw the scene, they mistakenly thought that Tatewaki had killed both their lord and Yahachirō. Twenty to thirty people now attacked him with swords and Tatewaki defended himself by fighting with them until he could get back to his men and explain what had happened. At which point, a page who had seen what had happened told his side of the story, and thus it was revealed that Lord Tatewaki was indeed telling the truth. Afterwards, a search of the traitor Yahachirō's pouch revealed a signed deed from Ishida's side. It promised that if he killed both Mizuno Sōbei and Horio Tatewaki, he would be given their domains in Mikawa and Enshū.

Musha Monogatari (1654)

Assassination was an accepted hazard that came with samurai status. Writing in the late sixteenth century, João Rodrigues observed that the samurai reserved their treachery for diplomacy and war. A target for assassination would be provided with generous entertainment, and then in the middle of the feasting, when their guard was down, they would be decapitated. However, Rodrigues does note that often an assassination was carried out to reduce political tension and avert war, which could actually end up saving lives. Before making their kill, samurai assassins would write a letter known as a *zankanjō* (斬奸状), in which they explained why the assassination was noble and necessary.

Plots to kill political rivals did not always succeed. In 1335, during the Kenmu period, when the two courts of north and south were fighting for supremacy, Saionji Kinmune and Hōjō Tokioki planned to assassinate the Emperor. Kinmune disguised himself as a priest to carry out his task, but the attempt failed and he was killed. Hōjō Tokioki managed to escape to a stronghold in the east.

When it comes to political intrigue, few periods of Japanese history can compete with the sixteenth century, and the powerful Tokugawa Ieyasu and his family were at the centre of the action. Ieyasu's grandfather, Matsudaira Kiyoyasu, was assassinated by one of his own retainers in 1535. Kiyoyasu's son (and Ieyasu's father), Matsudaira Hirotada, survived one attempt on his life when Iwamatsu Hachiya, known as 'the one-eyed', crept into the room where he was sleeping and attacked him with a spear. Having only managed to graze his target, the would-be assassin fled the scene to be captured on the castle bridge by a passing retainer, but in the struggle they both fell in the moat. Not long after, Hirotada was killed anyway – by some of his vassals, who had been bribed by the Oda clan.

Unlike his father and grandfather, Ieyasu himself lived into his seventies and died of natural causes, but he was targeted for assassination on numerous occasions during his career. It is said that Takeda Shingen sent a young man to kill him. The boy-assassin sneaked into Ieyasu's bedroom early one morning, but the room was empty as, luckily for him, Ieyasu was praying elsewhere. The youth was captured, but Ieyasu decided to send him back to Takeda Shingen unharmed because he respected the boy's courage in undertaking such a mission and did not want to waste the life of a dedicated retainer.

The *Mikawa Go Fudoki* (三河後風土記) document records another of Ieyasu's narrow escapes. It describes a battle in which Ieyasu, covered in blood, was fighting alongside his men. Because the battle was spread out, an enemy retainer was able to mix in with Ieyasu's troops and target him for death. However, two of Ieyasu's retainers, Amano Saburobei and Katō Masatsugu, brought the enemy down before he could do his job.

Dating from a later period, the *Hagakure* scroll relates another failed assassination attempt. A pair of samurai assassins crept up on their target, also a samurai, while he was having his feet washed. Before they could cut off his head, the fast-thinking target, sensing a presence behind him, turned and decapitated both of his assailants. Their heads were said to have landed in the washing bowl at his feet, although this sounds too good to be true.

The death of Oda Nobunaga – murder or assassination?

One of the most famous acts of betrayal in Japanese history is that of Akechi Mitsuhide, who killed his master, Oda Nobunaga – at the time the most powerful man in Japan. Nobunaga was getting ready to host an important banquet, to which he had invited the influential ex-Takeda retainer Anayama Baisetsu and Tokugawa Ieyasu. He had delegated the preparations to his trusted retainer Mitsuhide, but he was not at all happy with the samurai's efforts. It is reported that Nobunaga said that the food was rank, kicked over all the tables in a rage, stripped Mitsuhide of his duties and replaced him with someone else. According to some accounts, he also struck Mitsuhide in the fray.

Many years after this alleged incident, Mitsuhide and his men launched a surprise attack on Nobunaga at Honnōji Temple. The fighting pushed Nobunaga inside the temple and the attackers set fire to the complex. Those trapped inside the building, including Nobunaga, committed *seppuku* and his body burned to ashes.

It is still not fully understood whether Mitsuhide's motivation was emotional or political – whether he was murdering Nobunaga as an act of vengeance for his slight, or assassinating him in an attempt to gain power. It may even have been a combination of the two.

Whatever the reason for Mitsuhide's actions, the consequence was that the Oda alliance collapsed. With their kingpin now dead, the other main figures in the alliance retreated to the safety of their homelands. Those loyal to Nobunaga's memory reformed, hunted Mitsuhide down and exacted a bloody revenge, while Toyotomi Hideyoshi took command of all Japan.

Killing the messenger

Kawajiri Hidetaka had recently taken control of Kai province, which had been lost by the Takeda clan. His government was harsh and there was unrest among his subjects. Tokugawa Ieyasu decided to offer to meet Hidetaka to discuss how the new ruler could quell the anger of his people, sending his retainer Honda Nobutoshi to Hidetaka with this invitation.

However, Hidetaka saw this as a move by the Tokugawa to take his land away from him, so he proceeded to get the messenger very drunk and murder him. He then set out with a band of men to put down the revolt, but only succeeded in getting himself killed. It is interesting to note that, at this point, Ieyasu did actually move in and take Hidetaka's lands. Therefore, Hidetaka's spiteful decision to murder the innocent messenger and his cowardly method of doing so – by weakening him with drink before butchering him rather than challenging him to an honourable duel – were doubly punished.

Bloodlust

If an enemy was a political target or an object of revenge or even the object of justified anger, then to have them killed or to kill them personally was considered appropriate (although to do so carried the risk of reprisal). However, to kill someone out of uncontrolled bloodlust and brutality was not proper conduct for a samurai. It is not that anger itself was considered bad, but reacting violently while in a rage was shameful. The honourable thing to do was recognize your anger and restrain yourself from committing any grave deeds until it had blown over.

The sixteenth-century visitor to Japan Alessandro Valignano wrote that even implacable enemies would be extremely polite to one another, entertain each other and follow all the protocols of society. However, as soon as one saw that the other was off guard, they would draw their sword and set about killing the other. Afterwards, they would return their sword to their scabbard and carry on in a polite way. In Japanese society, to kill in cold blood was seen as more acceptable than to be rude and openly angry.

SHORT WORK
According to Alessandro Valignano, samurai swords and swordsmen were so efficient that normally the weaker opponent was dead after the first or second blow.

Allies who kill each other

Those who are killed by their own allies because they did not pay attention to clan emblems have died for nothing.
Bushidō Shoshinshū (c1700)

The prospect of being killed by an ally was a real threat for the samurai. At the battle of Okehazama, the samurai commander Imagawa Yoshimoto was unaware that his forces were being attacked from the rear by Oda Nobunaga. He had seen some commotion, but thought it was rivalry within his own ranks that had blown up into physical combat.

This idea of a commander having to judge whether a disturbance within allied lines was caused by an enemy attack or by fighters from the same side trying to kill each other is a recurring theme in samurai literature. Many samurai armies were uneasy coalitions comprising samurai from various clans. Not surprisingly, these forces were much less cohesive than those consisting of warriors from a single clan. This made them easier to infiltrate by enemy agents and far more volatile. The simple fact remains that when armed young men – products of a child-soldier culture – were forced to serve under harsh military conditions with people they did not know, violence was inevitable.

THE SUSPICIOUS BEHAVIOUR OF DATE MASAMUNE

During battle, the famous samurai Date Masamune fired at one of his own allies, Jinbō Sukeshige. When asked why he had done this, he said that he always fired upon anyone who was acting suspiciously, by which he might have meant resting at the wrong time or being in the wrong position. However, to his contemporaries it was Masamune's behaviour that was suspicious, not Sukeshige's.

INITIATION WRONGS

The *Bushidō Shoshinshū* describes low-level needling between samurai allies during times of peace. For example, existing members of a clan would enjoy watching newcomers make mistakes and instead of helping them get things right would further hinder and ridicule them.

SOURCES

I hear that those who have swords or wakizashi *with gold or silver fittings are sometimes beheaded by their allies for them while sleeping.*
Zōhyō Monogatari (1657–84)

Within our clan, any fighting or argument between allies is strictly prohibited, not only while we are in a battle camp but also whenever we are out on any form of manoeuvre. This law is in place because some people who have not killed [in battle] want to release their energy and you may find that trouble starts in the camp.
Zōhyō Monogatari (1657–84)

It is an issue if you have not killed a single enemy but have killed someone on your side, even if he is not within your clan. And remember this is an insult to the shōgun.

Zōhyō Monogatari (1657–84)

When rice is getting hard to come by, even allies may start to rob each other. Do not let your guard down or you will be robbed.

Zōhyō Monogatari (1657–84)

Some people, to cover up the fact that they have killed their own allies on purpose, collect as many heads as possible, cut off the noses and thread them around their neck like prayer beads, as they have too many to put under their breastplate.

Zōhyō Monogatari (1657–84)

Tomokuzure *(友崩) is a term used for when troops break formation when they mistake approaching allies as an enemy force.*

Ippei Yōkō (c1670)

According to Kōshū-Ryū, [temporary] warriors should be placed in the vanguard. This is done in case they betray or attack your allies. Do the same with those people who have surrendered themselves into your army from another army.

Ippei Yōkō (c1670)

CHANGING SIDES

According to the historian Thomas Conlan, there is no equivalent in Japanese to the pejorative term 'turncoat' because the samurai felt no shame in changing sides. Lifelong loyalty was a quality to be commended, but so was the ability to pick the correct side at the correct time.

At the start of the great war between the Minamoto and the Taira, the Minamoto clan was outnumbered. However, as the war progressed, Taira-allied samurai changed sides in droves. Some Taira captains even switched allegiance in the middle of naval battles. During one sea battle, the Minamoto captured the son of a powerful Taira retainer and forced him to tell them which ship the real Emperor was stationed on, leading to a number of Taira soldiers deciding to change sides.

The opportunity to jump ship did not stop once the Minamoto had defeated the Taira, as there soon developed a further war between the Minamoto brothers Yorimoto and Yoshitsune. Even the Emperor switched his support between the two brothers, naming each of them as 'public enemy' at different times depending on which of them was in the ascendancy.

There have been countless examples of retainers moving from one lord to another. The *Musha Monogatari* document actively recommended serving different masters as a *rōnin*, because it enabled samurai to get out and see the world and gain experience on the battle circuit. Ashikaga Takauji gladly accepted the defection of Yūki Chikatomo and rewarded him for his disloyalty. When Hōjō Ujiyasu died, his son Hōjō Ujimasa left the Uesugi clan to join forces with the Takeda. Namikiri Magoshichirō was an example of a retainer who rebelled against his lord, in this case Tokugawa Ieyasu, but later rejoined him. Famously, at the battle of Sekigahara, Kobayakawa Hideaki did not decide which side he was going to fight on until the very last second.

One high-ranking Sanada retainer moved from Takeda to Oda, Oda to Uesugi, Uesugi to Hōjō and from Hōjō to Tokugawa. It was said of him that he was the 'natural kind of freak' needed for these warring times when loyalty for a short period was accepted as the norm and all that mattered was ending up on the victorious side.

Alliances between clans were just as fragile. Tokugawa Ieyasu removed his support for Takeda forces at the same time as the Takeda were eyeing Tokugawa lands. The promises the two clans had made to each other were easily forgotten.

Simply put, the modern idea of scrupulously loyal samurai who would never dream of leaving their master was by no means universal. While such loyalty did exist, there are far too many accounts of disloyalty to allow the myth to continue. The following extended examples will help reinforce this point.

The mathematical samurai

Changing sides may not have been shameful, but getting caught could be disastrous. Tokugawa Ieyasu had a retainer called Ōga Yashirō, who rose up the ranks from the level of servant (*chūgen*) thanks to his particular talent for mathematics. He climbed so high up the social ladder that it was said that, 'the sun could not rise without his help.' However, he secretly sent word to Takeda Katsuyori offering to switch to the Takeda side. Katsuyori, excited at such a prospect, sent 13,000 men to take the castle Ōga was stationed at and bring him over to his cause. Unfortunately for both of them, the plot was discovered. Ōga was captured and his wife and children were crucified. He was then paraded backwards through the streets on a horse accompanied by banners and musicians that announced his treachery. Next, his fingers were cut off, his hamstrings sliced and a large board was put about his neck. He was then left for seven days to undergo execution by *nokogiri-biki* (鋸挽き), which involved all passers-by making a single cut to his body until he was dead.

The betrayal of a childhood friend

Ishikawa Kazumasa was another of Tokugawa Ieyasu's retainers. He came from a family that had served Ieyasu's clan for generations, which should have guaranteed his loyalty, and he was also a childhood friend and close battle companion of Ieyasu. His station was to guard the castle of Okazaki, but he took his family and men over to join forces with Toyotomi Hideyoshi in Osaka and invited others to do the same. This idea that even clans that had the status of generational retainers would desert a warlord chips away further at the mythology of the unfailingly loyal samurai.

The fall of the great Takeda clan

Kiso Yoshimasa was from a clan that had served the Takeda family loyally for fifteen generations; he had even married one of Takeda Shingen's daughters. After Shingen's death, leadership of the Takeda clan passed to his son Takeda

Katsuyori, as a result of which Yoshimasa decided to join Oda Nobunaga, taking the strategically important castle of Kiso-Fukushima with him. Katsuyori tried to take back the fortress with an army but could not do it. Even Katsuyori's cousin Anayama Baisetsu betrayed him and joined Tokugawa Ieyasu.

When the combined forces of Tokugawa, Oda and the rebel Takeda factions marched against the remaining Takeda forces, even more 'loyal' retainers chose to switch sides, including two uncles who fled to other provinces. This helped to bring about the downfall of the once powerful Takeda clan, which at its height had come close to ruling Japan.

Some generals and clans did remain loyal. For example, Nishina Nobumori held his fortress and his men fought so strongly that even Oda Nobunaga had to come down from his command post with sword in hand to join the battle. Secondary families, such as the Natori clan, remained with the Takeda until the end. Finally, Tokugawa Ieyasu spared the remnants of the Takeda army and offered them service in his growing powerbase. The ex-Takeda retainers who joined Ieyasu signed their names in blood in 1582.

The weight of the unseen samurai

Reading these accounts, you could not be blamed for thinking that most samurai were, in fact, outright traitors. This is not the case. To temper these examples of disloyalty, remember the unseen force of hundreds of thousands, if not millions, of samurai throughout all of Japanese history who remained loyal to their clan. History tends to spotlight the exceptional events and not the mundane reality. When a clan decided to change sides, that story entered history as a betrayal, but we must not forget that the faceless samurai who made up that clan were actually loyally following the decision of their leader.

It would appear that most samurai before the Edo period were either fully loyal clan members or they were *rōnin* for hire. These are the silent majority, not the recorded minority. We can conclude that, overall, loyalty was a common factor among subordinate samurai, but that it was not uncommon for leaders to redirect the loyalty of their clan as a whole.

TREATMENT OF NON-COMBATANTS .

Human shields

When the Mongols invaded Japan they used Japanese prisoners as human shields, reportedly tying women to the front of their ships as they advanced on the samurai. While the samurai considered this mistreatment of civilians as barbaric, they were themselves not averse to using low-ranking soldiers as 'cannon fodder'. Understanding that most casualties on a Japanese battlefield were inflicted by projectile weapons, samurai commanders would exchange *ashigaru* foot soldiers in gunfire like pawns on a chessboard until the two armies could get close enough for the glory of hand-to-hand combat. The Imagawa clan used up the retainers of their high-ranking hostages as forward troops against the Oda clan; this not only saved their own men, but weakened the provinces from which they had taken the hostages. However, as the following quote illustrates, the strategy of using comrades as human shields could be considered a cowardly action.

> *In a difficult situation someone may ask a warrior-comrade to shoot their bow or musket knowing that the act will get their ally killed. They leave the comrade's body on the earthen embankment as cover. This is considered distasteful and is an example of a stratagem used by a deviously skilled person. Do not fall for this.*
>
> *Ippei Yōkō* (c1670)

Hostages

Hostages were a major part of samurai life, which goes to show how little the samurai actually trusted each other's oaths and promises. We have been led to believe that a samurai's word was 'worth more than gold', but if that were really the case there would have been no need to exchange hostages as a guarantee of good faith.

In 1635, Tokugawa Iemitsu developed the *sankin kōtai* system of hostages to make sure that loyalty did not falter. This compelled all warlords and their families to spend a specific amount of time in the capital city of Edo while maintaining expensive residences. Imagawa Ujizane held hostages from all the clans he had power over, but as the Mikawa samurai under Tokugawa Ieyasu grew in influence, some of those clans decided to attach themselves to this new rising power even at the expense of their loved ones' lives.

Imagawa Ujizane also held hostages to ensure Tokugawa Ieyasu's loyalty, but Ieyasu launched a night raid to kidnap Ujizane's children and exchanged them for his own family members. In this complex system of giving and taking, Ujizane still made Ieyasu's father-in-law commit suicide and had twelve children who were hostages from Mikawa province impaled as an act of revenge for Ieyasu's disloyalty.

The mother of Toyotomi Hideyoshi was sent to Tokugawa Ieyasu as a political hostage. It is said that the rooms she was allocated were surrounded with bundles of brush wood. When she asked what they were for, she was told that they had been put there by Honda 'the Devil' Shigetsugu so that if any harm came to his master in his negotiations with Hideyoshi he would set fire to the brush wood and burn her and all of her ladies-in-waiting to death.

So much for a samurai's word.

Pillage

In Japan, they almost always take grain crops [when they pillage].
Luís Froís, *Tratado* (1585)

Known as *randori* (乱取り), pillage in Japan seems to have been far from the disorderly practice we think of in the West. There was a system in place allocating groups a set period of time to take what they needed, specifying which items were most important to take, and prohibiting certain actions, such as rape and random looting. Military gear was the most sought-after prize, because there was often a need to replace damaged gear that would have been expensive to mend. For this reason, clans avoided putting their crest on equipment that could easily be taken by the enemy. Crests were saved for armour and banners, because these were things that the samurai would only give up (literally) over their dead bodies. More dispensable objects carried the logo or emblem of individual samurai. The last things to be taken were gold and money, because in the heat of a campaign the most important items were those that could be put to immediate use, either to eat or to fight with.

Peasants

There are positive and negative aspects to the way samurai armies treated peasants in wartime. On one hand, there are accounts of peasant houses being demolished to build bridges or to prevent them being used for cover by the enemy. On the other hand, there were rules prohibiting soldiers from raping and stealing from locals. Peasants could even profit from an army passing through their village, as soldiers would have to pay for food and shelter under certain conditions, and, of course, the usual adult transactions would follow behind any army. Therefore, it is hard to know whether a village would have been happy at the prospect of an approaching army or if they would have run in dread.

Most armies would have been focused on destroying the enemy and would have wanted to keep the villages intact so that they could continue to produce for their new masters, if the invading force intended to stay. However, even the best behaved and most disciplined army must have greatly disturbed the normal tranquillity of village life.

DEALING WITH THE DEAD

From ancient times, the dead represented putrefaction, the body being an unclean object that needed to be disposed of, albeit with reverence. We often think of Japanese society as being divided into the famous four-tier class system of warrior, farmer, craftsman and merchant, but that does not account for royalty and outcasts, who existed above and below this spectrum. Known as *eta* and *hinin* among other often derogatory terms, it was the outcasts who dealt with the corpses of both animals and humans.

While outcasts did most of the work involved in funerary preparation, the samurai themselves often directly handled dead bodies in battle, particularly when taking their heads or looting their kit. They also sometimes repositioned the bodies of fallen allies on the ground to disguise the fact that they had been killed while running away. When Tokugawa Ieyasu did this after the battle of Mikatagahara it was to deceive the enemy, but it might also be done to ensure that soldiers received proper respect after death. There was a *yin–yang* aspect to the correct positioning of dead bodies, with male and female being associated with certain directions (the sky is the father and the earth is the mother). Minamoto no Yoshitsune gained great approval among his men for the respect he showed to his dead comrades of all social levels. He paid a monk with his horse and golden saddle to ensure that proper rites would be performed for the dead.

Away from the battlefield, the samurai almost never touched dead bodies. This even extended to meat, which always had to be eaten using chopsticks not hands, if it was eaten at all. As yet, there appears to be no explanation for this apparent contradiction.

STAYING OUT OF ENEMY HANDS

The last thing the samurai wanted was for their corpse to be acquired by the enemy. When they realized death was inevitable, they would sometimes retreat into a building, set fire to it and then perform *seppuku*, or they might throw themselves into deep water. If fire or water could not keep their remains out of enemy hands, they would hope that their comrades would carry their body – or at least their head – safely back home. However, if there were too many casualties for the surviving warriors to carry, they would at least arrange the bodies so that they faced the enemy to show they had died bravely.

The samurai head cult

As previously discussed, the samurai might be thought of as a death cult (see chapter 2), but, more than that, they were a head cult. While the samurai did not worship the human head as a divine object, they did consider it to have spiritual qualities and they prized above all things the capture of an enemy head. Heads were a currency that could be converted into land – often taken from the army that had just been defeated. When we picture the world of the samurai, we should see heads on spears, heads on pikes, heads on gibbets, heads on poles, heads on trees, heads attached to sword cords, heads attached to horse saddles, heads in bags, heads in boxes, heads wrapped in cloth, heads on display, heads in piles, and trenches full of buried heads. What else can this be called but a head cult?

This obsession with heads manifested itself throughout samurai history. Minamoto no Yoshitsune offered heads to Hachiman, but he also set fire to his own house to stop his enemy taking his head; however, this failed and his head was put on display. Taira no Kiyomori said his only dying wish was to have the head of Minamoto no Yoritomo hung above his grave. When they were captured, Taira no Munemori and his son were not killed immediately. Instead, they were made to walk closer to the place where their heads were to be put on display, so that the heads would be fresher for the inspection.

KEEPING A HEAD SAFE
The *sageo* cord attached to a sword scabbard could be used to secure not only a sword but also a decapitated head. The cord was passed through the mouth and out below the chin before being knotted and carried like a bag strap, so that no one could take this precious haul.

Head inspections

After battle, the victorious army would perform a ritual known as *jikken* (實撿), during which the most prestigious enemy heads to have been taken were presented for inspection. Other, lower-ranking heads would also be exhibited; in the wake of major battles such as Sekigahara, there would have been huge piles of heads on display. Head inspections were also referred to by various other names, including *kenbutsu* (見物), *taimen* (對面) and *mishiru* (見知る).

According to the *Ippei Yōkō* scroll of the Natori-Ryū school, the twelve reasons for a head inspection were:

1. To celebrate a victory in battle
2. To collect scattered soldiers together
3. Not to become lost in triumph and to stress the need for caution
4. To bring people back together so as to settle them down and follow the prescribed laws
5. To praise an achievement as there is no other way to approve them
6. For the lord-commander to acknowledge their soldiers
7. To enhance the dignity of the lord-commander in the eyes of the soldiers
8. To stimulate the discipline of soldiers by displaying fresh blood
9. To investigate and gain details of military achievements
10. To listen to the talk of the soldiers
11. To encourage those soldiers who are idle
12. To attack the enemy if they return and overwhelm them with your might

It was also believed that the ritual would protect the victors from any vengeful enemy spirits. To this end, holy men gave prayers to appease the dead and cast spells to safeguard the living. As with most other aspects of samurai life, there was a large amount of protocol involved in a head inspection, which covered the way that the participants were positioned and even extended to the choice of wood used to gibbet the heads.

The inspection itself was performed by the warlord. He would either be seated with protective bodyguards to each side or he would ride slowly past the gibbeted heads. Mutilated heads would be 'repaired' so that they could be inspected, or, if this was not possible, they would be cast away with a banishing ritual.

The following is a basic overview of the head inspection ceremony:

- A head must be clean.
- It must not have a malignant look.
- It must be from a warrior.
- It should come with its helmet or a section of its helmet.
- If two samurai have been involved in making the kill, the first one to make a cut is awarded the head even if the other dealt the final blow.
- A proper warrior should never steal another warrior's captured head.
- Samurai should take the heads of their allies who have fallen on the battlefield, but must be careful not to be accused of killing their comrade.
- Heads should have tags in the left ear.
- The tags should be written according to status.
- Heads of important enemies should be returned to their family.
- Samurai can receive a financial reward for confirmed head captures.
- When permission is given, the nose or skin from the face can be taken in lieu of the whole head. However, it must show either eyebrows or lip so that it can be identified as male.

Respect for the enemy dead

When Takeda Katsuyori lost his head, Oda Nobunaga was the first to inspect it. He was extremely disrespectful, shouting insults at the head, declaring how happy he was to see it in such a state and rejoicing in the downfall of this 'thorn in his side' and the mighty Takeda clan as a whole. The head was then presented to Tokugawa Ieyasu, who set it on a stand, bowed to it and commented sorrowfully that Katsuyori had ended up like this because his youth and inexperience had led him to ignore his councillors. He then took the remaining Takeda samurai into his own army.

This story highlights the samurai's responsibility to deal correctly not only with their own dead but also the dead of the enemy. This appears to have been a part of a chivalric attitude, but we can see from Nobunaga's conduct that even the greatest samurai were sometimes found wanting.

Preparing for inspection before and after death

Before entering battle, the samurai would make sure that they were well dressed for death. It was important that they were found to be dignified in defeat, should the worst happen. Tokugawa Ieyasu is said to have thought that a samurai should wear basic and robust armour but have a resplendent helmet because the head and helmet were what the enemy would inspect. Leaving a clean and scented head was said to increase a victim's reputation; to this day, the samurai Kimura Nagato no kami Shigenari and Naitō Kenmotsu are renowned for having left particularly splendid heads.

The victorious samurai would take care preparing enemy heads for inspection. A decapitated head was not only a great prize, but also represented the person it came from, someone with a certain position in society, so it needed to be presented in a way that reflected the original owner's status. The left ear lobe was pierced with a *kōgai*, an elongated spike which sits alongside the sword scabbard, so that a white paper tag could be attached to the head. On this tag was written the name of both the victim and the killer (the particular wording depended on the relative status of the two). In addition to this, the hair was oiled and the teeth of high-ranking victims were dyed black. If the warrior had died wearing a *horo* arrow cape – a sign of high status – the cape was folded and cut in a specific way and used to wrap the head. Finally, if the head was going to be returned to the victim's family, it was placed in a cylindrical or square container inscribed with prayers and sigils of power.

ARRANGING YOUR FACE

The *Bushidō Shoshinshū* says that when a samurai knows he has been beaten and is about to be killed, he should smile at the enemy and be kind when his head is about to be taken. It also states that a true warrior should make a 'definitive statement' before he dies.

SOURCES

The severed heads of our allies were gathered in the tower so that we could blacken the teeth and put name tags onto them; we did this so that we remembered who they were. 'Why was that?' asked the children. It is because those heads with blackened teeth were considered to be decent warriors and so we were told to apply the colour to those heads with white teeth. Remember, heads are nothing to be afraid of; back then, we even slept among the bloody heads.

Oamu Monogatari (17th century)

Our army now is told we are defeated and everyone in the castle is seriously depressed. Show this head to all of them and tell them that you have decapitated Lord Shingen. Tell everyone that our army has won.

Musha Monogatari (1654)

Kinshichirō was on the side of Nagatsuka Taizō at the battle of Sekigahara and he captured and dragged in ten enemies with a rake and had his allies cut off their heads, then he himself was killed in the battle.

Musha Monogatari (1654)

Just while he was going to take the head, we had an order from our lord to withdraw. He was half way through the beheading but we were told to get back right away, so he had to give up and leave the head. [...] It must have been a great disappointment to him. However, the troop commander said he would guarantee his feat, so it was almost as if he had taken the head.

Zōhyō Monogatari (1657–84)

> *I took that head for myself, like plucking a ripe fruit from a tree. My Master said, 'Remember, taking just a nose in battle is not allowed, because people cannot identify the man and they may think you have killed an ally. However, as lots of allies just saw you do this deed, [in this case] you may just take the nose off.'*
>
> Zōhyō Monogatari (1657–84)

> *Making severed heads appear as if they are of a vastly higher rank than they actually are is truly the work of a coward.*
>
> Heihō Yūkan (1645)

The worth of the body

For a samurai, honour was found in presenting a clean body and head for future inspection by the enemy or, better still, preventing the enemy capturing their body in the first place. However, of the tens of thousands who died in a major battle like Sekigahara, only a handful of high-ranking warriors would have been treated with respect. The rest would have had their gear stolen, their bodies ignominiously cast aside to be used as chopping practice for *katana*-wielding yokels, their noses removed, and their mutilated heads tossed in a pile or hung from a tree.

CHAPTER FOURTEEN

RITUAL SUICIDE

Everyone in the West is familiar with the Japanese concept of ritual suicide. Most people know it as *hara-kiri*, but an increasing number are now aware of its proper title of *seppuku*. In this chapter we will explore the origins of this grisly practice and seek to understand what inspired – or compelled – so many samurai to take their own lives.

THE KNIFE AND THE BELLY

> *The government of Japan may well be considered as the greatest and most powerful tyranny that ever was heard of in the world, for all are slaves to the Emperor* or, as they call him, the great commander, who, upon the least suspicion of, or anger at, any man, will cause him to receive a cut to his belly, which, if he refuse to do, not only he, but all of the rest of his race, shall feel the smart of.*
>
> Diary of Richard Cocks (1615–22)

Ritual suicide has a long tradition in Japan and in ancient China, where human sacrifice for the souls of dead lords, kings and emperors was also commonplace. What set Japanese *seppuku* apart from other forms of ritual suicide was the agonizing manner in which it was normally performed: by cutting open one's

---

* The 'Emperor' referred to by Cocks is most likely the *shōgun*, for many Western travellers did not fully understand the distinction between these two key figures.

own belly to die of blood loss. There may have been a Buddhist aspect to this. It was believed that you had to endure great pain in order to attain Buddhahood, so the agony of *seppuku* may have had a spiritually purifying function.

Seppuku started as a voluntary act, particularly as a way to avoid the ignominy of capture in battle. While some early examples involved belly cutting, they also used other techniques, including falling on a sword, leaping face first from horseback with sword in mouth, and running into a burning building (the last of these often in combination with self-disembowelment).

The first act of *seppuku* is often attributed to the great archer Minamoto no Tametomo, who killed himself in 1170 having been banished to the island of Ōshima. The document Hōgen Monogatari describes Tametomo administering multiple stabs to his stomach, after which a guard beheaded Tametomo's three children so that they would not fall into the hands of the enemy. To complete the bloody scene, the guard, in floods of tears, also committed *seppuku*.

Many of these early examples have entered literature and the popular imagination as displays of heroic self-sacrifice. However, as time progressed a second kind of *seppuku* emerged. No longer only a voluntary act, it could also constitute a death sentence meted out by a superior, a form of self-execution that samurai were honour bound to perform.

Human sacrifice

> *If the lord causes a wall to be built, either for the king [sic] or himself, his servants often at times beg that they might have the honour to lie under it, they do this out of the belief that what is founded upon a living man's flesh is subject to no misfortune.*
> Writings of François Caron (17th century)

Human sacrifice existed in Japan from prehistory and continued up until premodern times. When Chinese culture arrived in Japan, the idea of Chinese-style human sacrifice at the death of a lord or master arrived with it. An after-effect of this is seen in samurai who willingly performed ritual suicide to serve their masters in the next life (see below).

Stereotypical human sacrifice, involving an unwilling victim, was also a staple part of Japanese culture. It was often associated with the building of a new structure. For example, when a bridge was being built, a human sacrifice would be placed below one pillar so that the spirit of the person merged with the foundation of the bridge. This also extended to castle building. A retainer might sacrifice themselves by lying under a foundation stone at the start of a castle build, crushing them instantly but merging their soul with the defence of the castle. However, it must not be forgotten that Shintō does not allow for corpses to be kept in living areas or places of worship. In very early Japan, when someone died within a house the family would simply move out and build a new house, leaving the original home to become a shrine for the dead person. This is one possible reason why Shintō shrines are shaped like houses.

Following a lord into death

Following a lord into death was another old way that predated the samurai. Sometimes the retainers following a notable person into the afterlife were symbolic, not real. When Empress Hibasu-hime died in AD 3, a hundred potters made clay dolls of men (*haniwa*) and horses to accompany her soul. Sometimes, as recorded by the American historian Michael Cooper, followers would be buried alive with their master – possibly a carry-over from Chinese tomb sacrifice. Later, the rite became more aligned with the prevailing samurai tradition of *seppuku*. It became known by the terms *chūgi-bara* (忠義腹), 'loyalty stomach', and, more commonly, *junshi* (殉死), 'death by following'.

During the Sengoku period *junshi* became less common, but the rite returned to popularity during the period of peace starting in the seventeenth century. Writing at this time, François Caron reported that when a lord died those samurai who had benefited the most from his largesse would volunteer their suicide so that they could follow the lord into death. They would hold a great feast with their close relatives, after which they would cut open their belly to kill themselves. Caron noted that cutting as high up the belly as possible was to be particularly admired. In his diary from the same period, Richard Cocks wrote that he knew of two men who performed the fatal ceremony upon the death of Tokugawa Ieyasu in 1616. When the *shōgun* Tokugawa Iemitsu died in 1655, five *daimyō* warlords committed *junshi*, which no doubt had a knock-on effect for their own retainers.

Junshi had become so firmly embedded in samurai funeral ceremonies that in 1663 it was banned by Iemitsu's successor, Tokugawa Ietsuna, and severe penalties for the family of any samurai who committed the act were put in place. For example, when Sugiura Uemon performed *junshi* in 1668 following the death of his lord, two of his sons were ordered to commit suicide and his daughters were banished from their ancestral home. It may seem odd to use forced ritual suicide as a punishment for voluntary ritual suicide, but it certainly served as a strong deterrent. At best, it would lead to a dramatic loss of family income; at worst, it could bring about the extinction of the main family line and most likely the loss of future samurai status. However, *junshi* was still seen as a badge of honour for families whose ancestors had performed the act in the past.

Shortly after the Meiji Restoration of 1868, which brought an end to the Tokugawa period, a debate was held in parliament in which the clerk of the house, Ōno Seigoro, proposed a bill to abolish all forms of *seppuku*. Of the 206 people eligible to vote on the bill, 197 voted against it, six abstained and only three voted in favour. The following reasons for the continued support of *seppuku* were cited:

- It enshrined the national spirit.
- It was an ornament to the empire.
- It was a part of national policy.
- It encouraged the pursuit of honour and the ways of the samurai.
- It encouraged moral aspirations.

Ōno was assassinated soon after this debate. Although, by now, acts of *seppuku* were rare, the subject clearly still had the power to rouse strong feelings. Occasional instances continued into the twentieth century, including the suicide of a Japanese citizen outside the American embassy in Tōkyō in 1924 as a protest against harsh immigration laws imposed by the United States. There was even one official example of the long-outlawed *junshi*: in 1912 Count Nogi and his wife committed suicide on the death of Emperor Meiji.

> ## NO SHORTAGE OF VOLUNTEERS
> That Tokugawa Ietsuna considered it necessary to ban the ritual of *junshi* indicates just how many samurai there were who were willing to follow their lord into death. This is further evidence of the existence of a samurai death cult.

Other types of seppuku
The following are different types of suicide that can be categorized as *seppuku*. The term 'belly' in some of the translations refers to the traditional belly-cutting method of suicide adopted by the samurai.

追腹
Oibara

An alternative term used to describe someone following their lord into death.

諫死
Kanshi

Suicide in protest at a superior's decision or actions.

粗忽死
Sokotsushi

Death for stupidity or a mistake – literally a 'careless death'. This was a version of *seppuku* that became popular in the Tokugawa period and continued into modern Japan. An extreme example was that of a person who committed suicide in apology for having caused a delay to the Emperor's train.

詰腹
Sumebara

Literally, 'forced-into-a-corner belly'. It meant taking responsibility for an incorrect action while on duty or conducting samurai business.

無念腹
Munenbara
Literally, 'the regretful belly'. When a samurai was treated unjustly and unable to gain redress, he might commit suicide out of indignation at his mistreatment.

指腹
Sashibara
Literally, 'to point at another person belly'. Suicide through social pressure.

Seppuku as punishment

Seppuku had changed radically by the end of the samurai era. What started as a spontaneous act in a dire situation later became a system of highly ritualized execution. The cut to the belly became a symbolic action; the actual cause of death would be the *kaishaku* (介錯) beheading that took place immediately after. By performing this kind of punishment *seppuku*, a samurai was able to preserve his honour and save his clan from suffering further retribution for whatever misdeed he had committed.

A FITTING EXECUTION

Enforced *seppuku* was a far more respectable way to be put to death than the capital punishments endured by commoners – and, in some cases, it would actually be less painful. The notorious thief Ishikawa Goemon was the son of a samurai, which meant that when he was captured he should have received the samurai punishment of *seppuku*. Instead, he was boiled alive, a demeaning – and excruciating – commoner's execution.

Seppuku in society

Samurai boys as young as seven might be called upon to perform *seppuku*. That was the age at which they underwent the *genpuku* (元服) ceremony. As part of the ritual, they received a *wakizashi* sidearm, the weapon with which they would perform *seppuku* if required to do so. The full act of *seppuku* was taught during a later coming-of-age ceremony at the age of around 15. Women were also given a dagger called a *kaiken* (懐剣) with which to kill themselves, which they might need to do to protect their dignity if they had been dishonoured sexually. Rather than disembowelling themselves, as in the samurai *seppuku*, women would cut their own throat. However, first they tied their legs together so that they would fall into a dignified death posture.

Samurai children were told the story of Taira no Munemori being seized by Minamoto no Yoritomo. His captor laid out a carp fish and dagger in front of him as a not-too-subtle hint that he should perform *seppuku* instead of being executed like a criminal. However, the Taira samurai would not do it; he tried shamefully to avoid death until in the end he was executed anyway. This tale instilled in children the idea that they must commit *seppuku* instead of being killed by an enemy so that they would not be remembered as a dishonourable coward like Taira no Munemori.

Commoners mocked the samurai obsession with *seppuku* in satirical poems called *senryū* (川柳). These claimed that all that samurai wanted to do was teach their children how to die a proper death instead of prolonging their life.

THE CROSS CUT IS BEST

Alessandro Valignano, writing at the end of the sixteenth century, reported that the most esteemed form of ritual suicide was to be able to cut a full cross shape on the stomach. He also added that children actually performed the full act of *seppuku* at times.

SOURCES

In Japan, some cut their stomachs, but many cut off the tips of their fingers and toss them into the burning funeral pyres.

Luís Frois, *Tratado* (1585)

The Japanese in war, when they can do no more, cut open their bellies and expose their guts.

Luís Frois, *Tratado* (1585)

If the person is reluctant to commit seppuku *but is forced to do so, you should move closer to their right side and [crouch] with your right knee raised and your* wakizashi *short sword resting on your left hand. If they turn against you and attempt an attack, you should immediately stab and kill them. Otherwise, behead them in the normal way.*

Kaishaku Narabini Seppuku Dōtsuki no Shidai (17th century)

The proper way to perform kaishaku *is for the head to not be cut off completely but to remain connected [to the body] by the skin of the neck. However, cutting the head off completely in one blow will suffice [if you cannot retain the flap of skin].*

Kaishaku Narabini Seppuku Dōtsuki no Shidai (17th century)

When dealing with the seppuku *ritual of a young boy, the second should have them hold a folded fan and simulate a cut of the belly but without telling them that they are going to undergo actual* seppuku.

Kaishaku Narabini Seppuku Dōtsuki no Shidai (17th century)

TALES OF SAMURAI *SEPPUKU*

Suicide by drowning

In the naval battle of Dan-no-ura in 1185, the young Emperor Antoku was pushed into the sea to drown by his own family who also followed him into the water. Some jumped in with their armour on so that they would sink faster, others were pushed in because they did not want to die. The commander Taira no Noritsune held an enemy warrior under each arm before launching himself over the side.

The curse of the samurai in the tower

Nishino Nobumori was running a hard defence against the forces of Oda Nobunaga, but his castle was falling, no quarter was given and he had had to call on the women to join in the fighting. Upon realizing the castle was doomed, Nishino Nobumori ascended one of the towers, called out to Nobunaga that he was false and came from a family that practised patricide and that he himself was the killer of monks and civilians. Then he cursed Nobunaga and said he would die soon, before cutting open his belly from the top of the tower and perishing.

Domino effect

Takeda Katsuyori, the head of the once powerful Takeda force, was making his last stand in a rough, wooded area. Before he could be taken, his young wife killed herself. Katsuyori, acting as assistant, cut off her head and then he killed himself, helped by his son, who was in turn helped by others to kill himself in a chain of self-slaughter. This was the end of the powerful Takeda clan.

A risky ploy

When Tokugawa Ieyasu was ill with a cyst he refused to take the advice of his councillor Honda Masanobu to seek medical treatment, so Masanobu threatened to commit suicide. He argued that if his lord died from this illness it would be a dog's death and, as his adviser, he would not be able to bear the shame of it. Fortunately, Ieyasu agreed to get treatment so that his old comrade would not have to kill himself.

The ill-spoken messenger

João Rodrigues recounted an interesting incident sparked off by a messenger speaking out of turn or performing an incorrect action in front of the lord to whom he was delivering a message. In response to this faux pas, one of the lord's retainers instantly cut the messenger down and killed him.

However, the retainer realized that his action would create tension between his lord and the messenger's lord. One option would have been to kill the rest of the messenger's party so that they could not report back to their lord, but the disappearance of the whole group would have been suspicious. Therefore, to put an end to any possibility of future tension, the samurai who had cut the messenger down performed ritual suicide in front of the rest of the messenger party. With this, the matter was closed.

Rodrigues was amazed at this display, which was so different from anything he had witnessed in Europe. Here we have a dual example of *bushidō*: first in the fact that a samurai would instantly cut down another for incorrect behaviour in front of his master; and second that the same samurai would volunteer to end the matter through his own death – all in the name of preserving honour.

A Christian approach to seppuku

The warlord Arima Harunobu sided with Tokugawa Ieyasu during the Sekigahara campaign, but later he was caught in a scandal for which he was ordered to commit suicide. Because he was a Christian he could not kill himself, suicide being a sin, and therefore he instructed a retainer to decapitate him instead; the samurai Konishi Yukinaga also faced the same predicament.

Seppuku against the shōgun's wishes

Lord Inoue commanded Ishikawa Katsuzaemon to commit *seppuku* in his mansion in Edo. Upon hearing this the *shōgun* objected, because he did not want this act to take place within the capital. The rite was scheduled to continue, even with the complaints of the *shōgun* ringing out. However, the *shōgun* ordered that it take place outside Edo, but still it went ahead.

Suicide for love

Fujita Geki had inherited a 5,000 *koku* estate but he could not be truly happy because society prevented him from marrying the woman he loved, a geisha. So, they committed *shinjū* (心中), 'suicide for love', an act which allowed them to leave the system that kept them apart.

Something does not add up

The *Hagakure* scroll tells of a samurai whose ledger was wrong at the end of a day's calculations. The samurai at fault asked the officer in charge to lend him the missing money, because it would be terrible if he had to die for something so far removed from the warrior path. The officer agreed and gave him the money.

Post-samurai seppuku

While the samurai era officially came to an end shortly after the Meiji Restoration of 1868, samurai ways, including *seppuku*, continued until the generational shadow had passed on.

The dutiful wife

In 1895 – more than two decades after the age of the samurai – a lieutenant named Asada died during the First Sino-Japanese War. Having received her father's consent, Asada's wife prepared to follow him to the grave. First she cleaned her rooms, then she killed herself by cutting her throat with the dagger she had received as a wedding gift.

Alternative methods

Taken prisoner and later released by the Chinese in 1932, Major Kuga Noboru was so ashamed at his capture that he decided to perform *seppuku*. As his sword was damaged he had to use a pistol, but he wrote a note explaining that his act should still be considered as *seppuku*. Likewise, Suga Genzaburō, after losing his ship to a mine, committed *seppuku* with a razor blade.

Seppuku *as a form of protest*

Earlier, we touched on the idea of *kanshi*, a form of *seppuku* the samurai used to express their opposition to the actions of a superior. There are two notable examples of this in the post-samurai era. In 1891, Ōhara Takeyoshi performed *seppuku* over the grave of his ancestors out of concern at the prospect of Russian encroachment on Japanese territory. To draw public attention to this issue, he sent a death letter to the Tokyo News Agency urging the government to take action. Similarly, when Japan was forced by Russia, France and Germany to relinquish the conquered Chinese territory of Liaotung, it is said that forty military men committed suicide in protest.

SEPPUKU AND SPIRITUALITY

Seppuku is sometimes associated with the Buddhist tradition of achieving purification through suffering, but violence is not generally seen as being compatible with sacred values. The question arises, does *seppuku* defile an area with blood or elevate it with honour? The answer is both. Death is always seen as a contaminant in Japan, but the place of death also gains a spiritual significance as the site where, according to Daoist thought, the soul splits in two, with one part remaining on earth and the other part rising up into the sky. The sites of notable *seppuku* events often become famous, and relics such as the bloodstained floorboards from Fushimi Castle may be celebrated as symbols of honour (see chapter 12).

Following on to the afterlife

The samurai ritual of *seppuku* forms part of a wider tradition in China and Japan of following a superior or loved one into the afterlife. Some samurai may have believed that in the afterlife their spirits would continue as samurai. By following their lord into death, they would continue to have the honour of serving him. This belief may have originated in the ancient Chinese practice of sacrificing slaves when a ruler died so that he or she would still be attended in the afterlife.

This idea of providing service to a lord after death can be found throughout samurai history. When Hōjō Takatoki fell at the siege of Kamakura in 1333, a low-ranking retainer named Shiaku Shinsakon Nyūdō resolved to follow him into the afterlife. Before he killed himself, he told his elder son to remain alive, become a monk and serve Buddha. His son proclaimed that he could not do as his father wished, because he must repay the generosity of the lord who had sheltered him all his life. Upon which, he immediately cut his belly open. The father turned to his younger son, who was also about to commit suicide, and asked him to get a pen, ink and paper. Then he wrote the following death poem:

> *Holding my sword in hand I cut myself in two, in the midst of a great fire.*
> *Feel the refreshing breeze.*

Finally, he cut open his belly and his younger son beheaded him, using the same sword to open his own belly. This sent the whole male line of the family into the afterlife to continue in the service of their lord.

Similarly, when Tokugawa Ieyasu's son was taken hostage, a retainer of the Tokugawa family named Ishikawa Kazumasa volunteered to serve the boy in captivity and die if the boy died because it would not be proper for a samurai to go unaccompanied into the next life.

Other, less drastic expressions of this idea include women cutting off their hair when their husband or lord died and retainers chopping off a little finger and throwing it into their master's funeral pyre.

The samurai conception of the afterlife does not appear to match that found in the main religions of Japan. Buddhism told the samurai they would be reincarnated into a new body. Daoism said that their spirit would be divided into two parts, the *yin* and the *yang*, with the *yin* staying on earth and the *yang* ascending. Shintōism told them that they would become ancestor spirits that would look over future generations. However, as samurai they were led to believe that if they committed suicide they would live on in their present form and serve their lord in death as they had in life. The whole system is paradoxical, yet this does not seem to have bothered the samurai.

THE MONKS' WAY

Writing in 1621, the traveller Richard Cocks observed that monks followed a lord into death by hanging themselves near the funeral. They did not use the normal *seppuku* method because monks were not permitted to shed blood.

THE BLOOD OF LOYALTY

The selfless samurai willingly casting away their own lives to serve their lord for eternity in the afterlife is a perfect expression of honour and loyalty. However, the purity of this image contrasts starkly with the samurai who were forced to perform *seppuku* to avoid their entire family line being terminated. Loyalty that has to be enforced with such brutality is no loyalty at all.

BUSHIDŌ IN CONTEXT

In this part of the book, we will explore the nature of historical *bushidō* as exemplified by notable samurai of the golden age and Sengoku period. Then we will see how the decline of the samurai during the Edo period and their eventual phasing out in the late nineteenth century led to the growth of a mythical, idealized form of *bushidō*. To gain a proper appreciation of the samurai, it is necessary to return to the unsanitized reality of historical *bushidō*.

CHAPTER FIFTEEN

GREAT SAMURAI THROUGH THE AGES

Oda Nobunaga would kill a bird to force it to sing, Toyotomi Hideyoshi would coax it through manipulation, while Tokugawa Ieyasu would wait for the right time to hear its song.

Old Japanese saying

Bushidō is an ideal of samurai behaviour which changes depending on the time in question. In this chapter, we will look at certain major clans and historical figures of different eras and examine how closely their reported conduct conformed to the various aspects of what was considered to be correct behaviour at that time. Some of these people will be familiar from episodes recounted earlier in this book, but here we will focus on them through the lens of *bushidō*.

THE FUJIWARA - EARLY SAMURAI TIMES

It is important to remember that the samurai did not just 'pop' into existence. Their growth was gradual. The meaning of the term 'samurai' is servant; the samurai were originally treated as a separate category from the *bushi*, who were 'warrior gentlemen'. However, as the Chinese-style imperial army diminished in size during the second half of the first millennium, rural warriors would take up arms and consider themselves as servants (samurai) to more powerful lords, who in turn considered themselves as servants (samurai) to the aristocratic elite. By the end of the twelfth century, the distinction between samurai and *bushi* had dissolved.

Some old and powerful families existed before the samurai. One of the most influential was the Fujiwara. While the classic samurai idea was taking form, the Fujiwara clan was heavily involved in political life and orchestrating court events. They asserted their might over the Japanese imperial line and forced the sons of emperors to marry into their clan so that future emperors would have strong Fujiwara connections.

The Fujiwara were so embedded in the system that they could force a change of ruler simply by refusing to carry out administrative tasks. Indeed, at the height of their power, they served as official regents and so they could be said to have been the true rulers of Japan. The simple fact is this: even before the samurai were fully formed, proto-samurai such as the Fujiwara were displaying the same characteristics as the samurai proper. They were pushing for power without showing any genuine chivalric consideration for the general population. Beneath their highly developed sense of court structure and complex protocol, they were as self-serving as the countless generations of political players who succeeded them.

MINAMOTO NO YOSHITSUNE (1159-89) AND BENKEI (1155-89)

Minamoto no Yoshitsune and his retainer the warrior-monk Benkei became folk heroes of legend, akin to Robin Hood and Little John. They were staple figures in samurai romance and their exploits helped define what it meant to be a warrior.

Accounts of their meeting differ, but the most common version has them encountering each other on a bridge where Benkei was challenging passing warriors to duels. By the time Yoshitsune arrived, Benkei had captured ninety-nine swords from ninety-nine duels. He had vowed to capture a hundred swords, so Yoshitsune was all that stood between Benkei and his target. However, the mighty warrior-monk could not overcome the young but awesome Yoshitsune. Eventually, exhaustion conquered them both and a draw was called. Bound together in mutual respect, they decided to form a band of 'merry men'.

In some versions of the story the roles are reversed, but either way it sets the stage for warrior attitudes in plays and stories to come. The main issue here is the classic bridge challenge; it appears that the defeated duellists did not have to pay with their lives, only with their swords, as no severed heads are mentioned. Yoshitsune and Benkei were real historical figures, with a record of excellent military prowess. However, like King Arthur and Robin Hood, their adventures have crossed over into the realm of legend.

HŌJŌ TOKIMUNE (1251–84)

Eighth regent of Japan during the Kamakura shōgunate, Hōjō Tokimune is best remembered for defeating the Mongol hordes, which he achieved with the help of storms known as the *kamikaze*, or 'divine wind'. At his funeral, the following list was given as a summary of his greatness:

1. He lived up to his Buddhist vows.
2. He was a dutiful son.
3. He was loyal to the Emperor.
4. He cared for the welfare of the people.
5. He studied Zen deeply and grasped its truth.
6. He wielded actual power.
7. He gave no outward signs of anger.
8. He gave no display of joy after defeating the Mongols.
9. He established monastic houses.
10. He prayed for both Japanese and Mongol dead.
11. He honoured those who followed Buddhism.
12. He dressed correctly for death.
13. He wrote a death poem.

Whether these statements accurately reflected Tokimune's life is less important than the insight they give us into the values that were held in high regard by the samurai of his era. Tokimune may have prayed for the Mongol dead, but he is also said to have committed the apparently unchivalrous act of having five Mongol emissaries beheaded. This leads us to wonder whether the samurai of earlier times respected the 'do not shoot the messenger' principle or whether they deemed it acceptable to kill all enemies, no matter who.

KUSUNOKI MASASHIGE (1294–1333)

Few samurai have had as much influence on the idea of *bushidō* as Kusunoki Masashige. Having died following orders he disagreed with, while those who had issued them retreated to safety, he became the ideal samurai, a servant without dishonour. However, his status as the most loyal of all samurai and a beacon of chivalry was not established until well after his death. In fact, for many years the Kusunoki name was reviled and anyone who carried it was liable to be executed as an enemy of the state. According to the *Hekizan Nichiroku* document of 1460:

> *The records show that the Kusunoki family once held great military power and that they slaughtered untold tens of thousands of people, the majority of whom were innocent. Since the fall of the Southern Court, descendants of the Kusunoki have been taken by authorities and have all been put to death for their accumulated evils.*

In around 1560, Kusunoki Masatora successfully appealed to the court to rehabilitate his family's name, and so merely being a member of the Kusunoki clan was no longer a crime punishable by death. The name became respected once more and multiple schools of Kusunoki-Ryū emerged. During the 1660s, the Natori-Ryū school was renamed by Tokugawa Yorinobu as Shin-Kusunoki-Ryū, the 'New Kusunoki System'. This was the point at which the Kusunoki name really took root as an emblem of samurai loyalty and chivalry. In 1876, the American orientalist William Griffis wrote that Kusunoki Masashige stood above all others in the eyes of the Japanese nation as an examplar of loyalty. So great was the love of the Kusunoki ideal that the term *nankō sūhai* (楠公崇拝) was established, meaning 'a worshipper of Lord Kusunoki'. The value of a samurai's name must never be underestimated.

TAKEDA SHINGEN (1521–73)

One of the most famous of the samurai to have held actual power, Takeda Shingen, was from the generation just before the three 'great unifiers' of Japan – Oda Nobunaga, Toyotomi Hideyoshi and Tokugawa Ieyasu – and was the central character in the military classic the *Kōyō Gunkan*.

Shingen took control of the Takeda clan by overthrowing his father, Takeda Nobutora, in an act of familial disloyalty that appears to contravene the spirit of *bushidō*. Still, he met the crucial samurai criterion of leading his clan to great success. He went on to fight all the major leaders of the period at one time or another, including Uesugi Kenshin, whom he faced repeatedly at the battles of Kawanakajima, which took place over more than a decade (from 1553 to 1564). Shortly before this series of battles, Shingen had shaved his head and taken Buddhist vows; his monk's cowl became one of his defining features.

Just as he had usurped his father, so Shingen's son Yoshinobu sought to usurp him. However, Yoshinobu failed in his attempt and, according to contradictory reports, either killed himself or was poisoned, presumably at his father's orders. The matter is still debated.

UESUGI KENSHIN (1530-78)

Arguably Takeda Shingen's leading opponent, Uesugi Kenshin is notable for the following pithy definition of the way of the samurai.

1. Fate is in heaven.
2. Armour is upon your body.
3. Accomplishment is found in the legs.
4. Approach the battlefield sure of victory.
5. Engage in combat and be ready to die.
6. Leave your home knowing you may never see it again.
7. Fate has a determined point; believe in this.

ODA NOBUNAGA (1534-82)

The leader of Owari [Oda Nobunaga] would be about 37 years old, tall, thin, sparsely bearded, extremely warlike and much given to military exercises. He is inclined to works of justice and mercy, sensitive about his honour, reticent about his plans, an expert in military strategy, unwilling to receive advice from others, highly

esteemed and venerated by everyone, does not drink wine and
rarely offers it to others. Brusque in his manner, he despises all
the other Japanese lords and speaks to them over his shoulder in
a loud voice as if they were low-born servants. He is obeyed as an
absolute lord. He has good understanding and good judgement.
He hates the gods and Buddhas and all other pagan superstitions,
but he does nominally belong to the Hokke sect. Furthermore, he
openly denies the existence of a creator and the immortality of
the soul and the existence of life after death.

Luís Froís, *Tratado* (1585)

One of the most powerful samurai of all time, Oda Nobunaga had a fearsome reputation. He killed his own brother, massacred more than 25,000 people in his attack on the monasteries of Mount Hiei, destroying 700 years of Buddhist culture in the process, and, according to the Portuguese missionary Lourenço Mexia, is even said to have killed a maidservant for not cleaning a room correctly. We have already come across his boorish treatment of the decapitated head of Takeda Katsuyori (see chapter 13).

However, Nobunaga was undoubtedly a great military strategist. At Okehazama – one of the most decisive battles in Japanese history – he defeated the vastly superior but complacent Imagawa Yoshimoto. Nobunaga bamboozled the enemy by setting up dummy troops and flags and moving to the rear under cover of woodland and a thunderstorm to launch a surprise attack. In the ensuing victory, Imagawa Yoshimoto was killed. The enemy survivors joined Nobunaga's forces, and he embarked on a campaign that propelled him to the leadership of the whole nation. In the end, as we have seen, it was not defeat by an enemy that brought about Nobunaga's death but betrayal by one of his own retainers, Akechi Mitsuhide (see chapter 6).

Despite being famously irreligious, Nobunaga dedicated a temple to himself at Azuchiyama Castle, decreeing that people would be blessed if they worshipped him after his death. To attract pilgrims to the temple, he brought famous statues from other holy sites. Nobunaga may have not believed in the afterlife himself, but he understood the power of other people's belief.

Overall, Oda Nobunaga is a difficult character to evaluate in terms of *bushidō*. His tyrannical nature and wantonly brutal behaviour were far from chivalrous, but it could be argued that his steady accumulation of power and land and determined efforts to stabilize the nation were the actions of a samurai par excellence.

TOYOTOMI HIDEYOSHI (1537–98)

Born into the lower echelons of Japanese society – starting out either as a peasant or a low-level warrior – Toyotomi Hideyoshi tore up through the ranks of Oda Nobunaga's regime, eventually succeeding him as ruler of all Japan. One might have expected one of Nobunaga's sons to take over after their father's death, but instead Hideyoshi managed the remarkable feat of seizing control while also bringing the Oda clan with him. Central to this achievement was his defeat of Akechi Mitsuhide at the battle of Yamazaki, by which he avenged Nobunaga's death.

Hideyoshi is generally regarded as an extremely astute tactician, but in his invasions of Korea between 1592 and 1598 excessive ambition appears to have overtaken his good judgement. He sent hundreds of thousands of samurai war veterans over the Korea Strait with orders to kill every man, woman and child they could find and bring back their noses as proof of the genocide of the Korean people. His ultimate aim was to take the Chinese throne and become ruler of the known world.

Historians have speculated that Hideyoshi went mad with power toward the end of his life. The Spanish missionary Pedro Bautista Blásquez (canonized after his crucifixion in Nagasaki in 1597) wrote that Hideyoshi had told him that when he was a child a sunbeam had landed on his chest, which he took as a sign that his purpose was to unify Japan. He also said that he was destined to rule all that lay to the east and west. According to Blásquez, Hideyoshi's cruelty was renowned and so people told him only what he wanted to hear for fear of being punished. Just two days before the missionary's audience with him, Hideyoshi had had someone cut in half with a bamboo saw. On another occasion, he had two boys executed for writing graffiti.

After Hideyoshi's death, the famous craftsman Hon'ami Kōetsu – often referred to as the William Morris of Japan – stated that low-born people should not acquire so much power in one generation. He felt that peasants who were given too much authority did not have the breeding to carry it well. It is unlikely that Kōetsu would have ventured this opinion while Hideyoshi was still alive.

Toyotomi Hideyoshi is another difficult figure to assess in terms of *bushidō*. He was loyal to his lord, yet took power from the clan he served; he avenged his lord's death, but ordered the extermination of an entire people. The question remains, was all this permissible within *bushidō*?

RESPECT BY EXAMPLE

In a secret meeting, Toyotomi Hideyoshi is said to have asked for Tokugawa Ieyasu's help in earning the respect of his retainers. Having recently been one of their colleagues, Hideyoshi initially found it difficult to assert his authority over them as their master. Therefore, he asked Ieyasu to greet him with reverence to encourage everyone else to follow suit. If this is true, it indicates that the samurai were not overly keen on a person coming up through the ranks to take command and that such a person would have to rely on the support of other leaders to gain respect.

TOKUGAWA IEYASU (1543-1616)

The last of the three 'great unifiers', Tokugawa Ieyasu established the dictatorship that went on to rule Japan for more than a quarter of a millennium. He is arguably the most respected samurai of them all, but examination of his record reveals some less-than-respectable sides to his character.

Ieyasu's career provides many good examples of how *bushidō* can accommodate acts of deception, deviousness and treachery. As a young man, Ieyasu put down a rebellion by farmers and monks in his domain. Having signed a treaty agreeing that any temples and other properties damaged in the conflict should be returned to their original condition, Ieyasu promptly razed the affected buildings to the ground, arguing that that was their original condition.

Another example of Ieyasu's unreliability can be seen in his treatment of the warriors of Iga who helped him flee through their land after the assassination of Oda Nobunaga. Ieyasu hired a band of Iga samurai to fight with him and many of them died in his campaigns, but his only reward for their loyal service was to downgrade their status from samurai to basic castle guards. This is consistent with Ieyasu's tendency to allow men from other clans to bear the brunt of any action so that his own men were fresh for the victory later on.

When two brothers, Sakon and Naiki, came to assassinate Ieyasu their plot was discovered, but Ieyasu was so impressed by their daring that he allowed them to commit *seppuku* rather than be executed. However, less chivalrous was his decision to detain their younger brother, Hachimaro, who was just eight years old and had had nothing to do with the plot. He too was forced to commit suicide; the young boy watched his two brothers perform the act so that he could do it correctly and proudly be called his father's son.

One of the most important points for understanding of *bushidō* is Ieyasu's mistreatment of the Toyotomi family. After Ieyasu assured him that he would serve as an adviser to the Toyotomi clan, Toyotomi Hideyoshi died believing that his line would continue. It did not. Ieyasu swiftly broke his promise to the dying Hideyoshi by taking command of the nation away from the Toyotomi. He cemented his position by winning the pivotal battle of Sekigahara in 1600 and three years later was awarded the title of *shōgun*.

The Toyotomi provided the main source of resistance during the early years of Ieyasu's rule, until the *shōgun* laid siege to their stronghold, Osaka Castle, in 1614. Unable to break down the castle's defences, Ieyasu made another false promise: he offered to end the siege if the Toyotomi filled in their moats and took down the outer wall of the castle. They agreed and the siege was lifted. However, the following year Ieyasu returned to capture the weakened fortress. He killed the entire Toyotomi line, including Hideyoshi's eight-year-old grandson Kunimatsu, who was hunted down and beheaded. He even killed thousands of *rōnin* who worked for the Toyotomi. The clan was destroyed once and for all. Of course, some of Ieyasu's actions were in response to hostile moves made by the Toyotomi clan, but, nevertheless, it must be remembered that they were the rightful heirs to all Japan and Ieyasu took that from them.

Most of the actions described above can be defended as cold-blooded moves designed to increase the fortunes of the Tokugawa clan. However, Ieyasu was also prone to the kind of hot-tempered brutality more commonly associated with Oda Nobunaga. He is said to have killed a servant because the servant had damaged an expensive hawk and to have had an oil seller killed for his rudeness.

In another alleged incident, Ieyasu had reserved an area of hunting ground for his own sport, ordering that no one else was allowed to hunt there before him so that the game would be plentiful. However, when he arrived for his day's hunting he found that bird traps had already been set. Inquiring further, he discovered that two local magistrates had given permission for some other people to hunt and catch there. For this he almost had the magistrates executed, but they were saved by the well-chosen words of one of his advisers.

Similarly, when a samurai named Nonomura brought his horse too close to Ieyasu's and they pushed against each other, Ieyasu is said to have instantly drawn his sword and swiped at the samurai in pure anger.

In contrast, there are also accounts of Ieyasu's kindness, wisdom and generosity. During a head inspection, he was so impressed by a cut on a decapitated head that had gone clean through the teeth that he asked to see the sword. However, the samurai who had dealt the blow had been forced to sell the sword on, so Ieyasu bought it and gave it back to its original owner. He also awarded 16 *koku*, a small but good salary, to a poverty-stricken hermit he came across (though it must be said that this was not a very significant sum for a man who controlled the nation's millions of *koku*).

Ieyasu is said to have presided over a contest of theology between two priests from different sects. Before the debate, he asked each of them privately what should happen to the loser of the contest. The first said he should be beheaded; while the second said he should be defrocked. Ieyasu favoured the approach of the second contestant, stating that his more humane outlook was more fitting for a priest.

To help round off the image of Tokugawa Ieyasu, it is said that he was extremely thrifty in domestic matters – even if he spent fortunes waging war.

He believed that samurai should not be tempted by extravagances like the expensive peaches he was given by Oda Nobunaga (see chapter 4).

Along with Kusunoki Masashige, Tokugawa Ieyasu is probably the most revered samurai of all time, but whereas Masashige is remembered for his unfailing loyalty, Ieyasu is celebrated for his ability to rise above all others. If he were active today, he would certainly be called a dictator, but looking through the rose-tinted glasses of history his worshippers see him as an honourable samurai.

WORK NOT FIT FOR A SAMURAI

During his youth, Tokugawa Ieyasu was sent as a hostage to the Imagawa clan. Samurai prisoners were allowed to be attended by a retainer and were given a salary that came from a land allotment so they could maintain their samurai ways. However, the Imagawa misused this system and took most of the money for themselves. One hostage-retainer called Kondō had almost all his income taken away by the Imagawa. It is said that he laid his sword by a ditch and worked with the farmers to plant rice so that he could afford to survive. One day the young Ieyasu was walking near the fields so Kondō quickly muddied his face to avoid being recognized, but Ieyasu saw this. The retainer presented himself in dirty rags and with sword in hand, to which Ieyasu said that even though it was a difficult time it was still shameful to see a samurai forced to work the fields.

SING YOUR OWN SONG

It is said that when Tokugawa Ieyasu was given a bird that could mimic other sounds, he ordered it to be sent back to the person who gave it. He believed that people and creatures should be loved for their own nature, not for copying others.

> **NAIL-BITING SITUATION**
> Powerful though he was, Tokugawa Ieyasu was also apparently given to anxiety. He is said to have bitten his nails during times of stress.

ISHIDA MITSUNARI (1559–1600)

Ishida Mitsunari's rise to power under Toyotomi Hideyoshi came to a juddering halt when he led the Toyotomi loyalists to defeat against Tokugawa Ieyasu at the battle of Sekigahara. If he had been victorious, Mitsunari's name would be more famous among samurai enthusiasts today. Instead, after the battle he was captured and sentenced to death. In a possibly fictitious account of his pre-execution speech, he is said to have stated that he would have won the battle if it had not been for traitors within his camp, but his captors responded that he should have been clever enough to uncover those traitors. Mitsunari is also remembered for having refused a certain meal on the way to his execution because he feared it would be bad for his digestion. When it was pointed out that he need not worry about his digestion at this stage, he answered that any samurai who was still breathing had a duty to look after his health.

In terms of *bushidō*, Mitsunari can be commended for remaining loyal to the Toyotomi clan, although we will never know whether he would have seized control from them if he had won at Sekigahara. While he was fighting a rebellion against those who had dethroned the 'rightful' leaders of the country, it must be remembered that the Toyotomi had themselves dethroned the Oda clan, which in turn had taken that right from the clan that had gone before them, and so on back throughout samurai history.

MIYAMOTO MUSASHI (1584–1645)

We have encountered Miyamoto Musashi as a master swordsman (see chapter 11), but he was much more than that. His writings on philosophy and strategy are constantly cited in samurai research. Although he did not gain the political power of figures such as Oda Nobunaga and Tokugawa Ieyasu, his influence today is no less profound.

According to Musashi, the way of the warrior was like that of the carpenter; just as a great carpenter shapes and polishes wood to create something magnificent, so a samurai should create something greater than himself from his natural elements. Musashi focused on martial arts and strength of body and mind to learn how to defeat others. He advised samurai to carry themselves well, control other people with ease, use men in combat, hold society together and gain reputation. In his manual *Gorin no Sho* (五輪書), 'The Universal Book [of Swordsmanship]', he often criticized the samurai of his day for their lack of true samurai virtue and spirit. In his eyes, these samurai were just salesmen; their martial displays produced flowers but did not bear fruit, meaning that they were pretty to look at but no help in keeping a person alive.

Musashi set out his principles for a correct warrior life in his document titled *Dokkōdō*, a translation of which is given below.

Musashi's scroll for life

獨行道
Dokkōdō
Walking the Way alone
by
宮本武藏
Miyamoto Musashi
translated by
Mieko Koizumi and Antony Cummins

世々の道をそむく事なし
Never disobey the righteous ways of the world.

身にたのしみをたくます
Do not engage in pleasures of the flesh.

よろつに依怙の心なし

Never have a mind ruled by prejudice.

身をあさく思世をふかく思ふ

Consider yourself lightly [and with modesty] but consider the world [and other people] with depth [and consideration].

一生の間よくしん思わす

Never allow yourself to think with desire.

我事におゐて後悔をせす

Never regret what you have done.

善惡に他をねたむ心なし

Never view other people's fortune or misfortune with a jealous mind.

いつれの道にもわかれをかなします

Never feel sorrow when parting from any situation.

自他共にうらみかこつ心なし

Never harbour complaints about other people or yourself.

れんほの道思ひよるこゝろなし

Never dwell on the topic of love.

物毎にすきこのむ事なし

Never have likes and dislikes for anything.

私宅におゐてのそむ心なし

Never desire a [resplendent] house [but maintain simplicity].

身ひとつに美食をこのます

Never indulge in sophisticated food but stay within simplicity.

末々代物なる古き道具を所持せす
Never own antiques that have been passed down by your ancestors.

わか身にいたり物いみする事なし
Never fear superstitions or evil.

兵具は各別よの道具たしなます
Never focus on worldly goods except in the case of military weapons.

道におゐては死をいとわす思ふ
Never fear death when following the Way.

老身に財寳所領もちゆる心なし
Do not accumulate valuable treasures for your old age.

佛神は貴し佛神をたのます
The gods and Buddhas are holy but do not rely on them.

身を捨ても名利は捨てす
Never abandon your honour and pride, even if you have to sacrifice yourself.

常に兵法の道をはなれす
Never stray from the path of military ways.

正保弐年
1645

五月十二日
12th day of the 5th month

新免武藏
Shinmen Musashi

寺尾孫之丞殿
Given to Terao Magonojō

End of *Dokkōdō*

As can be seen, Musashi advocated practical experience, detachment from objects and love, a simple and purified mind, and faith in the Way. To cement these ideas, let us now look at one of his other most famous manuals, the *Gorin no Sho* (五輪書), 'The Universal Book [of Swordsmanship]'.

Musashi's scroll of principles

The following set of principles for training in martial arts is taken from the 'earth scroll' or *chi no maki* of the *Gorin no Sho* by Miyamoto Musashi.

よこしまになき事をおもふ所
Be without evil thoughts.

道の鍛錬する所
Forge yourself deeply in the Way.

諸藝にさハる所
Touch upon the various arts.

諸職の道を知事
Understand the way of various skills and professions.

物事の損徳をわきまゆる事
Understand the advantages and disadvantages of situations.

諸事目利を仕覺る事
Make judgements within all things.

目に見えぬ所をさとつてしる事
Understand things that are as yet unseen.

わづかな事にも氣を付る事
Observe even the smallest of things.

役にたたぬ事をせざる事
Never do that which is useless.

The following set of principles for training in martial arts is taken from the 'air scroll' or *kū no maki*. The term here is *kū* (空), which refers to emptiness as a concept in Japanese philosophy.

空有善
There is only virtue in emptiness.

無悪
There is no evil [in emptiness].

智ハ有也
There is wisdom [in emptiness].

利ハ有也
There is benefit [in emptiness].

TRANSCRIPTION ISSUE
In this last statement, the term *ri* (利) meaning 'profit' or 'benefit' is used. However, it could be a transcription error for *ri* (理) meaning 'reason', which would change the translation to: 'there is reason [in emptiness]'.

道ハ有也

The Way is found [in emptiness].

心は空也

The mind becomes emptiness.

These sections of the *kū* scroll are the most open to misinterpretation, being short and unspecific. Personal interpretation may lead to misunderstandings.

The Musashi paradox

Miyamoto Musashi is one of the most famous samurai of all time and his writings are revered by almost every samurai enthusiast. However, such devotion creates a conflict in the hearts of Musashi's modern-day followers.

As we have seen, Musashi not only taught his own brand of swordsmanship; he also denigrated the other samurai schools of his time, claiming that they had lost sight of the old way of real combat and now valued style over substance. If Musashi was correct, it would mean that he alone had preserved the older style of fighting. This would mean that the swordsmanship of all other samurai in the seventeenth century was incorrect, yet swordsmanship taught and practised by samurai has, by definition, to be regarded as samurai swordsmanship.

Musashi may well have had a point. It is not hard to believe that the samurai of his time, finding themselves in a period of peace, would have needed to make swordsmanship more appealing so that they could sell their skills to students to supplement an income that was quickly declining. It is also possible to detect an element of bravado in Musashi's statements. He entered into many duels on his extensive travels and he may have been belittling his conquered opponents by claiming that they had forgotten the skills of old. It is simply not possible to believe wholeheartedly in the words of Miyamoto Musashi while also respecting the traditional sword schools of Japan.

CHAPTER SIXTEEN

THE FALL OF THE SAMURAI
AND THE RISE OF ROMANCE

The unification of Japan under the Tokugawa shōgunate ushered in a prolonged period of peace. This brought prosperity and stability to the nation as a whole, but threatened the livelihood – and, indeed, the whole *raison d'être* – of the samurai. In this chapter, we will trace the decline of the samurai under the Tokugawa, from a vigorous warrior culture at the heart of political life to a faded vestige of a glorified past. We will then look at the growth of interest in *bushidō*, which gathered pace after the samurai era had drawn to a close in the late nineteenth century.

ADJUSTING TO PEACETIME

An idea shared by most samurai enthusiasts is that during the period of peace toward the end of samurai times the samurai evolved from bloodthirsty, land-grabbing military men into bureaucratic 'salarymen' who wore swords and spoke of combat but could no longer rightfully call themselves warriors. Already in the seventeenth and early eighteenth centuries writers such as Miyamoto Musashi, Natori Sanjūrō Masazumi, Chikamatsu Shigenori and Fujibayashi Yasutake were busily recording the ways of the warrior before they were lost forever.

Traditionally, samurai fathers handed over the family business to their eldest sons, which included teaching them the skills of the trade. Entering the Tokugawa period, the family business was, more often than not, fighting.

However, as it became apparent that the period of peace was going to be prolonged, the focus of most families shifted away from warfare and a peaceful samurai caste evolved.

We cannot conclude from this that *all* samurai turned away from combat. The first son of the family had to follow his father's trade, but younger sons could still focus on warfare. There were also the *rōnin* scouring the country for a living, always with a nose for trouble. However, as the decades wore on, and the iron fist of Tokugawa rule squeezed the fight out of the samurai, another source of income emerged. This period saw the growth of samurai *dōjō* culture; countless combat schools popped up in cities throughout Japan, and there was no shortage of students who wanted to be able to show off their samurai skills without having to test them in battle.

Peace always brings with it the glorification of days gone by. This was the time when idealized *bushidō* came into being, bringing with it the perfected idea of the samurai as noble protector.

Restricting membership

The samurai were never equal; some had royal blood, others were promoted foot soldiers. However, in the rigidly defined Japanese caste system there was a line that clearly divided the samurai from everyone else in society. During times of war, differences in wealth and prestige between samurai were less apparent. What mattered was that they all came under the samurai banner.

Once the warring was over, samurai began to live longer and land did not change hands as frequently as before. This meant that there were more samurai competing for the same amount of wealth, and they were no longer permitted to do so by taking up arms. Meanwhile, the merchant class was thriving.

One way to cope with this situation was to restrict membership of the samurai 'club'. In the warring period, lower-ranking categories such as *dōshin* (同心) 'lower samurai', *jizamurai* (地侍) 'country samurai' and so on had all been a part of the samurai system, but they started to be downgraded as the Edo period progressed. The *dōshin* were clearly marked out as being below samurai status, as they were allowed to carry only a single sword, not the two swords of the samurai.

New classes of honorary samurai also came into being, including the *koshi* (古士) of Iga. (The loose translation of this term is 'old warrior', but the actual translation is 'warrior from an old samurai family'.) Such people retained the trappings of samurai status – the swords, the clothes and the illustrious family names – but they no longer received a government stipend and so had to provide for themselves.

The rise of the bushidō myth

Some samurai managed to secure positions within local government in order to boost their income and prestige, but there were not enough of these jobs for everyone. Many other samurai found themselves with much less money and much more free time. These factors, coupled with a yearning for the glory days, created the perfect conditions for *bushidō* to evolve from practical guidelines for warriors to fanciful ideals for nostalgic romantics. The more time that passed since the days of actual warring, the harder it became to tell the difference between historical chivalry and idealized glory. By the twentieth century, the mythical samurai ideal had firmly embedded itself in popular imagination.

SAMURAI 'BECOME LIKE WOMEN'

The eighteenth-century scholar Sugita Genpaku stated that, living under peaceful rule, the samurai acted more like merchants and dressed like women, that they had no shame and were far from the ideal of chivalry. Yamaoka Shummei wrote: 'In these days of peace no one looks to prepare for war and even if they did there would be no one to teach them.' We have already seen that the *Hagakure* made a similar point, observing that men were becoming more like women. Other writers of the period of peace lamented the bygone days of warring, where weaker samurai were killed off and harder troops were battle ready.

THE END OF THE SAMURAI

By the mid-nineteenth century it had become clear that the Tokugawa shōgunate would not be able to hold on to power and maintain Japanese isolationism for much longer. Foreign powers, particularly the United States, were putting more and more pressure on the country to open itself up to overseas trade and influence. In the face of this pressure, rather than following the principles of *bushidō* loyalty and rallying behind the *shōgun*, the samurai split into two factions: those pro-*shōgun* and those in favour of moving on to a more modern era.

In 1868, more than two centuries of simmering resentment toward the Tokugawa boiled over into civil war. The *shōgun* was soon defeated; he refused to surrender his life, but did hand over Edo Castle, his navy and all government weapons. Having been taken away from the capital, he retired to a temple.

It is often, mistakenly, thought that the samurai era ended with the fall of the Tokugawa and the restoration of imperial rule in 1868. But that year marked only the start of the wrapping up of samurai rule, not the end of the position itself. The battle for the soul of Japan raged on even after this, but mainly in the far northern parts of the land, away from the political centre. Samurai warriors were storming the gates of modern army outposts as late as 1876 and a year after that they mounted a massive uprising in Satsuma. However, that was to be the last major show of resistance by the samurai. Had their allegiance to the *shōgun* not crumbled at the first test, perhaps they would have held on for longer. As it was, samurai loyalty was shown once and for all to be a myth.

A change of status

The samurai could not be extinguished overnight; they were phased out gradually. The feudal system was largely brought to an end in around 1870 and in 1876 the samurai lost the important symbolic right to wear swords in public. However, members of samurai and noble clans were given the titles *shizoku* (士族), 'warrior families', and *kazoku* (華族), 'aristocratic families'. So there remained a nominal distinction between commoners and the ex-samurai, even if former samurai were no longer directly paid by the state or given extra powers. They tended to integrate smoothly into the general population, and a new Western-style military force recruited men from all social ranks. In 1882, a new outline of military ethics was laid out in the Imperial Rescript to Military Men:

- His first duty is to be loyal.
- He should be upright in his demeanour.
- He should value health and strength.
- He should esteem fidelity.
- Frugality should be his basic principle.

BUSHIDŌ IN THE POST-SAMURAI ERA

After 1868, the story of chivalry took a new direction. Post-Edo-period Japanese history is not pertinent to understanding the values of real samurai within their own time, but it is extremely important in the story of the *bushidō* myth that grew during the twentieth century. The samurai was used as a symbol of national pride to support Japan's colonial ambitions in the lead-up to the Second World War. Since then, the emphasis has shifted to the idea of the samurai as representative of a spiritual quest. For a deeper insight into the post-samurai myth of *bushidō*, see *Inventing the Way of the Samurai* by Oleg Benesch.

Liberalization

At first, post-samurai Japan moved toward a much more liberal attitude. Having spent so long isolated from the rest of the world, the country eagerly embraced Western ways. For the first time, the samurai openly became a figure of fun. The reformist writer Fukuzawa Yukichi created a comic character called Kusunoki Gonsuke, a samurai who commits suicide over a trifling offence. The choice of the resonant name Kusunoki and the pointlessness of the death were meant to satirize samurai ways.

Just as Japan as a whole opened itself up to the world, so did the country's education system. A radical education act passed in 1872 brought in major changes, including a recognition that children needed to be taught about world events. In that year, a history of the world was published in Japan for the first time. For a brief moment, it looked like a new Japan with almost no connection to samurai militarism was about to rise.

A return to nationalism

The liberal dawn was to be a false one. By the 1880s, conservative factions were already making counter-moves to reinstate more traditional Japanese values. In the ensuing fight for ideological supremacy between the left and right wings of Japanese politics, there was a clear winner. School textbooks, which now had to be approved by the Ministry of Education, began to focus on victory and honour in combat with an emphasis on the great epics of military literature. Cruel, bloodthirsty emperors of the past were rehabilitated as figures of heavenly perfection, and the concept of Nippon Shugisha, a belief that Japan had a divine right to rule over other nations, took hold. Even the great liberal Fukuzawa Yukichi tacked to the right. Moving away from the policy of *bunmei kaika* (文明開化), 'civilization and enlightenment', he instead adopted the slogan *fukoku kyōhei* (富国強兵), 'strength of a nation through arms'.

During the 1890s, the conservatives tightened their hold even further. Liberal professors who questioned nationalistic ideas such as Nippon Shugisha were often forced to resign. Right-wing successes in education were mirrored on the battlefield as Japan conquered the Chinese in the First Sino-Japanese War of 1894. What had started as a liberal quest for a wider understanding of the world developed into totalitarian control of the state as Japan entered the twentieth century. Meanwhile, the idealized figure of the noble samurai loomed over everything.

The rise of the militant factions

The continued dominance of right-wing factions in the twentieth century was epitomized by the sorry tale of the first Japanese socialist party, which in 1901 was forced to disband on the day it was founded. Around this time the term *kokutai* (国体), 'national essence', reinforcing traditional notions of divine imperial authority, came into vogue. Victory over Russia in the Russo-Japanese War of 1905 did nothing to dent national pride.

Conservative control over the teaching of history tightened further. An extreme example was the attempt to rewrite the historical reality of the Northern and Southern Courts period in the fourteenth century, a time when there was a struggle for power between two rival emperors. In 1911, the *Yomiuri* newspaper lambasted schools that continued to teach children this part of Japan's history, arguing that it would foster disloyalty and a doubt over the legitimacy of the current emperor.

As we have seen, Nitobe Inazō's famous book on *bushidō* provoked great interest in the subject when it was published in Japanese in 1908 (see chapter 2). Following in Nitobe's wake, a scholar called Takagi Takeshi wrote a 1914 study comparing Western chivalry and Japanese *bushidō*. He concluded that in chivalry bravery was the highest virtue, whereas in *bushidō* loyalty was what counted above all. Historical samurai were divided into two camps: perfect hero figures such as Kusunoki Masashige, and disloyal traitors such as Akechi Mitsuhide. In 1934 the government minister Nakajima Kumakichi was forced to resign because he wrote an article that did not fit with the government agenda of cleaning up samurai history into a story of good guys versus bad guys.

By the 1930s, forty years' worth of children had been taught that Japan was divine, the Emperor was a god personified and unquestioning loyalty to the Emperor was the greatest virtue. When the Second World War broke out, the Japanese people were told that each and every one of them should give their loyalty just as the samurai had done. The soldiers of the Japanese army, desperate to emulate the noble warriors of the past, threw themselves into battle.

However, this zeal was not enough to deliver victory. After the war, General Douglas MacArthur, the supreme commander of the allied powers occupying Japan, skilfully managed to deflate nationalistic fervour without provoking a revolt. Central to this achievement was his handling of Emperor Hirohito. MacArthur protected Hirohito from those who wished to see him charged with war crimes, knowing that this would have caused uproar among the Japanese people. However, he also sought to demystify the figure of the Emperor by insisting that a photo of MacArthur towering over Hirohito be published and, most significantly, by compelling Hirohito to deny his own divinity. This shook the Japanese identity to the core. Ideas such as samurai being like cherry blossom – short-lived but glorious in the service of a god – became obsolete and Japan was forced to face the reality of its defeat.

Bushidō *stands alone*

Bushidō by its very essence requires a master to follow; without feudal lords to serve, *bushidō* has no focus. However, Nitobe Inazō turned this idea on its head. He maintained that *bushidō* itself could become the master, that instead of using *bushidō* as a framework by which to serve a lord, we can follow *bushidō* purely to improve our own lives. This is a key factor in understanding the modern version of *bushidō*, in which honour for honour's sake becomes the goal. With no lord, no clan, no war, the samurai ideal turns inward toward the spiritual.

The way of the peaceful warrior

From the 1960s to about the year 2000, Japanese *dōjōs* sprang up across the world and samurai-style posters, slogans and themes abounded in sports halls as children and adults alike dressed in Japanese clothes and practised martial arts, most of them oblivious to the brutal realities of samurai chivalry. This was the age of the peaceful warrior, the samurai knight as perfection personified.

Westerners were introduced to a bewildering array of martial arts disciplines, including Jūdō, Kung Fu, Wushu, Taekwondo, Aikidō, Kenpō, Karate-dō, Jeet Kun Do, Iaidō, Taijutsu and Kendō. What is often not understood is that some of these terms are Chinese and some are Korean. Of those that are Japanese, Karate is a constructed term created in the twentieth century and has no connection to the samurai, while Iaidō is a Zen-influenced derivation of a samurai discipline and Aikidō is a twentieth-century interpretation of samurai combat.

The golden age of spiritual *bushidō* hit its peak around the same time as the publication in 1980 of one of its finest expressions, Dan Millman's international bestseller *The Way of the Peaceful Warrior*. This was a time when countless books, documentaries and games presented the samurai as the perfect warrior and gave modern people a 'Disney-fied' version of medieval Japanese chivalry.

The myth of the samurai master

The classic image of the samurai master as an infallible figure with greying hair and stoic countenance, who with a single sword cut or arrow shot could strike down an evil doer, is misleading. The average samurai would have been considered battle ready by the age of 15 or thereabouts. Many gained fame and honour in their youth, and relatively few of them reached an age when they needed to worry about grey hair. The simple fact is that most samurai were educated to a lower level than monks, had some form of combat training, be it high level or not, and were expected to go to war upon a lord's order. Most samurai battle casualties would be the victims of bad luck in the form of a stray arrow, launched stone or gunshot; a much smaller number ever got to fight it out in heroic combat. There is no doubt that older, battle-hardened fighters did exist, and in all likelihood they would have been extremely proficient in military ways, but the Zen warrior remains a myth only.

Cage fighting

Around the year 2000, traditional Eastern martial arts began to fall from popularity. Previously rigorous training regimes had been softened for public consumption: belts and grades separated people, allowing each person to compete with someone of a more or less equal standard; bogus organizations were created; and home study courses proliferated, first on VHS and DVD and then online. The martial arts community of the late 1990s had become a slow, pulsating mass of over-indulgent warrior worship, weighed down by incompetence and corruption.

Many fighters had become sick of Eastern philosophy being pushed by often falsely accredited teachers and so they turned to hard training and hard fighting in caged areas, creating a new sport to rival the lucrative Eastern martial arts scene. Mixed Martial Arts (MMA) is based mainly on Brazilian Jūjutsu (BJJ), which was exported from Japan to Brazil before the Second World War and escaped the watering down of its skills that afflicted so many other forms of martial arts. Beneath the razzamatazz, and despite the heavy purses on offer to its competitors, MMA represents a return to a purer, harder kind of combat. Some may criticize it for lacking any chivalric code, but it is celebrated and followed from one end of the world to the other.

Modern dōjōs

The Japanese martial arts *dōjō* has become an established institution throughout the world. Rather than being permanent structures dedicated to teaching Japanese arts, most modern *dōjōs* are simply booked sessions held in a multi-purpose sports hall or gym. More often than not, the focus is on Karate, with a slight lean toward traditional Japanese aspects, but Karate purists will reach back into Okinawan history (the region where Karate was developed) and even further, to the Chinese martial art of Te. In this mix will often be found a synthesis of historical and idealized samurai values, including aspects of *bushidō* cherry-picked from *Bushidō: The Soul of Japan* and the *Hagakure*. The modern 'samurai *dōjō*' tends to teach a version of twentieth-century Japanese nationalism made palatable for a twenty-first-century audience and often does not take account of the reality of medieval samurai ethics.

Samurai: a laughing stock

To say the samurai warrior has become a cliché is an understatement. The samurai have been drained of all their worth and thrown on the heap. This lack of respect has been caused by the watering down of traditional schools and the spread of fake qualifications and misinformation. The rise of MMA has drawn naturally strong, aggressive men and women away from softer, Zen-related arts such as Iaidō (the way of Zen through the sword), Kyūdō (the way of Zen through the bow), Aikidō (the way of *chi* and harmony through movement), and traditional Jūjutsu, which has become a static and ritualized version of its cousin in MMA. Likewise, Karate is now the realm of children too young to enter into combat and veterans who are too old for combat and can enjoy the peace of Zen through *kata*.

If a samurai were to travel through time from the Sengoku period to the present day, he might recognize some aspects of MMA and the modern practice of traditional Japanese arts but he would be perplexed by the claim that these are the direct descendants of his craft. If such a man came forward in time, no one would tell him he was a cliché. They would not be laughing at him when they saw just how ready he was to burn them alive, decapitate them, gang up on them with spears, throw boiling water over them, lay traps and ambushes, attack them with explosives or simply infiltrate their homes and murder them in their beds or at the dinner table. No, they would certainly not be laughing then.

A return to the harsh reality of bushidō

The purpose of this book is to return the concept of *bushidō* to a form that would be familiar to the historical samurai. To strip it of all its modernizations and simplifications so that a detailed overview can be fully established. The aim is not to belittle those who follow the modern version of *bushidō*, but to explain the reality of samurai honour and chivalry in old Japan, to define that which was universal to all samurai but also to highlight the differences between the various times, clans and situations. There is no getting away from the fact that historical *bushidō* is complex, its values shift depending on the intent and it is based on showing loyalty to the dominant military power of the day. The way of the samurai is the way of proper behaviour, proper intent and proper progression conducted through the medium of war, be it glorious or horrific. It is time that we returned to the truth of historical *bushidō*, no matter how horrifying that truth may be.

BALANCING *BUSHIDŌ*

In this final part of the book, we will aim to reach some conclusions about *bushidō* by weighing up chivalric ideals against the historical reality of samurai behaviour. History tends to document the exceptional, dramatic events rather than everyday reality, and so we get a skewed picture of life in the past. Even taking this into account, the behaviour of the samurai does appear to have been less romantic and more brutal than is often imagined. Remember that the warrior class was patriarchal, young and often impulsive, in total control of the people, armed and prone to waging war.

Here we will break down everything we have come across so far into single points and list them in the following four main categories:

1. Chivalric ideals
2. Negative actions
3. Disputed actions
4. Historical reality

These categories have been further broken down into subdivisions to give a clear and accessible overview of samurai reality. By seeing the elements of *bushidō* laid out like this, you can decide for yourself how close the samurai came to following their own code of honour.

Before you start looking at these lists of samurai behaviours, bear in mind that the contents of this book have been drawn wholly from historical documentation and that they cannot reflect the millions of unknown people, actions and events that are lost to us. Some points in these lists may represent typical actions, others were not uncommon but not normal, while some happened only once.

CHIVALRIC IDEALS

The first section comprises points found in samurai literature that define how a samurai *should* behave. It is subdivided into: personal qualities; behaviour in public; relationships between samurai; war and combat; religion and spirituality; and death.

Personal qualities

Samurai should:

- be polite
- never lie
- always keep a promise
- be prepared
- have self-discipline
- take life at a slower speed
- keep their body clean
- be neat
- keep their living quarters clean
- lead a simple life
- be part of a clan
- feel pride toward both the clan crest and a samurai back banner
- restrict the treasures of the clan to military items
- value arms and armour
- have a distaste for money
- wear a sword correctly in both war and peace
- be respectful
- never complain about inconvenience
- have endurance
- follow the Way
- choose the way of righteousness over the way of self-enrichment
- cultivate will power
- have humanity
- have integrity
- be honest

- be constant
- respect justice
- refine their character
- engage in self-examination
- perfect their abilities
- have a good education
- engage in study
- study leadership
- study war

Behaviour in public

Samurai should:

- have total mental control
- show no fear
- be respected by peers
- stand out as an individual
- be an expert in a subject
- use the correct military vocabulary
- have a person whom they trust to point out their mistakes
- follow current manners and customs
- perform correct ceremony
- follow correct bowing procedure
- kneel down with their hands in front and on the floor when waiting for another to be seated
- adopt the correct seating posture for their rank according to the social situation
- accept the correct seating position assigned to them at a banquet
- clean away their own food tray and utensils
- wear clothes appropriate to the social situation
- dye their teeth black as a sign of social superiority
- have armour that prominently displays their prowess
- remove footwear indoors and in front of superiors when outdoors
- never gamble

- never borrow money (to do so would imply that they had mismanaged their estate)
- aspire to own a famous or high-quality sword
- understand the correct protocols for wearing swords, whether indoors or outside
- recognize the great honour of being allowed to wear the *horo* arrow cape
- never ride or push through an official procession
- never be influenced or intimidated by the threat of violence or death
- fight to the death if there is no way out of a situation
- know how to correctly decapitate someone committing *seppuku*
- correctly arrest and execute a comrade if ordered to do so
- erase a past mistake by an act of glory
- be born from a noble line with a glorious history
- be connected to the Japanese imperial family, by blood if possible

Relationships between samurai

Samurai should:

- show loyalty to all superiors
- never kill a senior or superior, such as a lord, master, father or elder brother
- be a good son
- spend the money allotted to them by their lord without either going into debt or hoarding
- be from a family that has served the same clan for multiple generations
- have a long line of ancestors who have died in action serving their clan

War and combat

Samurai should:

- be skilled in all the various arts of war
- be skilled in naval warfare
- announce their name to the enemy when appropriate
- aspire to be first into battle, first to strike and first to take a head
- strike deep into enemy lines
- know that to be second into battle is also a position of honour

- assist someone who has performed a great achievement
- give aid in combat to an ally
- test a new sword in battle
- fight in the 'tiger's mouth' – the most dangerous zone in a castle siege
- break open an enemy formation and send them running
- know the four outcomes of combat (in order of prestige): to kill an enemy; to kill an enemy but die in the process; to be killed by an enemy; and to walk away alive without having killed the enemy
- kill a superior or equally matched opponent single-handed
- gang up to kill a single target
- take the head of the enemy commander
- take the heads of socially higher enemies
- know the hierarchy of combat wounds
- continue to fight while wounded instead of retreating to base camp
- bring back a captured or fallen banner
- help a comrade retreat
- defend a retreat
- defend a baggage train
- defend a commander who has to retreat
- give their horse to a defeated commander who has to retreat
- take arrows to the body while shielding a superior
- fight against many opponents
- stand and die instead of fleeing
- die gloriously in a good combat
- use gongs and horns for war but stringed instruments for peace

Religion and spirituality

Samurai should:

- pay homage to the gods of war
- make promises before the gods and keep them
- study Zen
- venerate their ancestors
- realize their destiny

- recognize the symbolism of emblems such as the dragon (representing the leader) and the boar (strength and positivity)
- use magic and talismans
- worship divine ceremonial armour within a battle camp
- start each morning of a campaign with the correct ritual
- act according to the Five Phase theory of Earth, Fire, Metal, Water and Wind
- understand that the element of Earth is central to the structure of the army
- never touch the air vent of a helmet unless it is to remove it for suicide
- perform the correct ceremonies for the dead
- be on the lookout for omens and portents
- observe the *chi* of the enemy and read the future from it

Death

Samurai should:

- die in the service of a lord
- write a death poem
- commit suicide to atone for a mistake
- avenge the death of a family member
- take their own life and the lives of their family members to avoid being captured
- organize and present the decapitated heads of enemy samurai according to their status while living
- treat the decapitated head of any enemy with respect
- face up to the possibility of their own head being taken for death by preparing it with makeup, oils and a death poem hidden in the helmet
- rearrange the bodies of fallen comrades into positions of honour
- recognize that the dead are unclean and should be kept at a distance

NEGATIVE ACTIONS

The following are actions that were unquestionably negative in samurai culture and would always be frowned upon. They are divided into: personal qualities; behaviour in public; and war and death.

Personal qualities

Samurai should not:

- show anger
- be governed by desire
- be greedy
- exaggerate
- lie
- steal
- cheat
- be selfish
- surreptitiously read other people's correspondence
- focus on artistic pleasures instead of military ways
- make poor decisions
- be wrong minded

Behaviour in public

Samurai should not:

- show that they are hungry
- be panicked and rush
- be slovenly
- blame others for problems
- be guilty of favouritism
- show fear and react to it in a cowardly way
- try to save themselves no matter what, even when the situation is hopeless
- flee
- fail in arresting and executing a comrade
- avoid serving as an assistant in ritual suicide
- fail to correctly decapitate someone performing ritual suicide
- imply that a commander has lost the battle before it is evident that they have
- use inappropriate terms that either cause offence or display cowardice

War and death

Samurai should not:

- vomit at the sight of blood or killing
- die while retreating
- die while attempting to save their own life instead of fighting to the end
- have a disrespectful attitude during combat
- kill someone from within a conglomerate of clans
- kill a non-combatant and falsify their head as that of a warrior
- falsely claim a head to be higher ranking than it actually is
- steal another warrior's captured head
- kill a woman or a non-combatant monk in war
- kill a warrior who has been defeated by another samurai before they can deliver the blow
- lead an ally into a position where they will die
- fail in an attempt to kill an enemy target

DISPUTED ACTIONS

The following actions or patterns of behaviour have been viewed as honourable in certain historical sources and dishonourable in others. Some of them are given as opposing pairs, in which each contrasting half of the pair may be viewed either positively or negatively. Some of them are in one of the previous lists either as a positive or a negative action, but there are some cases where a contrary view is given and so they are also recorded here for balance.

- Seizing power from within the family (more likely to be seen as a positive if the usurper leads the clan to prosperity)
- Fighting a family member who is on the enemy side in a war or avoiding fighting them
- Having family treasures
- Crying in public
- Being thrifty or spending luxuriously
- Enjoying extravagant and rare things or dismissing them as frivolous
- Giving/receiving gifts

- Wearing high-status clothes or maintaining simplicity
- Engaging in pursuits that have nothing to do with the military
- Engaging in deception (usually accepted, but some samurai said it was not correct)
- Retreating and allowing fresh troops into the fray when ordered to do so
- Being Christian (acceptable at some points in history, forbidden at other times)
- Using sacred paper prepared for oaths for non-sacred writing or tasks
- Engaging in organized retreats from the front line
- Cutting off enemy provisions so as to starve them out instead of fighting man to man
- Letting a defeated enemy go
- Having actors and entertainers within an army
- Killing a monk (may be acceptable as many monks were either militaristic or ex-samurai)
- Insulting the decapitated head of an enemy
- Leading a lord's horse as a groom (it is unclear whether this is a position of honour or that of a lowly servant)
- Acting as a *shinobi* for the good of the clan

THE HISTORICAL REALITY OF SAMURAI BEHAVIOUR

The previous lists were made up of positive, negative and disputed actions as measured against the ideals laid out in samurai literature, but it is difficult to analyse actual historical behaviour against an ideal. Therefore, taking as much of known samurai history as possible for this book, the following lists contain a mixture of positive and negative points, being the actions of real samurai. While *bushidō* was an ideal, it should always be compared with historical reality.

This section on historical samurai behaviours has been subdivided into: behaviour in public; the samurai clan; relationships between samurai; relationships with the general population; war and combat; and death and killing. Remembering that these are highlights from history which may or may not have been the norm, and that there were countless samurai whose daily business went unrecorded, the following points reflect how samurai really acted in life.

Behaviour in public

- Samurai social standing was defined by land holdings, wealth, dress and speech.
- Samurai could wear colourful and ornate clothes.
- To repair clothes with patches was acceptable among all classes.
- It was unacceptable for samurai to put their hands inside their sleeves or *hakama* trousers in front of a superior.
- Samurai always wore a fan in their sash.
- To touch the hair of a samurai was an insult.
- To cut off a samurai's topknot was a dire insult.
- Hitting another person with the sword scabbard could trigger a fight to the death.
- Being able to draw back a more powerful bow was seen as more prestigious, while the weaker the bow-draw weight, the less honour and more shame. This later changed as the battlefield became more compact and the emphasis was more on speed than distance of firing.
- The *naginata* was once a weapon that denoted a certain rank.
- Spear type denoted the level of a samurai within society and there were various ways in which a spear could be carried, such as at the front of a parade.
- A red groove on a spear was a mark of honour.
- Samurai should always carry their shorter sword (there were a few social situations where this rule did not apply).
- The capture of another samurai's sword was prestigious to the victor, and such a dishonour to the victim that they might even commit ritual suicide.
- Certain swords and swordsmiths were said to be 'cursed' to excuse terrible acts done with their swords, shifting the responsibility from the human to the supernatural.
- Reckless or bloodthirsty lords were said to be under the influence of an evil spirit to excuse their deeds.
- Drawing a sword and attacking in emotional anger was dishonourable.
- Buying into samurai status was not unknown.
- Samurai visited prostitutes and had concubines.

- Samurai married for political gain.
- Homosexual relationships between samurai were accepted but not universal.
- Nepotism was commonplace.
- Epithets such as 'head taker', 'master of the spear' and 'the devil' were all seen as positive.
- Samurai could publicly make fun of disabled people.
- Disloyal samurai could be paraded through the streets with their shame being announced to all.
- Honour was given to a samurai who died trying to put out a fire.
- Battle scars seen in public were deemed as impressive unless they were on the back.
- Even though it might be detrimental to tactics, it was known for samurai to rebuild a famous bridge over a strategic river because they did not want the dishonour of being associated with the bridge's destruction.
- Samurai attempted to use the flimsiest evidence to connect themselves by blood to the Japanese imperial family.
- Samurai had parties, got drunk and sang loudly.
- Some samurai shared the hardships of their people; some did not and lived in luxury.
- Some samurai renounced military life and retired to a monastery.

The clan

- The clan had to survive at all costs.
- Loyalty was indoctrinated into the next generation.
- Clans sought to take power from other clans.
- Powerful clans sought to consolidate their influence by electing family members to positions of government authority.
- To ensure the longevity of the clan, the clan chief would often hand over power to his heir before he died.
- Power did not always pass on to the eldest son of the clan chief.
- In a dire situation, samurai would kill themselves and their children to avoid capture. However, they would try to ensure that at least one child was able to escape to carry on the family line.

- Some samurai killed their own siblings or fathers for personal gain.
- Some clan heads were so overbearing and cruel that their servants would only ever tell them what they wanted to hear, for fear of receiving undeserved punishment if they told them the truth.
- Samurai were entitled to kill their servants and family members and sometimes did.
- A clan might force an adopted son to kill himself to avert a war with another clan.
- Some samurai may have had their own sons poisoned.
- A dishonoured family name could be as good as a death sentence for future generations.
- It was known for a supposed ally to lure a samurai away from their clan castle and then take it.
- Sometimes a clan would split into two parts to ensure that one part of the family would be on the winning side of a war or political battle.
- Some samurai would sacrifice themselves by venturing on a death mission that would secure the future prosperity of their clan.
- It was imperative to avenge the deaths of male members of the clan, but the killing of female members could be overlooked.
- When a domain fell, subsidiary clans would find a new lord to serve.

Relationships between samurai

- Good service was often rewarded with a gift such as a weapon, pot or artistic implement.
- Some families who had served a lord for generations switched sides if it suited them.
- Occasionally samurai would assassinate their own lords.
- Doppelgängers were engaged to protect high-ranking people from assassins.
- Some samurai killed themselves to follow their lord to the afterlife.
- It was known for retainers to offer to sacrifice their lives to save a higher-ranking samurai from execution.
- A samurai could be beheaded by their lord without trial if it was deemed that he had acted incorrectly toward another person.

- Loyal samurai who tried to reproach their lords for bad behaviour might be killed for their trouble.
- Lords would test their samurai by observing how they reacted to being told they were to be executed or dismissed.
- It was acceptable to assassinate a lord who was out of control and engaging in evil deeds such as wanton murder and torture.
- Samurai often fought against their own lord's forces because of political shifts, but to actually enter into direct combat with the lord appears to have been dishonourable.
- It was known for samurai to rise high in the ranks of an army and then plot their commander's downfall.
- Samurai sometimes gave away the location of a superior to collect a capture reward.
- Samurai, despite being loyal, sometimes underwent a drop in salary and lost their true samurai status.
- Officials were known to be open to bribes.
- Samurai sometimes murdered each other at banquets, often by poisoning or beheading.
- Holding a samurai down and cutting off his hair brought shame on him.
- Some samurai would spread lies to discredit others.
- Samurai would threaten other samurai who did not come to help them.
- Samurai did sometimes push through an official procession even though it was rude to do so.
- Murder was common enough that laws against revenge killings were established.
- Victorious lords would seize land and redistribute it as a reward for good service or as an incentive for enemy samurai to join their force.
- Defeated samurai were uprooted from their ancestral lands and forced to live in towns.
- A samurai who failed in a task might be executed along with their family.
- It was known for a samurai to betray a promise given to someone on their deathbed and to murder the family they had sworn to protect.
- Local lords were forced to move to the capital on rotation at large expense to ensure they could not build up funds to launch a rebellion.

- A lord would cover his eyes as a gesture to demonstrate that he was 'turning a blind eye' to a negative action.
- Samurai sometimes stole each other's wives.
- It was known for a lord to promise the hand in marriage of a politically powerful bride to whomever could recover her from the enemy, but then to give her away to someone else.
- The wives and children of regional lords were sometimes brought to live at court as hostages.
- One samurai exchanged his daughter for the knowledge of how to engineer a European-style firing mechanism for a gun.
- Another forced a heavily pregnant woman to dance after killing her husband and then forced her into exile after she had given birth so that he could murder the child, which also happened to be his own nephew.
- Having made a promise to each other, samurai often exchanged hostages to ensure that they did not break their word.
- One samurai called a member of the imperial family a dog and shot an arrow at his carriage for no real reason beyond having fun.
- Some samurai would steal prized decapitated heads from others to claim the reward.
- Some samurai would falsify decapitated heads.
- A warrior was confined in a cage so small that he permanently lost the use of his legs.
- A samurai could be beheaded simply for wanting to leave Japan during the national lockdown period under the Tokugawa.
- Roguish samurai would deliberately hit other samurai with the tips of their scabbards to insult them and provoke a fight to the death.

Relationships with the general population

- Carrying two swords was not a samurai symbol until the very late sixteenth century.
- Some samurai had to engage in 'peasant work' to afford to live.
- Peasants who brought a successful legal case against their lord might still be executed for insubordination.

- Samurai taxed land on what it *should* yield, not what it actually *did* yield, creating poverty in the masses.
- Samurai used slaves in mining operations.
- Samurai put dwarfs in costume and used them as a form of court jester.
- One group of samurai behaved so badly in a foreign port that the locals attacked them and the crew of their ship, burning them out of a building and shooting at them.
- It was known for samurai pirates to attack foreign trade ships in response to trade conflicts.
- Foreign envoys sent to Japan were sometimes executed during the lengthy national lockdown.
- Some regional lords defied central government and set themselves up as an illegal local authority.
- Shrine maidens served as money lenders' agents so that samurai families could borrow money without losing face.
- Treasured religious buildings were sometimes destroyed along with the sacred artefacts housed within them. One temple was burned to the ground because a samurai had been refused permission to collect plants from its grounds.
- Holy stone idols were broken up to make the foundations of a castle.
- One samurai set himself up as a future demi-god with temples and a population ready to worship him when he died.

War and combat

- Samurai sons were indoctrinated with military principles and used as child soldiers.
- As part of their training for war, children were ordered to execute criminals.
- Samurai used lies and deception for many purposes, including to avoid capture.
- When given quarter after combat, a defeated samurai might promise to come quietly, but then, if the situation changed, kill his captor. Breaking one's word in such a situation brought no loss of honour.
- Some samurai would flee the battlefield.

- In all samurai forces, it was assumed that there would be a certain number of traitors.
- The bow was the primary samurai weapon before the spear and the sword.
- Samurai would prepare their body before battle so that, if the worst happened, those inspecting their corpse would praise it.
- What is termed in modern times 'dirty' fighting was acceptable in samurai times.
- Many samurai would absolutely fight to the death when in a hopeless situation.
- Samurai sometimes removed both their swords to grapple with a target for capture.
- Rakes, ropes and grabbing tools were common samurai implements.
- Samurai sometimes killed an ally and passed him off as an enemy kill.
- Samurai would chase off an ally who had just killed an enemy and falsely claim the head for themselves.
- Samurai would take a lower-ranking head and falsify it so it appeared to be higher ranking.
- It was not uncommon for samurai to swap sides at the offer of a more stable future and hereditary land rights.
- Wars often hinged on a conflict between loyalty to the Emperor and loyalty to the *shōgun*.
- Samurai would inform the enemy of a rival ally's movements to stop them gaining victory and renown.
- A city would sometimes be given an ultimatum: surrender or be destroyed; but when the city surrendered, it would still be destroyed.
- Entire villages or hamlets would be demolished to provide building materials or to stop the enemy using them as cover.
- On one occasion the besiegers of a castle promised the occupants that if they filled in the moats the siege would end and no harm would come to them. However, the attacking force returned to destroy the castle and kill the inhabitants.
- It was common practice to lie to an enemy envoy.
- Some samurai gave permission for things beyond their authority.

- In the Japanese invasion of Korea at the end of the sixteenth century, hundreds of thousands of Korean civilians were slaughtered.
- To be sent as an assassin and infiltrate deep into enemy company or sneak out of a besieged castle and get help from nearby allies were seen as great deeds.
- Wily commanders sometimes used fake soldiers and extra flags to confuse an enemy and appear stronger than they actually were.
- Keeping a vigilant watch in a guard tower was prestigious, but some samurai were said to be rowdy and inattentive.
- The style of flags worn by samurai was sometimes regulated to highlight men of prowess.
- It was prestigious for a samurai to be the first to throw his banner into a besieged castle.
- Besiegers sometimes showed mercy to the occupants of a doomed castle. For example, they might allow besieged samurai to see a performance by a famous actor before they die; permit items of significance to be safely removed before the castle fell; or let a samurai leave a siege if he possessed oral tradition that was deemed to be of cultural significance.
- It was important to be proficient at river crossing, both alone and with a military force.
- Samurai would often make tactical withdrawals.

Killing and death
- Historical examples of killings committed or caused by samurai include:
  - forcing innocent children to commit ritual suicide because of their sibling's crime
  - killing innocent people as a punishment for someone else's crimes
  - murdering a maidservant for not cleaning correctly
  - killing a servant for accidentally damaging property
  - killing an entire family because they could not meet an unreasonable tax demand
  - killing a samurai or forcing them to commit suicide for drawing a sword at the incorrect time

- ordering the death of someone in haste and then building a memorial to them
- killing a man because his sister had an affair with someone inappropriate yet allowing the sister to live
- killing innocent people who were under the protection of an enemy and burning down their dwellings
- burning down a temple despite knowing that there were women and children hiding inside
- locking monks in a temple and burning them alive
- burning people alive not for any crime but for their religious beliefs
- murdering a pregnant woman and using the unborn foetus as an ingredient in magical medicine
- stabbing a maid and carving open her mouth as a punishment for spreading rumours
- tying an innocent monk to a horse and having him dragged to his death (the monk just happened to be passing at the time the samurai who ordered his killing was feeling frustrated after an unsuccessful day's hunting)
- murdering a messenger
- sending messengers across the land to order the execution of various family members for a single crime committed by one member
- ordering a crack archer to shoot an enemy who was performing a ritualistic dance in that archer's honour
- killing a dancer because the dance was not of a high enough quality
- cutting the throat of a dying samurai before he had finished performing his own 'last rites'
- ordering the mass murder of tens of thousands of innocent women and children and also killing militarized and non-militarized holy men
- offering up a single family member for execution to allow the others to live
- Various samurai tried to assassinate the Emperor of Japan.
- Killing an innocent person could be overlooked, but to kill a fellow retainer was a dire offence which could start a clan war.

- For a samurai to be mentally ill and murder members of his family was overlooked.
- Samurai were well acquainted with dismembering the human body.
- Captured samurai were sometimes kept alive and decapitated as close as possible to the time and place where their heads were to be presented. This was done to ensure that the decapitated heads were fresh.
- When in a hopeless situation, samurai would go to lengths to ensure that the enemy could not take their body. For example, they might commit suicide in a burning building or weigh themselves down and jump into water.
- Human sacrifices sometimes took place in Japan, especially in connection to the construction of important buildings.
- Samurai sometimes moved dead bodies on the field of battle. For example, the corpses of allied warriors who had died fleeing might be rearranged into a braver posture to make it look as if they had died fighting hard.
- Samurai pulled out their entrails after they had cut open their stomach in the act of *seppuku*.
- Punishment was extreme and could be given for the slightest wrong: sentences of death by roasting, impalement, burning and other horrible execution methods were given out regularly.
- Dead warriors' teeth were dyed black.
- Monks sometimes committed suicide by hanging themselves at a samurai's funeral.
- Many samurai killed themselves willingly to follow their lord into the afterlife.

The truth of samurai behaviour

While many of the above actions were one-off examples performed by individual people, collectively they paint a far more complex picture of the samurai than is often imagined. The samurai did have a code of honour and that code did correspond in some ways with our modern-day ethics. However, the samurai were still a medieval people who bore as much responsibility as any other group for the brutality of their time. Actions that appear to us wholly barbaric may not have been considered unchivalrous at the time, and even those actions that would normally have been seen as dishonourable back then were accepted if they were carried out for the greater good of the clan.

BUSHIDŌ TODAY

Having delved deeply into the history of the samurai and *bushidō*, we are still left with one question, and that is what to do with *bushidō* today. For the modern-day student of the samurai path, *bushidō* still has to perform its function as a guide. In the past, the Seven Virtues of *Bushidō* outlined by Nitobe Inazō were hung on the wall of many a *dōjō* and held as the standard for those practising there, but these principles have been shown to be too simplistic as a practical guide to samurai philosophy. Therefore, to help those who have chosen to follow the way of the samurai through life, here is an updated version of the 'virtues of *bushidō*'. The samurai is one step away from the sage. The following points will help you to find your way.

Personal qualities and behaviour in public

- Keep life simple.
- Be aware of your own faults.
- Do the right thing for others.
- Be kind.
- Be honest.
- Be generous.
- Be consistent.
- Be focused.
- Be respectful to others.
- Talk, act and dress appropriately.
- Take responsibility.
- Do not dishonour people.
- Always keep a promise.
- Educate yourself.
- Take pride in your heritage.
- Be clean and neat in your person and your surroundings.
- Be prepared at all times.

- Value fitness and strength.
- Be mindful of where you place your loyalty.
- Have a keen sense of duty.
- Be brave in the face of danger.
- Maintain a controlled attitude.
- Do not complain.
- Never avoid a task if it is yours to do.
- Never use words that show fear.
- Never exaggerate.
- Do not tell people everything.
- Never lie unless it is to an enemy.
- Do not focus on money and wealth.
- Do not hoard things.
- Rise above the behaviour of the average person.
- Understand the manners and customs of your society.
- Understand the world you live in.
- Love your own religion and tolerate other people's faiths.
- Explore the mysteries of the world.
- Pay homage to the dead.
- Accept when it is your time to die.
- Consider the afterlife.
- Consider your place within the universe.

Military ways

- Maintain your individuality within a group.
- Work in teams.
- Announce who you are.
- Have respect for military knowledge.
- Have pride in your organization.
- Understand military vocabulary.
- Become an expert in your field.
- Own functional equipment.
- Maintain your equipment.

- Know how to use your equipment.
- Engage in combat training.
- Study weapons.
- Study tactics and strategy.
- Make decisions with thought.
- Be quick to move into action.
- Be aware of your position.
- Do not fear the enemy.
- Know and respect your enemy and their ability.
- Help your own comrades in need.
- Use the correct person for each task.
- Use deception and truth together.
- Do everything to win.
- Be fearsome.

These are the ways of the samurai condensed to the most salient points and represent a level of behaviour which is considered as positive if achievable. For those who wish to further dedicate themselves to the way of the samurai, see also *How to Be a Modern Samurai* by Antony Cummins.

ABOUT THE AUTHOR

Antony Cummins is the Official Tourism Ambassador for Wakayama, Japan (和歌山市観光発信人) and an author on historical Asian military culture, specifically Japanese. His intention is to present a historically accurate picture of both samurai and *shinobi* (ninja) to the Western world and lay down the foundations for a better understanding of their teachings and ways. With his translation partners, he has published an array of books on Japanese warfare, including translations of historical ninja manuals. Antony and his work can be followed on YouTube under 'Samurai and Ninja History' and 'Natori Ryu'. For more information see his website www.natori.co.uk

BIBLIOGRAPHY

Ansart, O., 'Loyalty in Seventeenth and Eighteenth Century Samurai Discourse'. *Japanese Studies*, 27:2, 2007.

Anshin, A., *The Truth of the Ancient Ways: A Critical Biography of the Swordsman Yamaoka Tesshū*. Kodenkan Institute, Redwood City, CA, 2012.

Archer, J., 'Understanding Samurai Disloyalty' *New Voices*, 2, , 2008.

Benesch, O., *Inventing the Way of the Samurai: Nationalism, Internationalism and Bushidō in Modern Japan*. Oxford University Press, Oxford, 2014.

Bennett, T., *Photography in Japan 1853–1912*. Tuttle, North Clarendon, VT, 2006.

Blomberg, C., '"A Strange White Smile": A survey of tooth-blackening and other dental practices in Japan'. *Japan Forum*, 2:2, 1990.

Carter, S. D. (editor), *Traditional Japanese Poetry: An Anthology*. Stanford University Press, Redwood City, CA, 1991.

Cleary, T. (translator), *Samurai Wisdom: Lessons from Japan's Warrior Culture – Five Classic Texts on Bushido*. Tuttle, North Clarendon, VT, 2009.

Cleary, T. (translator and editor), *Training the Samurai Mind: A Bushido Sourcebook*. Shambhala, Boston, MA, 2008.

Clements, J., *The Samurai: A New History of the Warrior Elite*. Robinson Press, London, 2010.

Cooper, M. (editor), *They Came to Japan: An Anthology of European Reports on Japan, 1543–1640*. Center for Japanese Studies, University of Michigan, Ann Arbor, MI, 1965.

Cummins, A. & Y. Minami, *The Book of Ninja: The First Complete Translation of the Bansenshukai*. Watkins, London, 2013.

Cummins, A. & Y. Minami, *The Book of Samurai: Fundamental Teachings (Book of Samurai* series, book 1). Watkins, London, 2015.

Cummins, A. & Y. Minami, *Iga and Koka Ninja Skills: The Secret Shinobi Scrolls of Chikamatsu Shigenori*. History Press, Cheltenham, 2013.

Cummins, A. & M. Koizumi, *The Lost Samurai School: Secrets of Mubyoshi Ryu*. Blue Snake Books, Berkeley, CA, 2016.

Cummins, A. & Y. Minami, *Samurai Arms, Armour and the Tactics of Warfare: The Collected Scrolls of Natori-Ryu* (*Book of Samurai* series, book 2). Watkins, London, 2018.

Cummins, A. & Y. Minami, *Samurai War Stories*. History Press, Cheltenham, 2013.

Cummins, A. & Y. Minami, *The Secret Traditions of the Shinobi: Hattori Hanzo's Shinobi Hiden and Other Ninja Scrolls*. Blue Snake Books, Berkeley, CA, 2012.

Cummins, A. & Y. Minami, *True Path of the Ninja: The Definitive Translation of the Shoninki*. Tuttle, North Clarendon, VT, 2011.

Cunningham, D., *Samurai Weapons: Tools of the Warrior*. Tuttle, North Clarendon, VT, 2008.

Dougill, J., *In Search of Japan's Hidden Christians: A Story of Suppression, Secrecy and Survival*. Tuttle, North Clarendon, VT, 2012.

Dunn, C. J., *Everyday Life in Traditional Japan*. Tuttle, North Clarendon, VT, 1969.

Friday, K., 'Valorous Butchers: The Art of War During the Golden Age of the Samurai'. *Japan Forum*, 5:1, 2007.

Gill, R. D., *Topsy-Turvy 1585: 611 Ways Europeans and Japanese Were Contrary – According to a Tract by Luís Froís S.J.*. Paraverse Press, Key Biscayne, FL, 2004.

Grimm, J. & W. (authors), J. Zipes (translator), *The Original Folk and Fairy Tales of the Brothers Grimm*. Princeton University Press, Princeton, NJ, 2014.

Hall, D., *Encyclopedia of Japanese Martial Arts*. Kodansha, Tōkyō, 2012.

Hojo Ujinaga (author), E. Shahan & K. Iida (translators), *Heiho Yukan: The Paragon of Military Strategy, Volumes 17–20 – A Critique of Merit & Departing for Battle*. CreateSpace Independent Publishing Platform, Scotts Valley, CA, 2016.

Howland, D. R., 'Samurai Status, Class, and Bureaucracy: A Historiographical Essay'. *Journal of Asian Studies*, 60:2, 2001.

Ikegami, E., 'Shame and the Samurai: Institutions, Trustworthiness, and Autonomy in the Elite Honor Culture'. *Social Research*, 70:4, 2003.

Kaibara Ekiken (author), W. S. Wilson (translator), *Yojokun: Life Lessons from a Samurai*. Kodansha, Tōkyō, 2008.

Katsu Kokichi (author), C. Teruko (translator), *Musui's Story: An Autobiography of a Tokugawa Samurai*. University of Arizona Press, Tucson, AZ, 1988.

Llull, R. (author), N. Fallows (translator), *The Book of the Order of Chivalry*. Boydell Press, Woodbridge, Suffolk, 2013.

Milton, G., *Samurai William: The Adventurer Who Unlocked Japan*. Hodder & Stoughton, London, 2002.

Miyamoto Musashi (author), T. Cleary (translator), *The Book of Five Rings: A Classic Text on the Japanese Way of the Sword*. Shambhala, Boston, MA, 2010.

Miyamoto Musashi (author), D. K. Groff (translator), *The Five Rings: Miyamoto Musashi's Art of Strategy – The New Illustrated Edition of the Japanese Warrior Classic*. Watkins, London, 2012.

Nitobe, I., *Bushidō: The Soul of Japan*. Kodansha, Tōkyō, 2002 (originally published in 1900).

Norman, F., *The Fighting Man of Japan: The Training and Exercises of the Samurai*. Dover, Mineola, NY, 2006 (originally published in 1905).

Perrin, N., *Giving Up the Gun: Japan's Reversion to the Sword, 1543–1879*. David R. Godine, Boston, MA, 1979.

Sadler, A. L., *Shogun: The Life of Tokugawa Ieyasu*. Tuttle, North Clarendon, VT, 1937.

Seward, J., *Hara-Kiri: Japanese Ritual Suicide*. Tuttle, North Clarendon, VT, 1968.

Shigenori Chikamatsu (author), K. Mori (translator), *Stories from a Tearoom Window: Lore and Legends of the Japanese Tea Ceremony*. Tuttle, North Clarendon, VT, 1982.

Song-Nyong Yu (author), C. Byonghyon (translator), *The Book of Corrections: Reflections on the National Crisis During the Japanese Invasion of Korea, 1592–1598*. University of California Institute of East Asian Studies, Berkeley, CA, 2002.

Suzuki, D. T., *Zen and Japanese Culture*. Princeton University Press, Princeton, NJ, 1970.

Tabata, K., *Secret Tactics: Lessons from the Great Masters of Martial Arts*. Tuttle, North Clarendon, VT, 2003.

Taira Shigesuke (author), T. Cleary (translator), *Code of the Samurai: A Modern Translation of the Bushido Shoshinshu of Taira Shigesuke*. Tuttle, North Clarendon, VT, 1999.

Turnbull, S., *Tokugawa Ieyasu: Leadership, Strategy, Conflict*. Osprey, New York, 2012.

Turner, P. S., *Samurai Rising: The Epic Life of Minamoto Yoshitsune*. Charlesbridge, Watertown, MA, 2016.

Tyler, R. (translator), *The Tale of the Heike*. Penguin, London, 2012.

Wilson, W. S., *The Lone Samurai: The Life of Miyamoto Musashi*. Kodansha, Tōkyō, 2004.

Yagyu Munenori (author), H. Sato (translator and editor), *The Sword & the Mind: The Classic Japanese Treatise on Swordsmanship and Tactics*. Barnes & Noble Books, New York, 1985.

Yamada, S., 'The Myth of Zen in the Art of Archery'. *Japanese Journal of Religious Studies*, 28:1–2, 2001.

Yamamoto Kansuke (author), T. Cleary (translator), *Secrets of the Japanese Art of Warfare: From the School of Certain Victory*. Tuttle, North Clarendon, VT, 2012.

Yamamoto Tsunetomo (author), A. Bennett (translator), *Hagakure: The Secret Wisdom of the Samurai*. Tuttle, North Clarendon, VT, 2014.

Yamamoto Tsunetomo (author), B. D. Steben (translator), *The Art of the Samurai: Yamamoto Tsunetomo's Hagakure*. Watkins, London, 2002.

Yamamoto Tsunetomo (author), W. S. Wilson (translator), *Hagakure: The Book of the Samurai*. Shambhala, Boston, MA, 2012.

Primary sources

Below is a list of the primary sources referred to or directly quoted in this book, along with their date and translator into English. Included in this list are many accounts of Japan by early European travellers to the country. The English titles of works in which the translations appear can be found in the main bibliography.

Álvares, Jorge, writings of, 16th century.

Ávila Girón, Bernardino de, writings of, late 16th/early 17th century.

Bansenshūkai (萬川集海), 1676, translated by Cummins and Minami.

Bishamonden (毘沙門伝), c1698, translated by Cummins, Minami and Koizumi.

Bushidō Shoshinshū (武士道初心集), c1700, translated by Thomas Cleary.

Carletti, Francesco, writings of, 1606.

Caron, François, writings of, 17th century.

Chasō Kanwa (茶窓閑話), written in 1739, published in 1804, translated by Kozaburo Mori.

Cocks, Richard, diary of, 1615–22.

Fernandez, Juan, writings of, 16th century.

St Francis Xavier, writings of, 16th century.

Fukushima-Ryū Shin'i Kufū no Maki (福嶋流心意工夫之巻), 17th century, transcribed in 1797, translated by Cummins, Minami and Koizumi.

Gorin no sho (五輪書), 1643–6, editions translated by Alexander Bennett, Thomas Cleary and David Groff.

Gunpō Jiyōshū (軍法侍用集), c1612, translated by Cummins and Minami.

Hagakure (葉隠), 1716, editions translated by Alexander Bennett, Barry D. Steben and William Scott-Wilson.

Heieki Yōhō (兵役要法), c1670, translated by Cummins and Minami.

Heihō Hidensho (兵法奥義書), 17th century, translated by Thomas Cleary.

Heihō Kadensho (兵法家伝書), 1632, editions translated by Tabata Kazumi and Satō Hiroaki.

Heihō Yūkan (兵法雄鑑), 1645, translated by Eric Shahan.

Heika Jōdan (兵家常談), c1670, translated by Cummins and Minami.

Heike Monogatari (平家物語), 14th century, translated by Royall Tyler.

Ichijō Kaneyoshi (1402–81), writings of, translated by Thomas Cleary.

Ippei Yōkō (一兵要功), c1670, translated by Cummins and Minami.

Ittōsai Sensei Kenpō no Sho (一刀斎先生剣法書), 1664, translated by Tabata Kazumi.

Jyōseishi Kendan (常静子剱談), 1810, translated by Tabata Kazumi.

Kaishaku Narabini Seppuku Dōtsuki no Shidai (介錯・切腹胴附之次第), 17th century, translated by Cummins and Koizumi.

Mexia, Lourenço, writings of, 16th century.

Mizukagami (水鏡), c1670, translated by Cummins and Minami.

Mizukagami Kuden no Oboe (水鏡口傳之覚), date unknown, translated by Cummins and Koizumi.

Musha Monogatari (武者物語), 1654, translated by Cummins and Minami.

Oamu Monogatari (おあむ物語), 17th century, translated by Cummins and Minami.

Okiku Monogatari (おきく物語), 17th century, translated by Cummins and Minami.

St Pedro Bautista Blásquez, writings of, 16th century.

Rodrigues, João, writings of, late 16th/early 17th century.

Saris, John, writings of, early 17th century.

Sekiguchi-Ryū scrolls from the Yamada Toshiyasu collection, translated by Cummins and Minami.

Shiba Yoshimasa (1349–1410), writings of, translated by Thomas Cleary.

Shinkan no Maki (心鑑之巻), transcribed in 1789, translated by Cummins and Koizumi.

Shoka no Hyōjō (諸家評定), 1621, translated by Cummins and Minami.

Shōninki (正忍記), 1681, translated by Cummins and Minami.

Suzuki Shosan (1579–1655), writings of, translated by Thomas Cleary.

Torres, Cosme de, writings of, 16th century.

Tratado by Luís Froís, 1585, translated by Robin Gill.

Uta no Maki (歌之巻), 17th century, translated by Cummins, Minami and Koizumi.

Valignano, Alessandro, writings of, 16th century.

Vilela, Gaspar, writings of, 16th century.

Vivero y Velasco, Rodrigo de, writings of, early 17th century.

Zōhyō Monogatari (雑兵物語), 1657–84, translated by Cummins and Minami.

INDEX